in camera

in camera

Secret Justice in Rhodesia

Peter Niesewand

Weidenfeld and Nicolson London

for my wife

Illustrations

Plainclothes police on official business have a way of entering a room which places them in control: loud knocks on the door, three men immediately walk in and fan out, as if expecting you to run.

The man in the middle takes charge, introducing himself and his colleagues so quickly you don't catch any of their names, flashing an identity card in front of you and withdrawing it before you can read what it says, then producing a search warrant which you are allowed to look at but not keep. They move quickly and efficiently. All three watch your face. One man holds a pencil and an open notebook to jot down anything you might say. The other, empty-handed, just stares.

The man in the middle keeps talking: 'We have a warrant to search your office and your house, and we propose doing so now. You will not communicate with anyone, or make any telephone calls. We are making inquiries into a possible charge under the Official Secrets Act over reports you sent to the *Guardian* and the BBC on 15 November. We want those reports.'

I said: 'Would you like some coffee?'

The man in the middle gave a thin smile. 'If you're making some.'

It was 26 November 1972: morning in the Rhodesian capital of Salisbury. My office messenger had gone down to the main Post Office to collect the overnight mail, and I was marking and cutting that day's edition of the *Rhodesia Herald* for my files.

I moved away from my desk and over to the shelf where I kept the stories I had sent to my clients over the previous month, but as I paged through the Leverarch file I knew what specific information they were after.

At the beginning of 1972, with the approval of the Portuguese Government, Rhodesian troops and aircraft began a series of raids across the border into Mozambique, pursuing black nationalist guerilla bands and attacking their camps. The Portuguese themselves had their hands overfull with the problem of combating the forces of FRELIMO (Front for the Liberation of Mozambique) in the territory, and so additional operations by Rhodesians were helpful. Yet the Portuguese wished – initially at least – to say nothing about Rhodesian involvement.

A point of pride was at stake. There had been suggestions that they were not able to cope with the guerilla situation in their overseas province, and these suggestions were founded in fact. Many soldiers in Mozambique were national servicemen brought from metropolitan Portugal to fight a hard and dirty war in a territory with which they did not identify, despite politicians' talk of 'overseas provinces'. They had little training in guerilla tactics and – to Rhodesian and South African eyes at least – showed themselves up as rather timid time-servers, unwilling to run risks.

There was much talk in Government and military circles in Salisbury about Portuguese inefficiency, and this was of more than passing concern to the Rhodesians. Outlawed Rhodesian nationalist organisations ZANU (The Zimbabwe African National Union) and ZAPU (The Zimbabwe African People's Union) were using Mozambique as a springboard for attacks into their white-ruled homeland. FRELIMO was providing bases in the thick bush of the Mukumbura district in remote north-western Mozambique for Rhodesian guerillas, recruits and instructors.

As the Portuguese army could not be relied upon to deal efficiently with the guerillas, the Rhodesians were anxious to have a try themselves – but they needed Portuguese permission. This the Mozambique armed forces were happy to give, as long as there was no suggestion that the presence of Rhodesians in the territory implied they were unable to control the situation.

So it was decided to say nothing officially. The Rhodesians quietly staged sporadic raids across the border, sometimes in hot pursuit of guerilla bands, sometimes to attack hostile bases. The Portuguese continued to lose their grip on the situation, FRELIMO activities increased, the Rhodesians privately made known their concern to the Mozambique authorities, and the Portuguese denied there was any reason for it. FRELIMO pushed downwards towards the Rhodesian road- and rail-links to the Mozambique port of Beira, making the Portuguese increasingly sensitive of any criticism of their military activities. Rhodesian operations in Mozambique began to carry an aura of implied criticism.

A Rhodesian military source told me: 'The trouble is, we can't make too much fuss about the Portuguese handling of the terrorist troubles, because if we do, they might stop us going across into Mozambique. Then we'd have to leave it entirely to them, and we'd really be in trouble.'

Early in November, I received information from a Rhodesian source that FRELIMO had attacked a railway line in Mozambique. I also received an unofficial briefing about Rhodesian concern over the situation in the neighbouring territory, and the part being played there by Rhodesian security forces. The FRELIMO attack was news: the rest of the information was merely background, having been published some months earlier in Rhodesia, South Africa and overseas.

I telexed reports to the *Guardian*, the BBC and other clients. My later trial on charges under the Official Secrets Act was based on these reports.

This was the *Guardian* story:

'FRELIMO guerillas in neighbouring Mozambique have launched a major new offensive on the railway line which runs from the port of Beira to Tete, site of the giant Cabora-Bassa hydro-electric scheme.

'According to Rhodesian intelligence reports, FRELIMO bands crossed the border from Malawi last Saturday [11 November] and laid landmines at about 20 points on the Tete line. The track had been cut in several places, the reports said.

'The guerillas are operating from bases in Malawi, a few miles from the Tete line. All attacks had taken place along a 100 mile front where the track runs close to the border, Rhodesian sources said.

'The Rhodesians are watching the security situation in Mozambique with growing concern. For months now, the road from Rhodesia to Malawi – which runs through Tete – has been officially considered 'unsafe', even for vehicles travelling in Portuguese military convoys. These convoys proceed at walking pace, while troops test the road for mines. But even so, a number of vehicles in the convoys have been blown up.

'The guerillas are staging hit-and-run raids on lines of communication in the area, and the Rhodesians fear that their vital supply routes to the ports of Beira and Lourenço Marques may soon be threatened.

'Military sources said the Rhodesians are already taking an

3

unofficial part in the Mozambique guerilla war – including supplying aircraft of the Rhodesian Air Force for specific tasks in the neighbouring territory, and sending patrols of soldiers across on request.

'In August, Rhodesia's Minister of Defence, Mr Jack Howman, said that if the Portuguese military authorities asked Rhodesia for help to fight terrorists in the Tete area, this would be granted.

'Mr Howman said: "They have, of course, a serious, a difficult situation up there. I think if our Portuguese friends wanted assistance, we would help them. But so far, they have given no indication of this.'

'Military sources say that although the Rhodesian Government is reluctant to officially admit its forces are already taking an active part in the Mozambique war, the true position is that security forces from this country have been involved for most of this year.'

At my trial, the Rhodesian Secretary for Law and Order, Mr John Fleming, confirmed the truth of this report, but said that the information on Rhodesian involvement was classified as Top Secret.

It was difficult to imagine a more widely-known secret, and the day my report appeared, the Portuguese Government in Lisbon, asked to comment, wasted little time in handing out a public rebuke. Prime Minister Marcello Caetano said: 'Some of our neighbours with less experience do not conceal their fears. They have been told more than once that there is no reason for their great fright.'

A few hours later, a Mozambique Government communiqué said that repairs to the Tete railway line were going ahead, following a FRELIMO attack. It was the first official indication that there had indeed been such a raid.

Minutes after receiving this confirmation, I was telephoned by David Williams, the Rhodesian Director of Information. A woman secretary in his office was listening on an extension, taking shorthand notes of our conversation which she later produced in court.

David Williams spoke rapidly. 'We're extremely concerned about a report on the BBC news at 8 p.m. last night – you quoted Rhodesian military sources, Rhodesian intelligence sources, and Rhodesian Government sources.'

'No,' I said. 'Quoting the Minister of Defence was the nearest I came to Rhodesian Government sources.'

'Can you give me the names of your sources?'

4

Mr Williams is an experienced man, and I couldn't believe he seriously expected a journalist to divulge that sort of information, so I laughed. 'Of course I can't tell you my sources,' I said, 'but they were pretty good, I'm absolutely confident about that. My story has been confirmed from Mozambique this morning.'

It occurred to me that Mr Williams himself might have been suspected of leaking the information on the FRELIMO raid to me, so I said: 'I certainly did not quote Rhodesian Government sources', and I went to get a copy of my BBC script from the files, and read short extracts to him. There was no reference to Government sources.

Finally, as his secretary took shorthand notes on the extension, Mr Williams said: 'Could you let me have a copy of your script as I didn't take notes or anything?'

'Of course you can,' I said. 'I'll send it up.'

I never did send Mr Williams the telex copies of the report. Over the years, I had submitted hundreds of queries, some of them urgent, to his Ministry of Information, and most of these were simply ignored. Others received an eventual 'no comment'. Perhaps ten per cent were answered. Now that the Information Ministry wanted something from me, it seemed appropriate for them to be promised assistance, and then ignored, and this is what I did.

David Williams, a pleasant, silver-haired Welshman, was a career civil servant, who despite his position as Director, gave the impression of exercising very little control over the workings of the Ministry. He always promised help, was always polite and friendly, and seemed to like journalists. But ranking both above and below him were men who made little effort to disguise their contempt for the Press, and who worked constantly to withhold information or create difficulties. It is a puzzle why the projection of Rhodesia's international image was placed in the hands of men who, in many cases, refused pointblank to give the Government's side of the story on contentious matters, and occasionally told straightforward, easily-checkable lies.

It was difficult to understand their reasoning, and, in the case of the British Broadcasting Corporation, their attitude.

Shortly after the Unilateral Declaration of Independence (UDI) from Britain in November 1965, the Rhodesians took exception to BBC broadcasts beamed to their country, which contained – among other things – information cut out of local newspapers by official censors. The BBC was declared *persona non grata*, and was ordered to 'withdraw its staff and impedimenta forthwith'.

5

Although I worked for the BBC, I was not a staff man – merely a freelance journalist (called a 'stringer') – and so, with the full knowledge of the Rhodesians, and using their communications facilities, I continued working for the Corporation. No attempt was made to stop me.

Instead, the Government and the Ministry of Information tried to ignore the existence of my BBC reports. They refused repeated invitations to take part in radio and television programmes sent out by me to London, because, they said, the Corporation was *persona non grata*. The fact that the programmes were being produced regardless of their ruling did not alter their judgement, and they would not even nominate a Rhodesian outside the Government who might be counted on to put across their point of view.

Occasionally, on major issues, I would approach André Holland, a Member of Parliament for the ruling Rhodesian Front party, and in desperation ask for help. Mr Holland farmed about fifteen miles outside Salisbury at 'The Ponderosa Ranch', and prided himself on maintaining good, paternalistic relations with his African staff. He was brighter than most of his RF colleagues, and had established friendly links with the Press. He also recognised the futility of the Information Ministry theory that reports about a situation could not be published until the Government had commented officially. No comment meant, of course, no story.

Several times, over the course of three years – usually during elections, RF party congresses and so on – I managed to persuade Mr Holland to be interviewed by me for the BBC. He would consider each request, make telephone calls to Prime Minister Ian Smith's office and the headquarters of the RF, and be told: 'Do as you think best. If anything goes wrong, then it's your personal responsibility.'

So after due thought, Mr Holland would change into a dark suit and tie, fetch and light his pipe, and we would begin. Because of his anxiety over possible misrepresentation, we'd go through the questions in advance, and he retained the right to order the deletion of any section which he felt had not gone well.

In the case of taped interviews, we would replay the recording two or three times to make certain he had got it right. For television interviews, I requested the BBC in London to contact friends of Mr Holland and ask them to watch the programme concerned. I also arranged to be sent an official transcript of the interview as broadcast, which I handed over to him.

As might be expected, Mr Holland was never dissatisfied, but

6

trying to get the white Rhodesian side of the story was a tedious and time-consuming business. In ordinary day-to-day coverage of events for the BBC and others, I merely performed the basic journalistic duty of asking the Government for comment, and if they failed to provide it, I sent out the story and lost no sleep. Publication of accurate reports or legitimate opposition opinions could not be held up merely because the Ministry of Information maintained silence.

The problem of obtaining the official viewpoint was not peculiar to me. Almost every journalist in Rhodesia has on record a long list of queries which went unanswered, opportunities to present cases which were passed up, and sheer Government bloody-mindedness. They, like me, have had to establish an elaborate system of contacts, which by-pass the Information Ministry machine, and provide tip-offs, background information, and glimpses of the official viewpoint. The Government is often angered by these leaks, and the Ministry of Information is piqued when 'unauthorised' news gets out.

The problem for the administration was, what to do about it?

Scores of journalists had been expelled from Rhodesia without unduly hindering the flow of information out of the country. So in 1972, Mr Smith's Government made the decision in principle to crack down hard on newsmen and intimidate them into a form of self-imposed censorship.

In September of that year, I heard about the possibility of action against the Press, and it seemed likely that, as one of the few stringers for non-Rhodesian newspapers and broadcasting corporations, I would be in the front of the firing line.

The first police raid on my office in November represented a warning shot by the authorities. Assistant Commissioner Ronald Eames and his two plainclothes colleagues, after their initial brusqueness, settled down to the search and cups of coffee.

I moved to a spare desk and continued cutting and pasting the *Herald* clippings. Occasionally one of the policemen would ask a question. Where are the keys to this cupboard? What do these notes mean? I answered helpfully.

Finally, Mr Eames said: 'You know what we're after, don't you? Who was your source of information?'

'Sorry,' I said. 'I can't tell you.'

'Can't, or won't?'

'Choose one of them,' I said.

They looked through notebooks, desk diaries, telephone pads and files. I said: 'You won't find out who gave me that information. It's

7

not written down. It's in my head, and I'm afraid it's staying there.'

I was not bluffing: there was nothing to find. Journalists can only work in Rhodesia on the assumption that all their reports are read, their telephones are tapped, their mail is opened, and every conversation is overheard. In my case, I also knew that one of my African employees was moonlighting for the Special Branch. My wife Nonie and I had stopped in at the office late one night after coming out of the cinema. We were a little surprised to find the night-shift messenger on his knees on the office floor, the contents of the waste-paper basket before him, piecing together bits of paper.

I said 'Good evening', stepped over the debris and went through to the telex room. I didn't mind the Special Branch employing one of my men. There was nothing seditious for him to find, nothing exciting to report, and I was glad to know the identity of the informer. My only worry was that they had chosen the least intelligent member of my staff, and I hoped he would give them a more reliable service than I was receiving, as my security depended on it.

The police search of my office began with a great show of thoroughness, but soon tailed off. They knew before they came that there was nothing there, and although I had detailed files going back two years, they glanced casually at these and only took away the specific Mozambique reports which I looked out for them. The main purpose of the search was intimidation and it didn't take me long to realise this.

I wanted somehow to get word to Nonie that we were being raided, and that the search would soon move to our house in the suburb of Northwood where she was looking after our six-month-old son, Oliver. It's an unpleasant feeling having the police arrive without warning, and simply take over, and I thought she should prepare herself.

When the phone rang, I answered it automatically. It was Nonie, and the three policemen stopped scratching through desks and drawers to listen. I hardly heard what she was saying as my mind was searching for a way to let her know what was happening. Finally I said: 'Are you going to be in this morning?'

'I was going out later,' she replied.

I moved the receiver slightly away from my mouth and said to Mr Eames: 'Do you want my wife to be at home?'

'No,' he said. 'It doesn't matter.'

I spoke directly into the receiver again. 'I'll be coming home in a little while with some men,' I said, 'but you needn't stick around if you don't want to.'

Nonie, who had heard everything, got the message and said: 'Oh, I'll stay.'

A few minutes later, she decided to take some peaches picked from a tree in our garden to neighbours across the road. At the gate, she noticed an unmarked car parked on the corner, with two plainclothes policemen watching our entrance. There was no point in getting the neighbours' house searched as well, so she turned back.

When the police had finished in my office, we walked down to their unmarked car, standing at an expired parking meter a few yards from the office. It had been ticketed, and I brightened up.

We drove the eight miles to Northwood, discussing gardens, the problems of buying new houses, and the weather. Assistant Commissioner Eames, it turned out, lived a short distance from us. As we drove up to the house I saw the second police car waiting at the corner, and as we pulled in to the drive, it came in behind us.

I introduced the policemen to Nonie, who offered them coffee, but by then they'd had enough. They obviously hadn't had any of their men going through the house before, as this search was thorough. I never bring work home, but Nonie had been freelancing as a writer so they went through her files with some care. One of them uncovered a novel I didn't know she was writing, and became engrossed in an article on abortion she had sold to a magazine.

Mr Eames concentrated on our bedroom, going through drawers, cupboards and my coat pockets. I tend to collect old cinema tickets and pieces of paper, so it took him some time.

While this was going on, the third policeman spent a long time by himself in our sitting room – so long that later I searched behind pictures and pelmets, and under chairs to find out if we'd been bugged, but if we had I never discovered it.

Finally, the police drove me to the main Salisbury charge office. One of them escorted me down into the concrete basement of the old building and took my fingerprints in triplicate.

Then I was led upstairs to the end of an echoing corridor, where a police photographer took full-face and profile photographs, with me holding up a sign saying 'Peter Niesewand'.

I asked if I could have copies of these. Christmas was coming up, and I thought they might make unusual cards.

'No,' said the photographer.

'I'll pay,' I offered.

9

'They're ours,' he said finally.

I saw the photographs nearly three months later, when I was detained without trial or charge. A Special Branch man showed them to me on the way to Gwelo Jail after I had told him the story of the first search. Actually, they would not have made good Christmas cards, because despite my supposedly unconcerned attitude, the tension showed in my face.

At the time, I believed that in terms of the State of Emergency Regulations, the police had the right to demand my fingerprints and take my photograph. I learned from my lawyer later that they had no such right, and should have applied to the Magistrates Court for an order to do so. A policeman told me subsequently it was doubtful they would have been granted one.

Finally, I was taken to Mr Eames's office, where he sat behind a big desk beneath a portrait of Queen Elizabeth: an ironic touch in a country which had rebelled against the Crown in 1965 and declared itself a Republic a few years later.

Again Mr Eames asked me to disclose my source of information, and again I refused, and signed a statement saying that I had refused.

Then he said: 'Well, we will not be detaining you at this stage.'

'I should hope not,' I said.

'But perhaps we'll see each other again.'

'No reflection on you, Mr Eames, but I hope not.'

He smiled. 'Perhaps socially,' he said, and I was driven back to my office.

chapter 2

There's not much to be said in favour of solitary confinement but it does give you time to think. I came to the conclusion that as a journalist, I had made two major mistakes.

In 1968, I was invited to take part in a Rhodesia Television discussion programme on the Freedom of the Press. It was RTV's first venture into controversy since UDI and, as it turned out, the series was abandoned shortly afterwards. White Rhodesians have always prided themselves on their independence of spirit – the dislike for the herd instinct shown, they believe, by people in countries such as Britain, and the determination to make up their own minds – so it's strange that for years, they allowed their lives and their thinking to be almost totally dominated by the Government. RTV, which is effectively state-controlled, decided that Rhodesians were not ready for controversial programmes, and the discussion series was taken off the air. Europeans accepted the decision passively.

Chairman of the programme was John Bishop, public relations officer for the University of Rhodesia and a freelance broadcaster. The panel was well-balanced: on the extreme right, was Ivor Benson, the South African propagandist who masterminded the campaign to persuade white Rhodesians to accept, firstly, the inevitability of a rebellion against Britain, and later that Ian Smith was a war hero and the saviour of his country, whose decisions should never be questioned by loyal men. Mr Benson's campaign worked brilliantly, and may well become a model for future generations of propagandists.

Next to him, also representing the right wing, was Harvey Ward, the head of the combined RTV/RBC newsrooms. Mr Ward seldom recalls the days when he was stringer for left-wing papers such as the *Daily Mail* in London. Indeed, listening to his later 'World Surveys' on the RBC, and his constant warnings against encroaching

Communism and the fellow-travelling Press, it's difficult to believe there ever was such a time.

Another freelance journalist, Reg Shay, and myself were left to defend the Press, and by Rhodesian definition, the political left-wing.

It was a heated discussion on predictable lines – Benson and Ward accusing the Press of deliberate distortion, Shay and myself denying this, and recalling Harvey Ward's old days as a stringer.

Then I made my first major mistake. I referred to white Rhodesian claims that the overseas Press was not giving a fair share of space to their attitudes, fears and hopes, and I agreed that this was broadly true. But the fault, I said, lay at the door of the Ministry of Information. When journalists tried to discover an official viewpoint, the Ministry proved unhelpful. Important queries on international and racial issues were usually ignored, or brushed aside with a 'no comment'. Yet the Ministry used up a lot of energy turning out Press Statements on matters which might interest an agricultural correspondent, but were useless to ordinary journalists. Of the pile of official releases delivered weekly, I said, a large proportion dealt with items such as the incidence of potato diseases, and helpful hints to farmers. Most journalists, myself included, merely dropped them into the wastepaper basket. If the Government felt misunderstood, it had only itself to blame, I argued.

The Information Ministry was furious. The Minister himself, languid, saturnine P. K. van der Byl – who despite his strong South African background has blossomed into a British-style aristocrat – drove down to the RTV studios to listen to a tape recording of the programme. He ordered that my name be stricken from the Press Distribution list, and for a year, I never received a single Information Ministry statement.

It is typical of Mr van der Byl's Ministry that it should concentrate on revenging itself on an individual. Although the Rhodesians had few friends, it was more important to the Ministry to stop sending me statements than to try, through me, to get their point of view across to the newspapers and broadcasting corporations I represented. Apart from the *Guardian* and the BBC, I worked for Agence France-Presse, United Press International, the London *Daily Mail*, the South African *Sunday Express* and the newspaper *Rapport* (which is a right-wing Sunday published in Afrikaans), and from time to time I was commissioned to report for the Canadian Broadcasting Corporation and the Australian Broadcasting Commission.

Professionally, I was not concerned which group was in power in

Rhodesia. My main task in that country was to act as a mirror, reflecting all points of view as accurately as I could. Occasionally, I would give my own assessment of a particular situation, but this represented perhaps five per cent of my output. I never joined any political organisation or took an active part in trying to influence events. I did not even enrol as a voter, believing that once you associate yourself emotionally with any political party, it is difficult then to stand aside and look objectively at it. The danger of close personal ties with groups or causes is that when a journalist is confronted with a story critical or damaging to these, he may feel inclined to indulge in a little self-censorship. This is particularly easy to do in Rhodesia, where journalistic competition is limited.

Rhodesia's main daily newspaper the *Rhodesia Herald* has fallen into the trap. The *Herald* proprietors, the Rhodesian Printing and Publishing Company, are anxious to purchase new printing equipment but are unable to do so while economic sanctions last and while there is a serious shortage of foreign currency. In addition the Rhodesian Printing and Publishing Company is operating at a steady profit and there are fears that the Government may step in and nationalise the company: so not surprisingly perhaps its policy is one of extreme caution. The *Herald*'s editor, Rhys Meier, is prepared actively to support settlement – apart from these reasons, no doubt he also genuinely fears eventual conflict between the five and a half million blacks and the quarter million Europeans, and sees an urgent need to provide jobs and security for African school leavers.

In his editorial columns Mr Meier has every right to espouse any cause he cares to name, but the *Herald*'s emotional involvement goes further than that. In 1971, during the final negotiations leading to the signing of the Independence Settlement Agreement between Britain and Rhodesia, the *Herald* instituted a policy of maintaining a 'low profile'. In other words, news reports which might damage the settlement chances were either played down or simply ignored.

The formation of the African National Council (ANC) – the group which spearheaded the black rejection of the 1971 terms – was reported briefly on an inside page of the *Herald*, despite its obvious significance. The ANC did not make the front page of the *Herald* until the Government launched a major attack on it. Many anti-settlement ANC statements were simply not printed by the paper. With this self-censoring outlook, one might reasonably expect Mr Smith's Government to have been well pleased with the *Herald*, but – in public at least – this was not so.

As soon as the Press starts retreating, so the authorities push their advantage. Publicly, Mr Smith's Government will not be content with anything short of unstinting praise, or as it's officially called, 'constructive criticism'.

In 1972, Des Frost, the chairman of the ruling Rhodesian Front, told the party's annual congress that he would like to see the Rhodesian Press nationalised, as he was tired of having to read left-wing propaganda every morning. Perhaps Mr Frost received a different edition of the *Herald* to the one which reached my home and office, but I have found no evidence to back up his complaint.

Privately, the Rhodesian Front sang a different tune. I learned from an RF backbencher that Rhys Meier was considered by the party to be 'the greatest editor in the history of this country', an accolade for which he has laboured.

Yet despite instances of private praise, it is useful for the Government to maintain the Press – local and international – as a whipping boy in the eyes of the ordinary white voter. If anything goes wrong, the Press can be blamed, along with the Communists and the United Nations. One might imagine that the mere fact of reading the *Herald* every day, and comparing it to the sinister newspaper of Government imaginings, would be enough to give white Rhodesians cause to examine the credibility gap. Perhaps few people read newspapers with any great concentration. Or perhaps – and I hope this is in fact the reason – many whites are merely confused because their only immediate point of comparison with the local Press is the output of the RBC and RTV combined newsrooms, which are effectively an extension of the Government.

For journalists not prepared to operate hand-in-glove with the Ministry of Information, there is little comfort. For journalists who criticise the Ministry, there is even less.

My television comments made me some powerful enemies. Apart from the Information Minister himself, I became aware of the active dislike of the then Secretary, Mr Leo Ross, and the Deputy Director, John Lewis.

I have only met Mr Ross once, face-to-face. In 1971, Agence France-Presse was in the process of negotiating a contract with the Information Ministry for the sale of a news service, and I accompanied one of the AFP executives during final meetings. I found Mr Ross to be a short, beetling man who scowled at me and refused to shake my hand when we were introduced. It was not a matter of great concern to me: AFP were entering into a commercial contract with Mr Ross's Ministry, and my part in the deal was merely to ensure that the Rhodesians received the best possible service. My office was to be the reception centre for telex radio transmissions emanating from Paris, and the signals would then be relayed to the Information Ministry's Press Section. My job was to see that the AFP service was received by them quickly and efficiently. The fact that Mr Ross did not like me personally was unimportant, so long as he paid the AFP bill.

I came into contact with Deputy Director John Lewis on a number of occasions, on none of which I found him impressive. A young trim man, dark-haired and not over-bright, he was alleged by his staff to be responsible for some of the stranger decisions of the Ministry. I should not be surprised if this was so. In November 1972, I was among a group of journalists in the Press Room of the Rhodesian Parliament, trying to persuade Mr Lewis to approach the Government and obtain clarification on the provisions of a lengthy new Bill, tabled that afternoon, which was to be rushed through all its Parliamentary stages the following day – the final day of the House sitting. Journalists were suspicious that, among other things, the Bill would effectively give the Government power to evict Asians and people of mixed blood from mainly-white suburbs.

For more than an hour, Mr Lewis refused point-blank to approach the Government for clarification. He said he did not understand what our hurry was. Why couldn't we wait a few days for an official reply, or perhaps see if the following day's rushed debate dealt with our queries? We tried to make Mr Lewis grasp that we were working for news agencies and daily papers, and that it was not unreasonable to seek urgent official guidance on complex matters, before writing our reports later that day. It would, we pointed out, avoid errors and misunderstandings. There was no expression on Mr Lewis's face as he listened to our arguments, and no hint of comprehension in his eyes. But perhaps he understood only too well: the Government wanted to rush the Bill through the House before the sixteen African MPs realised what was happening, and Mr Lewis didn't want them reading about its significance in the Press before the debate. I suspected that his job – typical of the Ministry – was not to give Information, but to suppress it.

P. K. van der Byl, Leo Ross and John Lewis – it was a trio unlikely to inspire journalists with confidence, but all were men of power and influence in Milton Buildings, the headquarters of Mr Smith's Government. For nearly three years, I believed that, although the

Information Ministry did not like me because of my television criticism of them, and because I did not rely sufficiently heavily on their Press Statements for my understanding of the Rhodesian situation, nevertheless, I had something of a friend in Ian Smith.

Mr Smith and I never met socially; only at formal or impromptu Press Conferences, but I had formed the impression that he did not dislike me, and that he rather enjoyed the odd probing question. Mr Smith made a name for himself when he came to power in the early 1960s by his handling of television interviews and conferences. He was a fairly skilled debater, and conveyed the impression of honesty and straight dealing. After UDI, the situation changed. It is difficult for a politician to score points during interviews in which tame, rehearsed questions are thrown at him, and not followed up. Mr Smith and his cabinet colleagues have had more than their fair share of this sort of programme, and it has left them mentally flabby. The Ministry of Information, in association with RTV, produced dozens of staged interviews, until even some white viewers who supported the Rhodesian Front found them cloying and unacceptable.

In May 1972, after black Rhodesians had rejected the independence settlement proposals signed by Mr Smith and British Foreign Secretary, Sir Alec Douglas-Home the previous November, the Rhodesian Prime Minister made it known he would welcome a televised Press Conference, with a small panel of journalists. Mr Smith had, it turned out, little to say. He wanted merely to project an image of himself as a strong, undeviating leader who, despite a minor setback, remained both trustworthy and in control.

The African rejection of the settlement had startled most whites, and even some of the black majority. A substantial body of opinion, myself included, had been taken in by the insistent propaganda of the Ministry of Internal Affairs that Africans in the designated tribal areas were largely content with their lot, and were prepared to leave politics to the white man. It was widely assumed that they would give an overwhelming 'yes' to the Pearce Commission when it sought their opinion on the settlement package.

But a body of right-wing Europeans had been startled by something apart from the black 'No' – the fact that Ian Smith, the same man who had unilaterally declared independence from Britain, could sign a settlement which, in their opinion, effectively sold out the white man to black majority rule.

In the opinion of the ultra-right, the African rejection of the

16

settlement was a stroke of extreme good fortune. Commander Chris Phillips of the Rhodesia National Party explained his relief in crude terms: 'The black kaffirs have saved us from the white kaffirs,' he said. The critics were not only from the ranks of other right-wing political organisations, but included leading members of Mr Smith's own Rhodesian Front.

Mr Smith worked hard in private to persuade his dissident colleagues that, of course, he had never had any intention of keeping to the multi-racial spirit of the settlement. He had merely signed the peace proposals in order to secure an end to economic sanctions. Once those were lifted and foreign exchange and investment was again coming into Rhodesia at an acceptable rate, the settlement could be forgotten. His assurances carried some weight.

At a report-back meeting in his constituency a few months later, RF backbencher Wickus de Kock said: 'When I first read the settlement terms, I nearly had a heart attack. But later I thought, well this is a package deal, and we have to compromise, so in the national interest we must accept it.'

Mr de Kock's transition from thrombosis-inducing disbelief to gracious acceptance appeared a little sudden, but clearly he had understood the Prime Minister's message: forget the details of the 1971 settlement. Once we've got rid of sanctions we can do what we like.

Mr Smith's disclaimers that he intended implementing the settlement terms fully could, naturally enough, be made only in private to selected individuals. For the ordinary, anxious white voter, the reassurance had to be oblique. A fighting Press Conference by the Prime Minister seemed to fit the bill nicely, and it was important that Mr Smith should emerge from the programme as an obviously strong and honest leader.

So RTV drew up a list of five journalists to ask the questions, Mr Smith approved it, and I found myself invited onto the panel. I researched and prepared a list of questions, which I was not required to submit in advance. On the morning of 8 May, I drove to Rhodesia Television where the programme was to be videotaped.

The panel seemed weighted in Mr Smith's favour: I was the only so-called 'left-wing' journalist to be invited; Rhys Meier, editor of the *Herald* was there, and so was Harald Pakendorf, editor of the right-wing weekly newspaper, the *Rhodesian Financial Gazette* which has links with the governing party. John Monks, staff correspondent for the London *Daily Express* – considered by the Rhodesians to be a

17

friendly British newspaper – had been asked, and so had Sandy Robertson whose *Sunday Mail* (a sister paper to the *Herald*) pretends to be left-wing but isn't. The sixth member of the panel was Harvey Ward, of the RBC/RTV newsroom.

In casual discussion while we waited, Harvey Ward, who along with the Board of Governors of the RBC and the ultra-right, seems to believe that Mr Smith is a liberal, mentioned that after the more serious questions had been dealt with, he planned asking about the high cost of extensions to the Prime Minister's official residence. So we agreed that Harvey would ask about the house, and I would ask about a racehorse given to Mr Smith by a South African financier.

The matter of the racehorse was, I thought, more interesting than the official residence controversy. He was given the horse, a two-year-old bay colt called French Moss, by a Mr Jaffee, a South African businessman, early in 1972. It was a generous gift, yet Mr Smith had been reticent about discussing it publicly.

In April 1972, the *Sunday Mail* asked him for comment, and Mr Smith replied: 'Who says I've got a horse?'

In fact, rather a lot of people said so, including the Jockey Club of South Africa who a few days earlier had granted the Prime Minister his racing colours, and had published the information in the Racing Calendar. We all presumed that Mr Smith did not plan running himself, and I hoped to elicit further details on the matter. As it turned out, I did not get round to it. Perhaps this was just as well – it would have compounded my second major mistake as a journalist in Rhodesia.

Mr Smith arrived for the videotaping shortly after 8 a.m. and walked straight to his seat in the studio. He began the conference by reading a prepared statement, which said that he would welcome constructive questions, consistent with the national interest, and that Rhodesians had to stick together in these troubled times. I was not among the first to ask questions, and was surprised to find that when I did, Mr Smith answered rudely. He was polite with the others, but I became his 'young friend' who knew all the answers, and who obviously hadn't been listening to his previous statements.

I was interested to see Mr Smith use this tactic. It was one he learned from South Africa's Prime Minister, John Vorster, who likes to pick on one journalist during a conference, and in his replies, try to show this man up as a fool. If asked a question, Mr Vorster replies with another, usually attacking, question. An unsuspecting journalist, confronted with such a tactic, tends to clam up. If he does, then Mr Vorster has won. His questioner looks silly, and remains silent for the rest of the interview. Mr Vorster looks strong and in charge. As it happens, I had watched the South African Prime Minister give a display of this tactic on the lawn of Mr Smith's official residence during a visit.

So when the Rhodesian leader tried it, and I was the target, I didn't feel unduly worried. It had become clear that Mr Smith had no special information to impart at this Press Conference, and was simply trying to project his image at my expense. It seemed to me that in these circumstances, the programme slipped from current affairs, into the realms of ordinary family entertainment, and I was entitled to defend myself against political manoeuvrings. Instead of shutting up and letting Mr Smith win by default, I asked more questions than I had originally planned, and the Prime Minister became increasingly agitated.

Towards the end, Harvey Ward got onto the matter of the extensions to the official residence. Why, he asked, had the cost been about £62,000 more than estimated? Mr Smith replied courteously that there had been a mistake in the original estimate. He explained that originally, the residence had only four bedrooms which was inadequate. When his family was at home, they took up all the available room, and there was not enough space for official visitors.

Mr Smith pointed out that it was, after all, a prestige residence which belonged to the nation. Extensions were undoubtedly needed. But the Prime Minister added, lest any blame be attached to himself, he had given orders that there should be no additions to the house until after economic sanctions were lifted.

'Regrettably, something else came into the picture, and that was security,' Mr Smith said. 'You see, things have changed. When I first moved into that residence, there was no security whatsoever. Those were happy days in Rhodesia, but the world has changed. Today we have to have security, not because I necessarily want it. Fortunately, this thing does not worry me a great deal, but I leave it to the people concerned, and for security reasons, additions had to be made to the residence.'

So I asked: 'Will two extra bedrooms make your residence more secure?'

Mr Smith stared at me in disbelief. 'What did you say?'

I repeated the question: 'Will two extra bedrooms make your residence more secure?'

I had never before seen Ian Smith lose his temper, but his face went white and he licked his lips. There was no mistaking the venom in his voice.

'Now as usual my friend here has got all the answers,' Mr Smith snapped. 'One room was built, you see, so he is twisting the facts, twisting the truth, Mr Chairman, and a man in his position should be more responsible, because that's a lie, you see, a blatant lie.'

Mr Smith went on at some length. The lie was two rooms, the truth was one extra room, and the explanation, it turned out, was that once builders come in and start working on improving the security arrangements (although I never did discover what security improvements had been made), they cause such disruption and mess that it is worth completing the entire job.

In the circumstances, I decided not to ask about his racehorse.

The programme ended soon after that, and Mr Smith left the studios without a word. It's not very pleasant being unpopular in a small country, and I expected to come under considerable social pressure because of the interview. But I was surprised at the reaction expressed to me.

Mr J. M. Helliwell, chairman of the RBC, who had pointedly ignored me before the taping of the conference, shook my hand warmly in congratulation. Others on the far-right were equally pleased, I attended a public meeting of the Candour League (an admirer of America's John Birch Society) two nights later, and the speaker said: 'Ladies and Gentlemen, we owe a debt of gratitude to Mr Peter Niesewand.' Everyone said: 'Here, here.'

The sudden leap from being a dangerous leftie to becoming the friend of the ultra-right was a little hard to take. Except for members of the Rhodesian Front and a sullen – but to my face, silent – section of the white population, a lot of people were glad that Mr Smith had lost his temper. The programme didn't provide very many answers, but at least some questions had been asked, and in the Rhodesian context, shielded from controversy and the rough-and-tumble of ordinary Western politics, this was quite a revolution.

Nearly a hundred whites wrote, phoned, or approached me in the streets about the programme, and only three of them wanted to know why I had been rude to the Prime Minister. They were not only supporters of the ultra-right, but moderates as well. It was my first indication of growing European discontent.

I was not at the time concerned for my future. I considered that Mr Smith had attacked me during the television programme merely for tactical reasons: he wanted to project an image. I had no idea that he actually disliked me intensely. In fact, it was not until late in 1972, when I received a report of a private conversation between Mr Smith and others, that I realised the extent of his feeling. Someone had mentioned my name. The Rhodesian Premier had flown into a cold rage, and denounced me at some length. 'His people' kept urging him to take action against me, Mr Smith said, and this was being done.

With enemies in the Ministry of Information and the Prime Minister's office, it was only a matter of time before I would be prevented from working in Rhodesia.

The Rhodesians began their campaign of intimidation in November with the police search of my office and home. Later the Government said unofficially that I was being followed by members of the Special Branch. This was not true: you can tell if you are being followed, and I was not.

After the November search, and the attempt to discover who had supplied me with information for the report on the military situation in Mozambique, I fully expected my sources to dry up, but surprisingly, I began receiving more information than ever before. Two days after the search, I was handed a genuine Official Secret: a three-page typewritten foolscap document stamped twice on every page with the state's green SECRET stamp.

It was a pretty dull secret, dealing with the report of a Rhodesian Front party caucus sub-committee on the expropriation of land in the Matetsi area of Rhodesia, near the Victoria Falls. This matter had been widely publicised already, and I couldn't even get a news story out of the document. But as it happened, a week before the November search, RTV had invited me to take part in another televised Press conference with Mr Smith. It seemed that the Secret document might come in useful if we could get the Prime Minister onto discussion of security matters, and the growing criticism that his Government was hiding unnecessarily behind a curtain of secrecy. Previously, Mr Smith had defended his administration against such charges, saying that they merely acted on the advice of their security chiefs, and were not using secrecy to withhold legitimate information from the public.

I hoped to get him to repeat this statement, and then produce the foolscap document, saying 'I have here an Official Secret, and I wonder if you could tell us why your security advisers suggested you give it this classification when it deals with the setting up of game hunting and photographic safaris in Matetsi? Could you say why this document deserves the green state SECRET stamp?'

I never got the chance to put this to Mr Smith. RTV withdrew the invitation to appear on the panel because of the police search, arguing that I might be detained between the time the programme was videotaped and its transmission, and that they would be guilty of contravening the Emergency Regulations if I then appeared on their screens. It was a thin argument, and they were obviously embarrassed. Subsequent inquiries showed that the Ministry of Information had suggested I be dropped from the panel, although Mr Smith himself denied all knowledge of this. The Prime Minister said he would have welcomed my presence on the programme, as it would have enabled him to show me up for what I was.

I made preparations for my sudden removal from the scene. I hired the best young lawyer in Salisbury, Anthony Eastwood, to look after my interests. We had tea in his offices on 22 November, shortly after the police search had ended. I outlined to him the courses of action I thought the Government would consider to get rid of me. Although I was born in South Africa, I had become a Rhodesian citizen by nationalisation at the age of sixteen. Mr Smith's government had since introduced legislation allowing them to deprive those not actually born in the country of their citizenship, and in 1972, the provisions of this Act had been widened to include people who, in the opinion of the Minister of Internal Affairs, had been 'disloyal to Rhodesia'. I told Anthony Eastwood I thought it was possible the Government might wish to move against me in this way, deprive me of my citizenship and then declare me a prohibited immigrant. The drawback to this was the fact that deprivation of citizenship tended to be a lengthy process, and I should certainly fight any such move by all means available to me. With appeals, and tribunals, the matter could be stretched out for two to three months, and although the Government would eventually get its own way, I would have time to sell my house and business, and clear up domestic and financial matters.

The second main possibility, I thought, was for the Government to detain me in terms of the nationwide State of Emergency Regulations. I was not a hero or a martyr, I said, and I had no political axes to grind. I thought that they might simply keep me in jail for about four weeks, and suddenly one morning offer to let me leave the country immediately providing I promised never to return. On the whole, this seemed their more likely course of action.

I spelled out to Anthony Eastwood the substance of my reports to the *Guardian* and the BBC on the military situation in Mozambique, and Rhodesia's involvement in it. At that stage, there had been no police or Government objections raised over the content of the reports, and I had merely been pressed to disclose my sources of information.

Anthony advised me that it was unlikely I could be compelled to identify my sources, even if I was brought before a magistrate and questioned on them, because the police search warrant provided me with the defence that to divulge such information might tend to incriminate me on a charge under the Official Secrets Act. Without this defence, thoughtfully provided by the police, any magistrate would be entitled to send me to prison for contempt of court for seven or eight days at a time, until either the authorities gave in, or I did.

I went to see my bank manager the following day, to arrange with him that my wife should take over the operation of my account should I suddenly be detained. He provided me with a yellow card, giving Nonie signing power, and I took this home to her for safe-keeping. If ever I was suddenly taken away, all she had to do was sign the card and insert the relevant date.

I wrote to overseas clients, telling them of the possibility of my detention, and outlining the emergency procedure which would come into effect. I had arranged with Ian Mills, the political corres- pondent of the *Rhodesia Herald*, that he should immediately move in to take over my business in such an eventuality. I didn't have to con- tact the Rhodesian clients of AFP and UPI who relied on my office as a reception and distribution centre for these agencies: they called me.

The RBC newsroom phoned in agitation to ask what would happen to these services in the event of my sudden departure. I assured them that contingency plans had been made, and that there would be absolutely no change as far as they were concerned. They wouldn't even know I'd gone. They seemed pleased.

Finally I contacted Thomas Cook's in Salisbury, through whom I received most fee and communications payments from British clients, and arranged that, in my absence, they would pay all monies received direct to Nonie.

Then there was nothing left to do but wait. It was coming up for Christmas, and neither Nonie nor I could shake the feeling that we were heading for a rough patch. The police search of my office and home was a topic of conversation at every party we attended, and we received several offers to send me cakes with files in them when I went to prison. A growing school of thought held that the search had been ordered by Mr Smith because he wanted to get me off the television Press conference panel. I didn't think this was true, but I did nothing to discourage the rumour.

I learned unofficially that the search had indeed been ordered by the Prime Minister's office, and it seemed to signal the beginning of the threatened Press purge.

chapter 3

Just before Christmas, the situation in Rhodesia changed suddenly. Unknown to the authorities, African nationalist guerillas had infiltrated into the north-east of Rhodesia from Mozambique six months earlier, and had been working among tribesmen in this remote area. Unlike previous infiltration attempts, this one secured the co-operation of ordinary Africans. The Rhodesians later claimed that the guerillas had succeeded purely by intimidation and the use of witchcraft. They had persuaded some tribal mediums – through whom the spirits of the ancestors were believed to speak – to back the guerilla cause, and influence the people to do the same.

No doubt, there is truth in both these Rhodesian allegations, but it is not the whole truth. Most Africans in the area had already been emotionally prepared to turn against the white man. If this was not so, the Rhodesians, who rely for between 80 and 85 per cent of their intelligence information on tribal informers, would surely have been tipped off about the presence of guerillas. Thousands of Africans knew they were there, but over a period of six months, not one man or woman came forward to say so.

Europeans in the area were too blind, and too over-confident, to discover for themselves that the situation had changed. The blame for this rests on the shoulders of the Ministry of Internal Affairs – the same Ministry which mistakenly persuaded the Rhodesian and British Governments, and many other people, that the Africans would accept the 1971 settlement terms by an overwhelming majority. Internal Affairs men hold regular meetings with tribal chiefs and elders, and find that the Africans are most respectful towards them, and always provide the required answer. This is perhaps not surprising when the Government has the power, and has used it in the past, to depose obstinate hereditary chiefs and take action against other dissidents. Chiefs receive a salary from the

Government, and most don't want to lose it. So if the Government wants a 'yes' answer, the chiefs will courteously provide it. Back home in the kraals and villages, the tribal leaders sing a different tune, and few Africans blame them for their official subservience.

One chief who went into a Salisbury township for a visit, was accosted by young and angry African men who demanded to know why he did not stand with his people. The Chief replied: 'My children, I am an old man, and the Government gives me money. Let me spend my last days in peace and comfort.' The young men left him alone, and went away.

The Internal Affairs Ministry has not been able to see that 'yes-men' do not necessarily represent the views of the majority. District Commissioners refuse to accept that the old tribal system is breaking down, and that despite white efforts to turn the tide, the days are long gone when the opinions of the tribesmen can be ignored. Whites aren't so interested in finding out what Africans think, as in telling them through the chiefs, what should be done. In this way, the chiefs have been turned from hereditary leaders who represent the black consensus view, to a political extension of the white executive, and the new system is not working.

The white Government has been faced with two alternatives: either face up to the reality of the situation and try to reach an honest accommodation with the Africans, or else try to change the reality by a show of white strength and determination. The Ministry of Internal Affairs, and the Rhodesian Government itself, has chosen the latter course.

The policy of 'Africans will do as they're told' has worked for generations, and they believe it still works. So in the second half of 1972, the Internal Affairs officials in the north-east went about their normal business confidently, and did not notice the absence of men in some villages. If they had, and if they had followed up this clear sign, they might have discovered that the men had been recruited for guerilla training in nearby Mozambique, or were helping carry arms across the border into Rhodesia and bury them in small caches over a wide area.

They never imagined Africans would turn against them so suddenly, and it came as a surprise when the guerillas finally announced their presence with an attack on Altena Farm in the European tobacco growing area of Centenary, and it became clear that they had massive tribal support.

I later found myself accused in court of aiding the guerillas by my reports for the *Guardian* and the BBC, and the Government hinted at a link between my work as a journalist and the guerilla offensive in the north-east.

As 1972 drew to a close, pressure on me began to mount, and as so often happens in Rhodesia, it came in the form of a spate of rumours impossible to check back to source. The rumours began in the farming district of Centenary, and although they could have been officially-inspired, I have no direct evidence of this. However, I appeared to be the target of a smear campaign.

I was a stringer for the BBC, and although the Corporation also subscribes to the world's major news agencies, people in Rhodesia tended to hold me personally responsible for their real, or imagined grievances against the BBC.

When rumours began circulating that the BBC had carried reports of Centenary farmers leaving their homes and fleeing to Salisbury because of the guerilla offensive, it seemed to many Rhodesians, both inside and out of Government, that this was my work. I received a number of calls asking what I meant by it, as it was untrue. I took the precaution of telephoning David Williams at the Ministry of Information to see if he could supply me with details of the alleged reports, as I had not sent them out but was apparently being blamed for them. The Ministry of Information employs a man to listen to BBC programmes and news bulletins and report daily to them, and Mr Williams said he would check on this matter. He phoned back later to say they knew nothing of such BBC reports. I also telexed Broadcasting House in London, asking the BBC to carry out a thorough check of all External Service transmissions over the period in question, and again received a negative reply.

Yet the rumours continued to circulate. I spent a fruitless morning telephoning Centenary farmers to see if any of them could say where they had heard the allegations. They all knew what I was talking about, but none had first-hand knowledge of such reports. The closest I came to an answer was in conversation with a farmer who had heard the allegations in a bar, from a man who said he had personally listened to the offending reports. When pressed, the farmer admitted he could not be sure the transmission was alleged to have come from the BBC. It could have been Radio Zambia, or perhaps it had really been a report carried in one of the British papers.

The rumours gathered strength. The Johannesburg *Sunday Express*, on 31 December, said a BBC report that the morale of troops

27

and farmers in the Centenary district was low had 'caused anger' in Rhodesian army circles. The paper quoted a Rhodesian army officer as saying: 'I don't know what the hell they are trying to get at. Our spirit has never been better. Are they deliberately trying to undermine us? If so, the BBC should be told that we are in excellent fighting spirit.'

January 1973 was a busy news month. The guerilla offensive in the north-east increased in intensity, with new attacks on white farmsteads in Centenary, and the first civilian deaths being recorded. On 9 January, Premier Smith announced the closure of the border with Zambia, as a reprisal for Zambian assistance to black nationalist guerillas operating against the South. Mr Smith said the border would remain closed until he received satisfactory assurances from President Kenneth Kaunda that guerillas would no longer be permitted to use his country as a springboard into Rhodesia.

It was a major mistake by Mr Smith – compounded by the fact that he had neglected even to notify friendly South Africa of his intentions, although the closure of the Zambian border meant a sudden halt to South African trade with the black-ruled north.

Inside Rhodesia, the border closure meant that Zambia was inextricably linked in white minds with the guerilla offensive in the north-east. Europeans were led to believe that the guerillas had come from Zambia, so they naturally expected any assurances obtained from President Kaunda to result in almost immediate peace in the Centenary area. In fact, the Centenary guerillas infiltrated from, and had been trained in, the Mukumbura district of north-western Mozambique, and most had not been to Zambia at all.

Mr Smith reopened the Zambian border twenty-five days later, claiming he had received satisfactory assurances from the north, and immediately lost considerable face when President Kaunda denied this, refused to reopen his side of the frontier, and made plans to divert Zambian trade through other countries. Worst of all, the security situation in the north-east continued to deteriorate.

The *Guardian* carried a report of mine headlined 'Smith in the fool's role', which quoted Pat Bashford, President of Rhodesia's multi-racial Centre Party, as saying: 'It makes Mr Smith look a right Charley.'

I wrote: 'The image of a strong white Government bringing a recalcitrant black neighbour to heel is rather dented by the refusal of that neighbour to enjoy the rewards of their changed behaviour.'

It appeared, I said, that Mr Smith had suffered a major strategic and diplomatic defeat.

With the Ministry of Information attitude towards me chilling noticeably, two errors were made by clients of mine which hastened the approach of official winter. Mistakes happen in the best organised households: for me, their timing was unfortunate.

A sub-editor for United Press International in London received a report of mine quoting the ultra-right wing party, the United Front, as calling for a tougher line against Zambia, including the cutting off of hydro-electric power to the north from the jointly-owned Kariba dam on the Zambezi river frontier. The power station is on the Rhodesian bank, and such a cut-off move would be easy for Mr Smith. The United Front is a small, and internationally little-known organisation, so the London sub-editor thought I must have meant the governing party, and he substituted 'Rhodesian Front' for 'United Front'.

The report was received simultaneously in my office, and the RBC newsroom. Harvey Ward was on the phone to me while it was still coming over, and I was on telex to London within three minutes. The report was, of course, corrected swiftly, but I was not altogether surprised to receive a call from David Williams the following day asking why I'd quoted the governing party as calling for the cutting off of Kariba power to Zambia. I explained what had happened, and that a correction had been made, and I apologised. Mr Williams – a former newspaperman himself – was sympathetic. 'I hoped you'd say that,' he told me. But for Mr Smith, and other Information Ministry officials, it was one more strike against me.

I was also blamed for an error made by a telex operator working for a completely separate organisation. Three Africans had appeared before a magistrate in a small Rhodesian town, charged with aiding terrorists, and the case was held 'in camera'. What this usually means is that the Press are allowed into court to 'see that justice is done', but members of the public are excluded. In return, the Press are ordered not to divulge information such as the names of the accused, the names of their contacts and so on. The Rhodesians hope in this way to keep the guerilla tacticians guessing on which of their men have been captured, which have been killed, and which have simply disappeared.

In the Rhodesian context, it was a straightforward story, but I missed it entirely. My contact system failed, and as I was not alerted to the fact of the trial, I did not write a story about it.

But a competing agency in Salisbury did. IANA (Inter Africa News Agency) wrote an accurate account, and handed it through to their telex room. The telex operator who sent it out mistakenly typed 'Americans' instead of 'Africans'. So the report of three Americans on secret trial in Rhodesia for aiding terrorists went to the South African Press Association in Johannesburg, where Reuters picked it up and transmitted it to London. The BBC used it in three consecutive news bulletins. When the error became known, everyone sent out corrections. Meanwhile, my telephone rang constantly with the RBC and others wanting to know what I meant by sending out this report I'd never even seen. Curiously the Ministry of Information did not phone, so I called Mr Williams and explained what had happened. He did not seem particularly interested.

In ways both roundabout and direct, the Government made sure they let me, and my clients, know that they objected to me personally.

On 23 January, a BBC Current Affairs television programme 'Midweek', asked if I could film a documentary on the security situation, and I wrote immediately to David Williams: 'I do not think it would be possible to deal adequately with this complex and emotive situation without Government assistance and to this end I ask your help.'

I requested permission to take a camera team into the areas where security forces were operating, and said I would be happy to be accompanied by an Information Ministry official, or a member of the security forces, as I realised that I might not be allowed to film certain aspects of operations. I also asked if I might interview the Prime Minister for the programme.

Mr Smith rejected the requests out of hand, but the Government then underlined the fact that the refusal was based on personal dislike. Although the BBC had been declared *persona non grata* in Rhodesia, staff correspondents were occasionally allowed in for specific purposes, providing they received prior Government approval. The BBC's new Southern Africa man, John Osman, had been given permission to fly up to Salisbury for a few weeks, and he arrived only hours after the Rhodesians had rejected my request. David Williams telephoned Mr Osman on arrival, and – unasked – offered him the facilities denied me: an interview with the Prime Minister, and permission to shoot some film in the north-east.

I can't say I minded especially. The BBC got the facilities they wanted which was the important thing, and although I got another snub, I was used to working without official cooperation and it made little practical difference.

The Ministry of Information then began neglecting to give me official Press Statements, particularly over weekends when the normal messenger service was not operating, and the duty Press officer had to telephone individual journalists and organisations. However, I had established a reasonably efficient intelligence system, and even if the Ministry withheld specific statements from me, they were usually on my desk within twenty minutes of release. This made the Ministry angry.

On the last day of January, Mr Smith held a general Press Conference in the Ministry of Information's television studio just outside the city. Although no one had specifically invited me, I felt sure this was an oversight and went along with notebook and tape recorder to join the other seventy or eighty journalists assembled there. Ministry officials did not greet me with great warmth, but didn't stop me going in.

We extracted from Mr Smith two fairly significant admissions: he agreed that tribal assistance for guerillas in the north-east might in some way be connected with grievances against the white Government, and he admitted that new regulations, allowing entire communities to be fined by civil servants for the suspected offences of individuals, did not apply only to tribesmen but could also be used against white Rhodesians.

The Collective Punishment Regulations had been introduced with a Ministry of Information fanfare claiming that they were aimed at the tribal areas, where villagers were aiding subversion, and that the principle of community fines was traditional in African life. The Ministry also indicated that the tribal leaders had asked for collective punishments to be introduced, and would be responsible for carrying them out.

As it turned out, the Ministry could hardly have been more incorrect. Africans I spoke to knew nothing about a tradition of collective punishments. They said that tribal custom allowed an accused individual to be tried by an entire village, but any punishment was borne by the individual himself. The Collective Punishment Regulations were not to be carried out by tribal leaders, either, but by white Provincial Commissioners belonging to the Internal Affairs Ministry.

And finally, at his Press conference, Mr Smith admitted that the

Collective Punishments, imposed without trial or charge by civil servants, could be turned against groups of white Rhodesians too. Mr Smith did not claim that this was part of the European tradition, and I could not think of a precedent in civilised Western society since the days of the Third Reich, but he said rather snappily that people had to decide whether they were on the side of the law-breakers and the revolutionaries, or whether they supported law and order.

After the conference, John Osman and I returned to my office and wrote the initial stories, then made plans for shipping BBC Television film to London the following day, as he and other journalists were to be taken on a Government facility trip to the Centenary district. I had not been included in the invitation, but would not have gone even if asked: there was no point in two men from the same office being away for a day on the same story, and leaving the main office unmanned.

I was therefore a little surprised to receive a strange telephone call from John Morton, the Chief Press Officer at the Ministry of Information. John Morton and I have always got on well. In the early 1960s, he flew out from England with his family to join the *Rhodesia Herald*. At the time, I was working for the *Herald* and was sent to Salisbury Airport to welcome them in and see them installed in temporary accommodation provided by the Company. It was a sad family group that came off the aircraft. The flight had been long and uncomfortable, and the children had been sick. But the Mortons settled in, and after a year or two of struggling along on the low *Herald* salaries, John joined the Ministry of Information. Although he never said so to me, I sensed he was uncomfortable in his position of official 'no commenter', yet there was apparently nowhere else he could go in Rhodesia to be offered better work and the same money. He had his family, and security, and comfort, to think of, and I couldn't blame him.

On this afternoon, however, John Morton had been given a disagreeable task.

'Hello Peter,' he said. 'There's a facility trip going up to Centenary tomorrow morning, and up to Chirundu (on the Zambian border) on Friday.'

'Oh,' I said, 'that's very interesting.'

'Yes,' said John Morton, 'and I've been instructed to tell you you're not invited.'

I felt my anger rising. 'Well then, don't waste my time by telephoning me,' I said, and put the phone down.

I waited a moment or two before calling David Williams to protest about 'telephonic nose-thumbing'. It was, I suggested strongly, a juvenile tactic by a Government Ministry. As usual, Mr Williams knew nothing of the matter, but said he would make inquiries. He did not call me back.

That weekend, Saturday 3 February, the Rhodesian Government cut its losses and reopened the Zambian border, claiming victory. The Press Statement announcing this was not delivered to my office, and the duty Press Officer did not telephone me. There were two other important statements issued at about the same time. One told of another clash between security forces and guerillas, and the other gave background information to guerilla operations in the north-east. I received the statements through unofficial channels at the time they were officially released, so I was not inconvenienced, although I made a note to contact Mr Williams after the weekend.

On Monday morning, I received well-sourced information that the security forces had sealed off the Chiweshe Tribal Trust Land, which lies south of the Centenary area, and that schools, churches, shops and even some hospitals had been closed. No reason was given for the action, nor did the authorities say when the restrictions would be relaxed. Strangers in the area were ordered to leave; cars and buses were searched. It looked like a variation on the Collective Punishment theme, as guerillas had received support from many tribesmen in Chiweshe, and the Government apparently thought that infiltrators were still being sheltered and aided there.

I was satisfied that my information was correct, but I did not use it immediately. Instead, I asked the Information Ministry for comment. The Ministry then telephoned other journalists in Salisbury, reminding them that penalties for 'rumour-mongering' included several years' imprisonment, and saying that 'in the national interest' the information on Chiweshe should not be used.

I heard of these warnings to others that afternoon, but no Information official phoned me asking me not to use the story, and I received no reply to my request for comment.

It was clear that I was being set up for some Government action, but I felt that I should ignore such intimidatory tactics, so I went ahead and filed the reports. As far as I know, no other journalist did so at that time.

I also phoned Mr Williams to complain about the Ministry's failure to send me the weekend Press Statements on the reopening of the Zambian border and the security situation. He didn't know anything about it, he said, but in reply to questions, agreed that my name was not, in fact, on a special weekend list for receiving such releases, and that he would see I was included in future.

The following weekend, when again I had not officially been sent Saturday statements, I made an early morning telephone call of protest to Mr Williams at his home. The weekend after that I protested again, wondering aloud who I should buy a drink for to get my name on the list. He said he would personally write it in without delay. The following weekend, I was in solitary confinement in Gwelo Jail, and my name had been permanently removed from all Ministry distribution sheets.

In the last few days of working in Rhodesia, relations with the Ministry were particularly unhappy. I learned that the Prime Minister had asked RTV to arrange another television Press conference, with five or six invited journalists asking the questions. The arrangements were made under a veil of unnecessary secrecy, but I heard about them fairly quickly. I was not one of those invited, but to cheer myself up, I phoned John Morton and explained that I was preparing my questions for the television Press conference which was being recorded at RTV at 8.15 a.m. the following morning. I said it occurred to me that I should also set up facilities for broadcasting extracts to the BBC in London, and would like to know the embargo time for the programme.

There was a long silence, then Mr Morton said he would call me back. He did so within five minutes.

'I have been instructed to tell you that there is no Press conference at RTV tomorrow morning,' he said.

'Want to bet?' I asked.

'I am not a betting man,' he replied.

I telephoned RBC/RTV headquarters and asked for permission to record the conference at 8.15 the following morning. They agreed almost immediately, but perhaps no one had thought to tell them it was a secret.

At the conference, Premier Smith claimed the reopening of the Zambian border was a victory for Rhodesia. He also indicated that it would have no effect on the guerilla situation in the north-eastern district. None of his questioners asked him to reconcile the two statements.

The Ministry of Information collection of 'evidence' against me was swelled by an interview I recorded for the BBC with the leaders

34

of a pro-settlement African group, the African Settlement Convention. The Convention came into being early in 1973, but its black organisers explained they had actually been working quietly in African areas for some months. The Convention handed out a number of extremely impressive documents, including a Constitution, and a lengthy explanation of why the black majority should now accept the independence settlement terms. The Convention said it had already received the support of about 10,000 African business and professional men throughout Rhodesia, although it had not yet begun enrolling members, and curiously, did not have the names of those who had expressed support. What the Organisation did have, however, was a fair amount of financial backing – sufficient to pay for rooms in one of Salisbury's prestige office blocks, and the professional typing and duplicating of their documents.

I was initially interested in four aspects of their operation: who was the author of their documents, who was giving them financial backing, how precisely had they counted 10,000 African supporters in the business and professional field, and why they had not enrolled these people as members, or even bothered to collect their signatures.

I was not able to get satisfactory answers. The documents were extremely erudite, and included references to 'G. K. Chesterton's little book on St Francis of Asissi'. The Convention insisted that a committee of four Africans had been the authors. It is usually easy to spot the work of any committee, black or white. The Convention's Constitution was the work of a committee, and read like it. Their lengthy explanation of why the settlement proposals should be accepted appeared to be the work of one rather intellectual individual, and I suspected he could be found in the leadership of a white pro-settlement body in Salisbury. I thought I recognised the style.

On the question of financial backing, the Convention leaders were unhelpful, although they did agree that European money was involved.

I was puzzled by their explanation of how they had managed to get 10,000 Africans to support their aims. They said they had held a series of meetings in hotels and halls in different parts of Rhodesia, to each of which they invited about 120 selected African business and professional men.

I asked if they had received official permission to hold these meetings. No, they replied, this was not necessary because they had limited their numbers to 120 at a time. I was intrigued by this reply because in terms of Rhodesia's State of Emergency Regulations a

35

gathering of more than three or four people for a political purpose requires not only prior authorisation by the police, but the conveners have to insure any hired hall or room against riot and damage – an expensive business. The Settlement Convention wanted me to believe that they had managed to hold a series of illegal meetings in different parts of Rhodesia, without this coming to the notice of the authorities, a claim I considered unlikely. Nor were the organisers altogether clear on their reasons for failing to get the names or signatures of the 10,000 Africans who, they said, wanted the 1971 proposals implemented without delay.

I taped an interview for the BBC, and airfreighted it to London without comment. It was broadcast over the African Service, and was monitored by the Rhodesian Government, who were not pleased.

A few days later, I spoke to leaders of the African Businessmen's Association in Salisbury. They said they had never heard of the Settlement Convention, and had no knowledge of any pro-settlement meetings held in the capital or elsewhere which could be linked with the organisation.

Mr Smith's Government was anxious to convince the world that the black majority had changed their minds over their earlier rejection of the settlement, but the African Settlement Convention, for all its good intentions, appeared to deal a blow to their campaign.

The last straw which decided the Rhodesian authorities to detain me without trial was even more curious. Rumours flashed around the African townships of Salisbury that white soldiers of the Rhodesian Light Infantry had raped some African women in the Chiweshe Tribal Trust Land, which was still a 'closed area' by order of the security forces.

I tried to check out the rumours with bodies such as the Salvation Army, which runs schools and hospitals in Chiweshe, but without success. As a matter of routine, I phoned the Information Ministry, told them of the rumours, and asked for an official comment. I emphasised the importance of the matter, particularly in view of the currency being given to the reports in the townships. Three times within as many days, I telephoned the Ministry to ask for comment on similar Chiweshe rumours, but I received no direct response.

In Milton Buildings, near the statue of Rhodesia's founder, Cecil John Rhodes, my requests enabled senior Information Ministry officials to go to Mr Smith's office and report that Peter Niesewand was passing round stories that white troops were raping Africans.

36

Information Secretary Leo Ross also advised the Government that my detention without trial or charge would not have serious international repercussions, as I was not well liked by my colleagues.

In his first-floor office, Mr Smith considered all the Information Ministry's reports, and said 'Right!'

Two weeks after my detention, John Morton phoned my wife. A Zambian Government official had been reported as saying that white Rhodesian troops had raped African women in Chiweshe. Morton said: 'Our reply to this is that the remarks are too fatuous to be taken seriously.'

'Well, what do you want me to do?' Nonie asked, bewildered.

'You really ought to know,' said Morton.

'I can't think why,' Nonie replied. 'No story was ever sent out from Peter's office about it.'

She was perfectly correct. The Chiweshe reports had been unsubstantiated as far as I was concerned, and I had not referred to them in any news story or feature article. After unsuccessful preliminary investigations, I had simply put in a query to the Information Ministry, and there, for me, the matter rested.

chapter 4

On Monday, 19 February, I failed to keep an appointment, and I had cause to regret this later. It was not written down in any diary or notebook because – with an informer working out of my office – I carried sensitive information in my head. On this day, I had a sudden urge to complete all outstanding work, so I stayed in my office through lunch hour, writing a feature on the guerilla war for an American magazine. My meeting was to have been with a man I had known for some years – a person who I would reasonably have expected to know of my impending detention, and would almost certainly have tipped me off.

But I stayed in working. I've wondered since then what I would have done had I been warned in advance of the Government's intentions. An aircraft was leaving for South Africa that night – would I have been aboard? Or would I have stayed and allowed the authorities to take whatever action they wished?

On Monday, the Detention Order was signed by the Minister of Justice, Law and Order, Mr Desmond Lardner-Burke, sending me to Gwelo Jail, 182 miles south-west of the capital.

That night, the authorities experienced their first difficulties, when they found it was not easy to get senior Special Branch men to come and arrest me. I learned later that a number of men had been contacted between the hours of 9 p.m. and 11 p.m., and had refused to take part in the detention. It was well known to the Special Branch that I was not a security risk, and when Mr Smith decided to remove me from circulation, he disregarded the advice of his top security officials, and acted in accordance with the recommendations of the Ministry of Information.

At 11.30 p.m. on Monday night, the telephone rang at the home of Geoffrey Quick, a young British-born policeman, ordering him to report to the police headquarters at 5.30 a.m. He was not given the reasons for the order. Another junior Special Branch officer, Brian Oberholser, received the same instructions, as did a young, dark-haired woman, Helen Bryce. Mrs Bryce had previous experience in detentions without trial: in 1972, as Miss Helen Pronk, she was in the police party which arrested former Rhodesian Prime Minister Garfield Todd and his twenty-eight-year-old daughter Judy, and took them to solitary confinement in separate prisons.

The three reported to the Railway Avenue headquarters before dawn, and were told of their assignment. Geoff Quick was given the November police 'mugshots' of me, and Brian Oberholser placed the Detention Order in his black briefcase. All it needed to become effective was for him to insert the date and the time it was served on me, and sign it, with Quick acting as witness. Helen Bryce's job was to cope with Nonie if she became hysterical, as wives and families sometimes do when the police arrive to take their men away to prison without trial or charge.

The arresting detail then drove through the empty streets to Northwood in an unmarked grey Alfa Romeo – one of the batch of sanctions-busting car kits assembled in Rhodesia – and arrived at our home just after 6.30 a.m. Nonie had been woken early by the hungry crying of our baby. Padding through the house in her dressing gown, she prepared Oliver's bottle and brought him through to our bedroom where he finished it and lay playing. Then she went outside to collect the morning newspaper and gave it to me. She left the front door wide open as it was a warm sunny morning.

Nonie was laying the breakfast table, when she looked up and saw the two young men and the woman standing at the open front door watching her. She thought immediately that they were members of the Jehovah's Witness sect: they did not look like police to her. Geoff Quick wore an apricot-coloured shirt, Brian Oberholser had a pink shirt, and both carried black briefcases. Helen Bryce stood in the rear, her face composed sympathetically.

Quick spoke: 'Is Peter Niesewand here?'

'Yes,' said Nonie. 'Just a minute.'

She walked through to the bedroom and said, 'There are two men and a woman at the front door who want to speak to you. Who are they?'

I said: 'Probably the police.'

I put on a white towelling dressing gown, and carried Oliver through to the hall where the three stood.

'Hello,' I said, 'Can I help you?'

'Are you Peter Niesewand?' asked Geoff Quick.

'That's right.'

He introduced himself and his colleagues. 'We are from the CID, and we'd like to speak to you.'

'Come in,' I said, and led them into the lounge. 'Please sit down.'

Brian Oberholser immediately opened his briefcase and brought out a roneoed piece of paper. Quick watched me, and Mrs Bryce looked interestedly around the room.

Oberholser began talking, but his voice was not steady. 'I have here an order in terms of the Emergency Powers Regulations' . . . and I knew that I was being detained . . . 'The Minister of Law and Order has decided that it is in the interests of public safety or public order to make an Order against you.'

I couldn't think of very much to say, so I said: 'Gracious.'

Nonie came into the lounge, having dressed quickly, and he continued: 'The making of this Order is based on a belief that you are likely to commit, or to incite the commission of, acts in Rhodesia which would endanger the public safety, or disturb or interfere with the maintenance of public order.'

I said: 'Where am I going to be held?'

'In Gwelo Jail,' Oberholser replied.

Nonie asked: 'What's happening?'

'I'm being detained without trial in Gwelo Jail,' I told her. She took Oliver from me and walked quickly out of the lounge, with Mrs Bryce close behind.

The policewoman caught up with her at the end of the passage. 'Is there anything I can do to help you Mrs Niesewand?' she asked.

'Just keep out of my way,' Nonie said, and went into the bedroom.

I said to Quick and Oberholser: 'Can I offer you some tea or coffee?' They looked at each other.

'Thank you,' said Quick. 'Coffee would be fine.'

'I'll organise it,' I said, but went through to the bedroom. Mrs Bryce was hovering indecisively outside the door. 'Excuse me,' I said as I passed her and went in to Nonie, shutting the door.

She was sitting on the bed, holding Oliver, and crying. I felt numb as I sat beside her. 'Why?' she asked me. 'Why?'

'It's only a game,' I said.

After a few minutes I went out to organise the coffee and found Quick, Oberholser and Bryce grouped uncomfortably together round the bedroom door.

'Coffee?' I said to Helen Bryce.

'I don't think so,' she replied.

Later I dressed and Quick said: 'We have orders to search your house and your office.'

'Have you a search warrant?'

'No,' he said. 'We don't need one. I must also tell you that you were a detainee from the moment you were served with the Order. You are allowed to speak to your wife, but you cannot speak to anyone else, and you are not allowed to use the telephone.'

'Can my wife phone my lawyer?'

'Yes, if she wants to.'

Oberholser stood with an open notebook and ballpoint pen, taking down everything I said, including instructions I gave to Nonie, asking her to tell other journalists of my detention, and to advise my mother – who was on holiday at the South African coast – not to come back early on my account.

Nonie phoned Anthony Eastwood at his home, and read him the Detention Order. He told her he would meet me either at my office, or at the Police Headquarters before I was taken to Gwelo.

Quick said to me: 'He won't be allowed to talk to you at the charge office.' Then he noticed our telephone directory had the names of friends and relatives written on the cover. 'I think we'll take that,' he said.

They began the search, going thoroughly through drawers and cupboards, rediscovering Nonie's half-written novel and copies of articles she had completed. At the back of a drawer in the spare room they found a small plum-coloured box and opened it with interest. It contained miniatures of the medals Nonie's late father had won in the Second World War. He had been in the 237 Rhodesian Squadron of the Royal Air Force – the same squadron in which Ian Smith served. In fact, her father had been one of those who carried Mr Smith from the shattered cockpit of his Hurricane when he crashed at the end of the military runway. Mr Smith's poor airmanship nearly cost him his life, and he spent months in hospital recovering and undergoing plastic surgery. It was on such incidents that Mr Smith's reputation as a war hero was founded, and accounts no doubt for the paucity of detail on his wartime exploits.

Quick and Oberholser examined the box of medals. Nonie said: 'They're my father's medals from World War Two. He was away for seven years fighting for freedom and democracy. It doesn't seem to have done much good.'

Oberholser looked incuriously at her.

The policemen enjoyed a laugh as they looked through my chest of drawers and discovered a Valentine's Day card Nonie had sent me. They were also amused when I packed a bag to take to prison and included a book on Yoga.

I wasn't sure what to take to jail, and Oberholser and Quick were of little help. They suggested a pack of soap flakes so I could wash my clothes. 'Better take some jerseys,' added Quick. 'It will be winter in three months, and it gets cold in Gwelo.'

Nonie asked: 'Are you a Detective-Inspector?'

'No,' said Quick. 'I haven't risen to those dizzy heights yet.'

When I had finished packing, they came and searched the bag. Nonie organised breakfast for me, but my stomach had tightened and I could not eat.

I said goodbye to my baby son, and Nonie took him across to the neighbours. When she returned she picked up a book and said: 'Why not take this to jail? It's about life in a Russian detention camp.' She handed me Koestler's *Darkness at Noon*. I was cheered by her spirit, but the conditions and discipline in a Rhodesian prison were a mystery to me, and I doubted they would allow me to keep the book. Indeed, I thought it would probably antagonise them, so I left it at home. Nonie stayed at the house to make some telephone calls, and I left with the Special Branch trio for my office, where she would meet us later.

As we drove into Salisbury, I reflected about Desmond Lardner-Burke, and Gwelo. Nonie was born in this small midlands town, unkindly described by critics as 'a layby with lights'. She and her family lived near the Lardner-Burkes for some years and were on friendly terms. When Nonie and I were married in 1969, we had a small wedding with about thirty guests, including Desmond Lardner-Burke and his kind and gracious wife, Maisie.

At the reception, Mr Lardner-Burke drew me aside: 'Take care of her, won't you?' he said.

'Of course, Minister.'

'If you don't I'll have you restricted.' I looked at him, amused, expecting him to laugh, but he didn't. As it happened, I did take care of my wife, so instead of restricting me, he had me detained.

I subsequently met the Lardner-Burkes socially on two or three occasions. Nonie and I were invited to a dinner party at their home in December 1971, held to welcome Lardner-Burke's son David and his wife Virginia, who were on holiday from Britain. David Lardner-Burke is a senior member of the Anglo-Rhodesian Society, and despite his public criticism of life in permissive, socialist England, has lived and worked there for many apparently happy years, returning to Rhodesia only for short holidays.

This was one such occasion. After supper, Desmond Lardner-Burke stood up to propose a toast to his son and daughter-in-law. He spoke of the splendid work David was doing in the Anglo-Rhodesian society, especially in counteracting the lies and distortions of the overseas Press. Every eye was fixed on me as the Minister spoke, and I murmured a quiet 'Here, here,' but I couldn't help thinking it was strange behaviour on the part of someone who was, after all, my host.

On another occasion, we met on neutral ground, and argued quite heatedly about censorship, the permissive society and national service. On the latter issue, I felt on particularly secure ground, as I had done my required national service in the Rhodesian army, while as far as I knew, the Minister had not donned a uniform in his life, not even during the war, and could not therefore speak with authority on the character-building properties of spit-and-polish and route marches. Although I did not underline this aspect of the case, I enjoyed the discussion. Mr Lardner-Burke apparently did not. After my detention, his daughter Cherry was asked by friends why this action had been taken against me. It was the first she had heard about it, but she said: 'I'm not surprised. He was *very* rude to Daddy.'

Desmond Lardner-Burke is a stern-faced man with white hair, glasses and a high opinion of himself, who always wears a rose or a carnation in his button hole. He is a firm advocate of censorship, an opponent of the permissive society, including long hair, and I once listened to him preach a lunchtime sermon from the pulpit of the Anglican cathedral in Salisbury in which he took as his lesson a reading from the Bible: 'In my father's house are many mansions. I go to prepare a place for you.' Mr Lardner-Burke wove around this an argument in favour of racial segregation, and clearly expected to be in a whites-only mansion in heaven some day.

I did not believe him to be a particularly clever man, and I also had information that – like most members of the Rhodesian cabinet – he was dominated by Premier Smith. Many decisions, including my detention, were taken by the Prime Minister himself, and Mr Lardner-Burke was merely instructed to carry them out.

As we entered the city centre, I said to the Special Branch: 'I know how to get my revenge on Desmond Lardner-Burke.'

'How?' asked Quick, interested.

'When I get out,' I said, 'I am going to reveal to the world that every morning he drinks a glass of salt water through his nose.'

The car rocked with laughter.

'Does he really?' asked Quick.

I nodded. 'He says it clears his tubes.'

Quick said: 'Well, that's not his only trouble. I heard this morning that he has gout, and was having difficulty putting his shoes on.'

'How terrible,' I said, and the atmosphere in the car became quite jolly, considering I was on my way to solitary confinement.

We stopped in at the office for the second part of the search, and this time the Special Branch packed cardboard cartons full of documents, notebooks, and scores of recorded tapes of interviews I had done for the BBC, to take them away for examination.

My mouth and throat were dry, and I had to struggle to stop myself gagging, so I made some coffee.

Nonie arrived at the office and when she was in, Oberholser locked the door. A few minutes later, there was a loud knocking and the Special Branch opened it cautiously.

I looked through the crack and said: 'Hello Anthony.' Then to the police: 'It's my lawyer, Anthony Eastwood.' Rather grudgingly they let him in and relocked the door.

Anthony was splendid. His face was hard and his eyes were glittering, and he smiled. He asked the names of the Special Branch team, looked at the Detention Order, and turned to me as I perched on the edge of a table.

'You are going to be taken to Gwelo Jail, where you'll be held indefinitely. You are entitled to appeal to the Minister of Law and Order within seven days, asking him to revoke the Order.'

'I want to use every appeal facility that's open to me,' I said.

'Fine,' said Anthony. 'We'll also put in an application for your case to be reviewed by the Review Tribunal within three months. You will be subject to prison discipline, although you are not a convict and are not required to do any labour at all. You are entitled to at least a letter a week, and a minimum of one visit a week, but I suggest Nonie gets in touch with the Gwelo Prison superintendent to see what he will allow.'

Then he swung round to the policemen who had slowed down their search and were listening, it seemed to me, a little apprehensively.

'May I see your search warrant?' Anthony said.

'We don't have a special search warrant,' said Quick. 'We are carrying out orders.'

'You don't have a warrant? Why not?'

'We don't need one,' Quick was nervous. 'We've been ordered to search here, and we are doing so.'

'You should really observe the niceties, Mr Quick,' Anthony said. 'It wouldn't have been too much trouble, would it? Why are you holding Mr Niesewand here? The Order says he should be detained at Gwelo Jail, not at his office in Salisbury.'

He turned to me: 'You are perfectly entitled to walk right out the door if you want to,' he said. 'They've got no right to keep you here.' Quick and Oberholser looked at each other. 'But I don't think I would advise it.'

Nonie said: 'He's packed clothes, some books and soap flakes.'

'You should also take writing paper, carbons, envelopes and stamps, and some pens. You may only be allowed to send one private letter out a week, but you can write to me, as your lawyer, at any time you like,' Anthony said. 'Also take your typewriter. You may be allowed to keep it. What about goodies? As a detainee you are allowed sweets, fruit and so on.' We talked for a while longer, and then Anthony said he'd go off and buy a 'goodie bag' for me. He came back with brown paper packets of things to make prison life a little more pleasant.

Anthony left soon afterwards to draft the Review Tribunal application, and the police finished in the office. Nonie rode down in the lift with us, and we said goodbye outside on the pavement in Union Avenue. I watched her walk up towards the *Rhodesia Herald* offices to give them the news, and I felt numbed, as if this was happening to someone else. The following day, the *Herald* printed a short news item, buried on page four, saying that a Salisbury freelance journalist had been detained under the Emergency Powers Regulations. The Emergency Regulations prohibit the publication of the names of detainees, and the *Herald* abided by this ruling for some weeks. An editorial on the same day asked why the new detainee could not be charged and tried in open court. The *Herald* said: 'Rhodesia is going through a dangerous and difficult phase. Drastic action is unavoidable if the new terrorist campaign is to be contained and defeated. ... That the journalist was not the Government's favourite reporter was not surprising after some of his comments and messages broadcast or published overseas. Some will consider that he had been silly: but was he more than that?'

The *Herald* played down my detention as far as possible until after the Government charged me under the Official Secrets Act, when I was suddenly promoted to the front page, and my name was used, making Rhodesia's major daily paper almost the last news publication in the world with an interest in the story to take the leap. In its desire not to offend the authorities, the *Herald* went to lengths which were bizarre even by its own standards. It carried part of an editorial from the conservative British newspaper, the *Daily Telegraph*, on my detention. The *Telegraph* commented: 'The arrest and detention of Mr Niesewand is another particularly ugly manifestation of the way the Smith regime is drifting. Mr Smith's Government is stumbling from one blunder to another.'

The *Herald* reported the editorial, but omitted not only my name, but also all references to me and my detention: quite a considerable feat in the circumstances. An official censor could hardly have done a more thorough job.

The Special Branch drove me to the echoing concrete corridors of the Railway Avenue police headquarters, and my fingerprints were again taken in triplicate. Then I settled down to wait for an hour or two before being driven to Gwelo Jail.

'I take it you're not in any hurry?' Geoff Quick asked.

'My time is yours,' I said.

The drive to Gwelo takes nearly four hours, and we were to have a meal on the way. Quick came into the office where I sat, concentrating on relaxing the tension out of my body. 'I've been given $20 to buy you lunch,' he said. 'You must be important.' He thought for a moment. 'Maybe we should stay in Salisbury and go through the menu at a Chinese Restaurant. But if we do, we won't get to Gwelo until late, and the prison officers won't be very pleased. You don't want to start off on the wrong foot.'

We began the long drive to the midlands, leaving Mrs Bryce behind at headquarters, her part in the arrest completed: another family had been separated in a manner whose morality was questionable; another person detained without trial or charge; she could go home to her husband that night in the knowledge that she had done her job well.

The plainclothes CID men who conducted the November search of my home and office said defensively three or four times: 'We're only doing our job,' a statement which surprised me as neither Nonie nor myself had attacked or criticised them in any way, and on the morning of my detention, Quick said the same thing. I wondered if

African detainees had heard similar disclaimers of responsibility from those depriving them of their freedom and plunging their families into something resembling a nightmare, and I wondered if – after years of detention without trial – the future black political leaders of the country would emerge from prison intent on securing social justice, or whether they would be burning for revenge. I decided that I should not like to be a Mrs Bryce, or a Geoffrey Quick in the Rhodesia of the future – not to mention an Ian Smith, or a Desmond Lardner-Burke. Once power has slipped or been wrested from their grasp, can the Europeans responsible for the present treatment of Africans reasonably expect a fairer deal from their former victims?

As we drove towards Gwelo Jail before noon on 20 February, with Oberholser driving and Quick leaning over the front seat chatting, apparently casually, to me, I felt neither anger nor resentment, only unreality.

Quick said: 'How do you think you're going to like solitary confinement?'

'I don't know,' I replied. 'You never really know how you're going to react to a situation until you're actually in it. I can't stand being alone, normally, but I'm pretty adaptable, so I'll just have to get used to it.'

'I hope you brought enough jerseys, because it gets very cold in Gwelo during winter. When do you think you'll get out?'

I considered the question, then said: '1984', as it seemed an appropriate date, and the policemen laughed.

I knew that the friendly conversation we were holding at 70 m.p.h. on the Gwelo road was in fact an interrogation, and Quick confirmed this later. 'When I get back to headquarters,' he said, 'they're going to ask me for a report on what you said when you were arrested, and on your way to jail. What do you want me to tell them?'

'Tell them that I know the Special Branch has nothing against me, because there's nothing to get, and I've always worked on the assumption you know everything I do. My detention is a political matter – the Government is moving against the Press, because they're starting a campaign in the tribal areas to persuade Africans to say "Yes" to the settlement, and they don't want it published – especially not how they're going about it. They want the Press to censor themselves, and they've chosen to make an example of me because Mr Smith can't stand me and wants me out of the country. Politics is a game, and what's happened today is part of the game.

47

'It hasn't come as a complete surprise, of course. But the thing is, I'm a journalist, not a politician. I've been prevented from carrying on writing by my arrest, but I've no political points to make by staying in prison and becoming a martyr.

'Last November, after the first search, I spoke to my lawyer, and told him I thought that if I was detained, the Government would probably leave me in prison for four or five weeks, and then come to me one day and offer to let me leave the country on condition I didn't come back.

'I've got my wife and family to think about, and you can tell the Government that I'm perfectly prepared to sign a document agreeing to leave in exchange for my freedom.'

Quick asked: 'Why do you think they'd be interested in a deal like that?'

'Because they've got nothing to gain by keeping me in jail,' I said. 'The longer I'm in, the more bad publicity they're going to get. They wanted to stop me working in Rhodesia, and they have.'

'Would you be prepared to reveal your sources of information in exchange for your release?'

'I could never do that,' I said. 'There are no circumstances in which a journalist can reveal his sources and stay in the business. It's out of the question.'

'Well,' said Quick, 'I'll tell them.'

We stopped at the small town of Hartley to get a Coke at a garage, and allow me to buy a box of tissues. Oberholser followed me into the chemists while I made my purchase with the small amount of money I had brought with me, and when we returned to the car, it would not start. The starter motor had jammed.

'I think we're going to have to jump the clutch,' I said. Quick had gone across the road to get the soft drinks, and Oberholser asked an African standing on the pavement to help push the unmarked Alfa Romeo.

I had an idea which seemed worth trying. I had no intention of escaping, because the chances of success were small and once you're in the grip of the police or the prisons, there is little point trying to beat the system. A directly-affected individual can seldom win by standing against such state machines, only by attempting to work within their confines. But the temptation of getting behind the steering wheel of the Special Branch car, starting it and driving off at speed leaving the police behind, was almost irresistible. I only intended going around the block and then picking them up again.

'I'll jump the clutch if you like,' I said helpfully, but Oberholser, after a pause for thought, shook his head. 'I don't like the idea of filling in reports about how you got away in our car,' he said.

So a rather sullen African and a political prisoner pushed the police Alfa down the main street of Hartley, while in the driver's seat, Oberholser concentrated on simultaneously trying to get the car started, steering it, and watching me in the rear view mirror in case I stopped pushing and suddenly headed off down a side street. I thought he could hardly report that I had been unco-operative.

When Quick rejoined us I said: 'I think it's a bit much having to push my way to prison,' and he agreed. We stopped for lunch at a modern motel in the midlands town of Gatooma, and with the compliments of the Special Branch, I drank my final beer. I hadn't been able to eat breakfast, but thought I should make a positive attempt at lunch, although I was not hungry, because I didn't know what the food would be like at Gwelo Jail. I ordered a simple, but substantial meal of pâté, fish and ice cream.

It was a relaxed and friendly luncheon, and anyone listening to our conversation would not have guessed that I was the prisoner of my hosts. I began to forget this myself, until I decided to go to the lavatory, and they followed me in to make sure I didn't squeeze out of a window and run off. Afterwards, Quick and I pushed the Alfa to get it started again, and I sat silently in the back for an hour, watching the Rhodesian bush moving past.

Rhodesia is a very beautiful country. Out of the towns and cities, the horizons widen and the view becomes cinemascopic, with miles of veld and bush trees with gnarled trunks. I watched intently, because I did not know when I would see it again. I felt a sadness, not only because of my own situation, but because of the condition of the land. A major drought had gripped the country, and fields of maize, which normally stood higher than a man, were dry and stunted. The Government had described the failure of the rains as 'a national disaster', and they were right. Not only would there be a loss to the country in foreign exchange earnings but, more important, there was the real prospect of hunger among subsistence farmers and their families in the tribal areas. It was one more major problem for a country already heavily burdened, and I hoped Mr Smith and his cabinet colleagues would deal properly with it and its human implications, and that it would not be an occasion for further deterioration in race relations. Over the preceding few months, I had watched the gap between black and white widen quickly, and although there had been no apparent change in the peaceful atmosphere of Salisbury, below the surface the racial pot was on the boil.

African anger and mistrust of whites, usually hidden behind smiles, or subservience, or expressionless eyes, surfaced more readily in private conversations. Most grievances had originally been laid at the door of the Rhodesian Front Government, but increasingly Africans felt the blame should be shouldered by all Europeans.

An African man explained their viewpoint to me: 'It's the white electorate which voted the Rhodesian Front into power, and it's the whites who keep Mr Smith in office. If they are not prepared to come to the Africans wanting to talk and compromise then who can condemn us for thinking there is no difference between them and the RF?'

The first months of the guerilla campaign accelerated the trend. The security forces were obviously having difficulty containing the situation, and unexpected unity among tribesmen in the north-east behind the insurgents was causing concern in both the army and political circles. Although the Ministry of Information tried its best to keep details from the public, the efficient African grapevine meant that stories of attacks were known in the townships around Salisbury within a few hours, and the atmosphere of interest and in some cases, excitement, which they generated provided a fertile bed for rumours as well as factual reports.

Some Europeans with contacts in the township noticed the change. A day after guerillas attacked a police post, an army encampment, administrative buildings and two bridges in the Mount Darwin district, north-east of the capital, a white woman commented to me: 'I've never seen Africans looking so smug.' The Europeans did not know what had taken place a few miles from their doors, because the Government had not announced details of the attack, but Africans knew.

Yet the tranquil surface of life in Salisbury was scarcely ruffled, and it remained possible for most whites to continue oblivious of the changing times, although some found it difficult to suppress a sense of unease. I had noticed that on social occasions, during the routine discussions on what might happen next, someone would eventually begin wondering aloud where to go after Rhodesia.

If Prime Minister Smith had felt the stirrings, he gave no public sign. He continued simultaneously operating two widely divergent policies: on the one hand, the country's legislation was becoming increasingly committed to a form of South African-style apartheid, and on the other, Mr Smith was anxious to implement the 1971 Independence settlement terms, which were multi-racial in spirit. Which did Mr Smith himself genuinely believe in? Having covered the Rhodesian political scene for eight years, I had no idea, and nor I suspect did the ordinary white voter, who apparently looked at the Prime Minister's stern, fearless expression, and listened carefully to the tone of his voice, yet paid little heed to the words themselves. Mr Smith could – and sometimes did – contradict himself completely in the same prepared speech, without many people noticing. It was a politician's paradise.

The Special Branch car reached the outskirts of Gwelo, and Geoff Quick looked over his shoulder and gave me a friendly smile.

'You'd better get some insect repellent,' he said, 'otherwise the mosquitoes will keep you awake at night.'

So we stopped at a supermarket, and Quick and I went in to buy a can of aerosol spray on a Special Offer stand.

Back in the car, Oberholser said: 'I wonder if I can find the jail?'

'Don't worry if you can't,' I said. 'I'll check into a hotel.'

But he found his way without difficulty, across a railway track a few yards from Gwelo Station, and past a sign saying Gwelo Prison and surmounted by the official blue crest. We stopped at a barrier, and Oberholser said to the African guard: 'Special Branch, Salisbury,' the boom lifted and we drove through the twelve-foot-high security fence topped by barbed wire and parked the car.

I got out and looked at my new home. There was another security fence between us and the cream-painted, rather grim walls, and to the left was the main brown wooden door with a brass knocker and a peephole. Quick walked to the inner perimeter fence and said to the guard: 'Special Branch with a European detainee from Salisbury' and the padlock was opened. Quick and Oberholser helped me carry my suitcases and packages into the prison, and the brass knocker made a loud crashing sound before the peephole opened and Quick announced us once more.

A small inner door opened, and Quick said: 'After you.' I stepped into jail, feeling quite unreal.

chapter 5

We stood in a concrete entrance area, with the administration offices leading off one side, and the gate control and a search room off the other. Directly opposite the main prison door were heavy steel bars from floor to ceiling, and through them we could see a large concrete quadrangle, bordered by small cells. It was about 3.30 p.m., and dozens of African convicts were finishing their day's labour, sitting quietly in queues waiting for a warder's shout, before standing up and quickly stripping off their prison shorts and singlets to stand naked while their clothes were searched.

We moved towards the administration offices, where two young European warders waited behind desks. I was surprised when no one shouted at me, or abused me. In fact, for a few minutes, no one spoke to me or even looked my way. It was almost as if I had become invisible. Quick handed over a copy of my Detention Order, and then he and Oberholser left. The warders began filling in forms. The Prison Superintendent walked past and into his office without even a glance in my direction. I waited patiently, trying to check the rising apprehension I felt. There's no hurry, I told myself. I no longer had to care about ringing telephones, or newspaper deadlines, or telex machines. I had all the time in the world. Outside, a siren started up – a low rumble building up into a high pitched wail, and then fading away after a minute or so

At last, one of the warders looked directly at me – a short, slim, fair-haired man with a new scar running down his chin from his lower lip. His eyes were impersonal. 'We'll have to make a list of all your personal effects,' he said. 'You're not allowed any jewellery or money. We'll keep your watch and any rings you have and your money, in a safe here.'

'I've got a bag of sweets and fruit which my lawyer brought for me. Can I keep those?'

He looked at the other warder. 'We'll ask the boss.'

'I'd also like to keep my typewriter and my radio and my clothes.'

'We'll have to ask the boss.'

They began making the list. Niesewand Peter. Eur. Male Det. Three pairs slacks. One suit. One belt. Six shirts. Two pairs shoes. Personal articles belonging to someone who officially had become a non-person. I glanced round the office to a blackboard listing the number of prisoners at Gwelo, and the breakdown of offenders. There were no Europeans listed, but while I watched, an African warder came up with a piece of chalk and wrote in: '1 E.M. Det' and that was me. I saw there were 42 A.M. Dets (African male detainees) on the board, and I felt ashamed that, as a former working journalist in Rhodesia, I did not know the name of even one of them. When most Africans are detained, they simply vanish. Their families – perhaps through fear – say nothing to the Press, and local newspapers are forbidden by the Emergency Regulations to use their names, even if they knew them.

The prison superintendent came back into the office, and the blond warder Mr Lowe, said: 'He wants to know if he can keep some of his stuff with him, sir.'

Supt Durand said to me: 'What have you got?'

'I'd like to keep my typewriter, because I'm left-handed and my ordinary writing is illegible,' I said, and he nodded.

'I've got a bag of fruit, biltong (sticks of dried spiced meat), chocolate and so on – which my lawyer bought me.'

'All right.'

'I'd like to keep my own clothes.'

'We'll lock them up for you. Just ask when you want to change.'

'And I'd like to keep my radio.'

Supt Durand hesitated. 'I don't know about that,' he said. 'I'll have to ask if you can have it.'

The list of belongings was completed, and I signed my name beneath it. An African prisoner was called in to help me carry the suitcase, typewriter, radio and packets to my cell block. We walked out into the reception area, but instead of then going through to the concrete quadrangle bordered by cells, we went out the main door of the prison building, and walked around by the side of the jail, until we reached a second large wooden door.

Mr Lowe banged the brass knocker, the peephole opened and an eye stared out at us, then disappeared. A heavy key turned in the lock and the door swung open. We were in another entrance area, leading onto a dirt courtyard and cells. We walked through this, turned left and headed for a small door set in the side of a high concrete hall. The other cells had windows facing the front beside their entrances, but there were no windows here. My heart sank and I thought: 'Oh no, they're not going to keep me in a hole like that.'

When the door was unlocked, it opened not into a cell, as I expected, but onto another courtyard, with grass and a bed of lavender. In the middle stood a jail block, near whose locked main door grew a very beautiful flamboyant tree, its leaves a sheet of green, rippling in the breeze. Mr Lowe opened a padlock, swung wide the double doors, then led me down a wooden passage and into a cell.

It was not as bad as I had imagined: a large room, with a wooden floor and two windows, heavily barred. There was a bed against one wall, with a small, low, white-painted wooden cupboard next to it, and a table. In one corner was a metal bucket with a bottle of khaki-coloured disinfectant – for use as my lavatory between the time I was locked into the cell at 4 p.m., and the time I was unlocked at about 7 a.m. I swore never to use it, and I never did.

Mr Lowe opened a nearby cell and my clothes and radio were locked in it. Then he and the African prisoner went out, leaving my cell door open but locking me into the building.

I looked around. At the end of the corridor was a lavatory and a bathroom. Next to them was a kitchen, with an electric stove and a sink, but otherwise abandoned. All the remaining cells were locked, and I peered through the peepholes at their emptiness. A room near the main door was open – it contained a cheap wooden table and a chair, and like the others, its windows were fronted by thick steel bars.

I went back into my cell and sat on the bed. The government blankets folded on top of the mattress felt and smelled oily. Out of the windows I could see a lemon tree, and, twelve feet away, a high wall, although not high enough to hide a sentry tower in the middle of the jail enclosure from which an African warder stared down trying to see the European detainee.

A key rattled in the main ʾoutside lock, the doors opened, and four men walked in – Supt Durand, Mr Lowe, a chaplain in the khaki prison uniform and dog collar, and leading them, a man nearing his sixties, with a furious face. He stalked down the corridor carrying a swagger stick and glaring at the locked doors on either side, then past me without a glance, and on towards the kitchen and bathroom. A quick look into each room, a long stare into the

54

lavatory pan, then a stalk back, never once looking at me, a glare into my cell, then a pause while the others stood uncomfortably around him.

I said: 'Good afternoon, gentlemen,' but no one returned my greeting, and the leader glared in another direction. I gathered he was the senior prison official. After a second or two, the group turned and walked away. I heard Supt Durand murmuring to the man about the reopening of this block, then the door banged heavily and the padlock rattled, and I was alone again. I decided I would have to get used to being invisible.

A few minutes later, rattle of keys, banging open of door, and Mr Lowe returned.

'You've arrived a bit late for dinner,' he said, 'but would you like me to see what we can fix up?'

'Don't worry,' I said, 'Special Branch bought me lunch and I'm not very hungry. Besides, I've got fruit if I change my mind.'

'All right,' he said. 'I'll lock you in your cell now.'

I went into my cell, and he locked the door, and I heard his boots going down the passage, then the bang and rattle of the main door being locked, and I went and lay down on my bed.

Quick had asked how I thought I would react to solitary confinement, and I said I didn't know. Well, here I was, and I felt no emotion, and no panic. Outside, a Rhodesia Railways train shunted past unseen, its steam engine puffing smoke and noise, and its whistle high-pitched and discordant. The guard in the watchtower fifty yards away had become tired of staring into my isolation block, and now had his back to me, peering over the edge at the ground below. My watch and wedding and signet rings had been taken from me, and I felt strange without them. I wondered how slowly time would pass. It was just after four o'clock, and I had at least two hours to wait until sundown. I lay back on the bed, smelling the greasy, dark-grey blankets, and tried to clear my mind of the clutter of thoughts. I had been working hard over the past few months, and I told myself it would be good to have a rest. Yet I could not relax. I swung my legs off the bed and began walking. Seven paces to cross the space between the windows and the locked wooden door, with its four-inch-square peephole.

I became conscious of silence, and hummed to myself. Not only was I alone in the cell block, but there was no one around who could even hear if I began to shout. Perhaps the guard in the watchtower would hear, but I doubted it.

I had never been content with my own company. On the few occasions when Nonie was away from home overnight, I found it difficult to stay in the house by myself, knowing that no one else was there and that empty hours stretched ahead. On these occasions, I would drive into town for a meal, or go to the cinema, or have a few drinks in Salisbury's Quill Club – the meeting place for journalists and advertising men – and simply return home late at night to sleep.

How would I fill empty, solitary weeks? I resolved the problem by instinct, rather than by an intellectual decision. There was no advantage to be gained by my being unco-operative to the prison authorities. I was in their power, and I had to accept it with as much dignity and as little whining as possible. Kicking against the prison system would not make the slightest difference to them, but could well damage me personally, and I could not afford to lose control of myself, or be eaten by rage. Anger is a luxury which the free can afford. Outside the prison, Nonie, fuelled by her anger, waged a relentless campaign to have my conditions improved, and to secure my release. In jail, I could merely make requests, and if they were refused, I had to accept this immediately and not let official pettiness get me down. She accepted nothing, but a new challenge, and used her freedom to force changes in interpretation of the prison rules, particularly after I was transferred to Salisbury Jail, and to publicly spotlight the questionable morality of official actions against me.

Inside jail, I was surrounded by prison regulations, implemented on occasions by people lacking compassion and intelligence, and I had to work within the strict confines of the system. Yet, at the same time, I instinctively shied away from admitting to myself that I was in prison at all. As far as possible, when I was alone, I blotted from my mind all thoughts of cells, or bars, or warders, and I lived initially from day to day, but later from week to week. Memories of home and family were painful, as they entailed the intellectual admission that we were separated. I tried to accept my situation without thinking too deeply about it, except in the abstract. I tried not to consider why it was I spent hours lying on my back staring at the ceiling, or why I was locked in an empty building for most of the day, and a cell for all the night, or why I played thousands of games of patience.

This switching-off process was occasionally interrupted by visits from Nonie and members of my family, and meetings with Anthony

56

Eastwood. With Anthony, our discussions were naturally on legal and detention matters, and I managed to talk about these things academically – at least initially. In effect, I was reporting to him about the prison conditions of a certain journalist – not myself – who was being held in solitary confinement, and I was discussing with as little emotional involvement as possible, tactics for getting him out.

It was not as easy to deal with visits from Nonie and my family. The most difficult thing I found about solitary confinement was coping with kindness, which re-established the emotional links I had instinctively suppressed, and made me realise my predicament.

I looked forward to our short times together, and virtually lived from visit to visit, but a special kindness – particularly a kind word – could cut immediately through the barrier I had thrown up to cover us, and end for a while the pretence that there was nothing unusual about brief meetings behind high walls and barbed wire, with a prison officer listening in. My mother said: 'I'm proud of you,' and her words hurt more than listening to a magistrate impose a two-year prison sentence. It was a strange experience.

There are problems about living in prison, with locks and warders, and yet pretending you're not in jail at all, but there are ways of maintaining the illusion for a time. I called no prison official 'sir'. If I knew their names, I called them 'mister'; if I did not, I called them nothing. If I was out of my cell when the keys rattled at the main door, I immediately returned to sit or lie on my bed and wait there for whoever was coming in, although sometimes I would contrive to walk towards the entrance to the cell and meet them at the door. I avoided situations in which I felt myself to be like an animal in a cage – my life revolving around who walked in and out, waiting on the whims of my captors. I preferred to appear independent of them, and self-contained, treating the warders in a friendly, but not subservient manner, remaining as far as possible unmoved by the humiliations of prison life, in the hope that they would feel like visitors and not landlords when they entered my isolation block. I think I succeeded in making some of them uneasy at losing the psychological advantage, or uncomfortable at the implied switch in roles. I did manage to manoeuvre one European warder into the position where he began calling me 'Mister' Nicsewand – a form of address you lose in prison even when you haven't been tried or charged.

But it was only a minor victory. I *was* dependent on the warders

57

for most of my human contact – perhaps lasting three or four minutes a day when they opened the door so that another prisoner could bring me meals, and this had its dangers. Nonie remembers meetings we had in Salisbury Prison where she got the impression I had formed an alliance with whichever warder was in charge of my cell block, with me looking to him for approval when she handed over food parcels, and sometimes including him in our conversations, when I should have ignored his presence completely.

Trying to retain a degree of independence, and at the same time keeping a fairly friendly relationship going with those directly in charge of me: here were the seeds of the collapse of self-respect. Looking back, I wonder how long it would have taken before I started sounding like other European remand prisoners I had heard, addressing warders in the coaxing, slightly whiney manner of small boys trying to wheedle a favour from a schoolmaster. Yet all the time, with my warders censoring our conversations, Nonie could say nothing of her fears. I was probably lucky that I did not remain in prison long enough to discover whether I would be able to retain my self-respect. Being friendly to warders, as distinct from being distant but polite, was the first false step on a slippery slope, and it was no secret that in solitary confinement, I was going mentally and physically downhill.

Night took its time coming on my first evening in Gwelo Jail, but at dusk, I heard the bang of the door at the outer perimeter wall signal that someone was coming, and a few seconds later, there was the rattle of keys at the main door to my block, then the tramping of boots down the wooden passageway, the scrabbling of keys in my lock – two wrong keys first, a pause, then the right one – and a warder turned on the switch in the passage which controlled the naked light in my cell.

'You all right?' he said.

'Yes thanks, I'm fine.'

'Do you want the light on? You can have it on until eight o'clock.'

Instinctively I said: 'No thanks, leave it off.'

'All right. Goodnight.'

'Goodnight.'

Throughout my imprisonment, I refused to have the light on at night. When the sun went down, I went to bed and lay staring into the darkness. There were two reasons for this. I knew the light would attract mosquitoes, and even with my cell in darkness, I had trouble with these insects. But more important, I hated the thought of lying awake waiting for someone to come and turn out my light. If I couldn't control the switch myself, I wasn't interested in having it on at all.

That first long night, I came to realise some of the drawbacks of Gwelo Prison. Trains shunted nearby, or thundered past, their noise amplified by the night, and at a level crossing which appeared to be just outside my window, engine drivers played tunes on their train whistles.

A warder came to unlock my cell at about 7 a.m., but relocked the main door to the building when he went away. I went to the bathroom and while I washed my face, I considered how I might fill the hours ahead. Obviously, it was necessary not to rush anything, so I walked from the bathroom to my cell to collect my toothbrush, which I took back to the basin and laid carefully on the ledge. Then I went back to fetch the toothpaste. At the basin, I cleaned my teeth carefully, and after a few minutes, took a slow walk down the passage, still brushing. I didn't have a watch, but I imagine I made it last for ten minutes. When I had finished, I rinsed the toothbrush, dried it on a towel, and replaced it in a plastic box, which I carried back to the cell. I returned to the bathroom. I screwed the top onto the toothpaste, put the tube carefully back into its box, and carried it to the cell.

Shaving was next. One trip to fetch my razor, another to get the shaving cream, and a third to find the shaving brush. There was no mirror, so a careful job filled a few minutes. Then individually, I returned each article to the cell. Finally I went to fetch a hairbrush, and when I'd completed everything, I dressed slowly. I had filled probably half an hour, and outside, the siren started its low, growling buildup to the wailing sound which signalled the official beginning of another prison day.

A few minutes later, the crash of the outer perimeter door announced the approach of a warder, and I stopped my aimless prowling up and down the corridor and went to sit on my bed.

A face appeared at the door and I looked up.

'Breakfast,' said the warder.

'Thanks,' I said, and walked down the passage to the end room where a tin plate had been placed on the table by an African prisoner, together with a tin mug of coffee. I waited until they had gone before tasting the mealie meal (maize) porridge. It was cold and unappetising, and I pushed it aside untouched and drank the coffee. I didn't know if I was allowed to leave food uneaten, so I

59

took the plate through to the kitchen, and washed the porridge down the drain, pushing lumps through with my finger.

It was about 8 a.m. and I had eight hours to fill before I was again locked up for the night. I ate some biltong sticks and fruit, and afterwards went for a walk. Seven paces along my cell, five paces across, then out the door and up the passage and down the other side. I ran down the passage, then played a game of hopscotch along the boards. I tried to remember all the tunes from West Side Story, and their words, and the same with South Pacific and Oklahoma. I am a very poor singer, but there was no one to hear and my voice echoed in the virtually empty building.

Then I went back to my cell, sat on the bed and stared around. There was something familiar about the room, and I puzzled over it for a few minutes before I remembered that it reminded me of the office I used to have in London when I worked for the BBC External Services at Bush House. Brown and cream – perhaps the same colour co-ordinator had been employed by the BBC and the Rhodesian prison service – and both buildings had high ceilings. The similarities ended there, but it was enough to let me pretend that I was back at the BBC, waiting for someone to come and ask me to do some work.

I did have a job to do that morning: I had been turning over in my mind what to say in my formal appeal to Mr Lardner-Burke to reconsider my detention, particularly as I had never been given reasons for the action against me. At around 9 a.m. I took my portable typewriter down to the end room in the block.

'It is very difficult for me to know quite what to say to you,' I wrote to Mr Lardner-Burke; 'The Order says my detention is deemed to be in the interests of Public Safety and Order, but it gives no details. I have not been questioned by any police or government officials on any matter concerning Public Safety or Public Order, so I do not know on what lines your mind may be running.'

I recalled the police search of my office and home in November, on suspicion that I had contravened the Official Secrets Act. 'I have not heard from the police on this matter since then,' I went on, 'and presume – because of the time elapsed – that there is no basis for a prosecution. But I cannot believe that this incident has formed any part of such a serious matter as my indefinite detention.

'I recall that in many previous cases where the reasons for detention have never been publicly disclosed, the officially-encouraged inference has been that the individuals concerned know in their hearts what prompted the Government to take such an extraordinary step. Indeed, until it happens to oneself, there is always that outside chance that some secret nefarious deeds have been performed by those involved. However, I have searched my conscience and I can think of no act of mine, planned or committed, which would involve anything more serious than a fine for speeding. Oh, and Judy Todd sent me an autographed copy of her book, *The Right to Say No*, but I think that distribution of this is an offence, but possession is not.' I said the suggestion that my continued freedom in Rhodesia might constitute a danger to Public Safety or Order could not be substantiated.

'At the same time,' I wrote, 'I do not believe you ordered my Detention lightly, or on a whim, but I cannot think what evidence has been presented to you which would justify such a move, and of course in this I am offered no official enlightenment. I can only suggest that the information at your disposal deserves more thorough checking.' I said I was aware that the Government did not like me, but I pointed out that, even within the ruling party, people who had actually worked with me from time to time had been satisfied with the honesty and impartiality of my reports, and I outlined to Mr Lardner-Burke how I viewed my job as a journalist in Rhodesia.

'I have never been a member of any political party or organisation,' I said. 'Similarly, I have never registered as a voter, or taken part in any election. I do not feel that, as a journalist, I should identify with any political standpoint. I do, however, maintain fairly close contacts with different political parties and organisations. My job is fairly and accurately to represent all credible political viewpoints in this country, and from time to time, make my own assessment of the situation as an uncommitted observer.

'I am the first to admit that the Rhodesian Government point of view gets a pretty bad showing overseas, but I am afraid this is the fault of your extremely poor Ministry of Information.

'Journalists can only reflect points of view if they know what these are. The Rhodesia Party, the ANC, the Centre Party, the United Front and other opposition groups are only too happy to have their say, privately and publicly. The Rhodesian Front, and the Government itself, like the Tar Baby, "just ain't saying nuttin".' I cited the controversial Zambian border closure, and its later reopening, as examples of poor public relations, in which the official policy of saying too little, too late, had reflected badly on the Rhodesian Government.

But I noted: 'As you see, I am merely casting blindly round for possible reasons for the Detention Order against me. I may never find out: as you know better than most people, the Review Tribunal is not obliged to give me details of the charges, or confront me with my accusers, in the manner in which justice usually functions in a Western Democracy. Nonetheless, I plan to take all available opportunities to appear personally before Tribunals to end this detention.' I said I hoped this would not be necessary. The Minister had removed my freedom and my livelihood, and had placed me in solitary confinement, but he had not relieved me of my responsibilities to my wife and family. I had to provide for them, and if he did not immediately release me from detention and allow me to pursue my business as a journalist, then the only way I could be able to meet my obligations was to leave Rhodesia for England, where I would have no difficulty in finding a job. If the Minister did decide to let me leave the country, I said, I would like two or three days' freedom in Salisbury to wind up my business affairs, and decide what to do about the house in Northwood which Nonie and I had bought six months earlier.

I kept a carbon copy of the letter, and put the original in an envelope addressed to Anthony Eastwood at his Salisbury offices, together with a covering letter asking him to approve it before forwarding to Mr Lardner-Burke. Later that morning, I handed it to a prison warder for censoring and posting. It was logged out of Gwelo Jail at 9.00 a.m. on Thursday but for some reason, did not arrive in Salisbury until the following Tuesday – five days later – by which time the permitted seven day appeal period had expired. I was glad about Anthony's advice that I take carbon paper to prison, as I was able to hand him a copy of the letter when he visited me at Gwelo on the Saturday. So despite the strangely erratic post, my appeal was in Mr Lardner-Burke's hands on time, and he turned it down a few days later.

I had expected him to do this. To release me would have involved a tacit admission that the detention had been unjustified in the first place, and this would have meant an official loss of face. I anticipated being held for between four to eight weeks, to make it appear that there had been grounds for action against me, but that the unspecified danger was now past, and I could be freed providing I left the country. This estimate did not take into account the Government's later decision to try me under the Official Secrets Act, which stretched the period of solitary confinement to just over ten weeks, but in substance, it was accurate.

Crash went the perimeter door, rattle the keys to the main door of my block, and a prison chaplain came in – dog collar, khaki uniform with prison insignia, a man in his early thirties with hair cut short-back-and-sides, and a friendly smile.

'I'm Padre Spong,' he said, putting out his hand. 'Bishop Mark of Matabeleland phoned me this morning and asked me to look in on you and give you his best wishes. He hopes to be able to come up and see you in a few days. Is he a friend of yours?'

'Yes,' I said. 'My wife and I knew him when he was Dean at the Cathedral in Salisbury. It's very kind of him.'

'Well,' said Spong, 'I'm the Anglican prison chaplain for the area which includes Gwelo, and we'll be seeing quite a lot of each other.'

I was glad of company, and Spong seemed a pleasant man. We chatted for a few minutes, and I asked why he wore a prison uniform if he was a priest. Surely, I said, it placed him under suspicion of being a government informer. He agreed that there was often suspicion, but he believed the uniform was necessary because it enabled him to move freely around Rhodesian jails, without being accompanied by warders, while priests outside the prison service were usually forbidden to get near prisoners.

He finished with some advice. 'This prison block used to be the women's section, but it was closed about twelve months ago and the women were moved to Salisbury. It's seen a lot of unhappiness and there have been many people who made things worse for themselves by counting the days until their release. You're in a different position of course, because you don't know how long you'll be here, but the principle is the same,' Padre Spong said. 'It might be difficult for you to see this now, but you can turn this into a useful experience for yourself. You have lots of spare time, and you might be able to use it to turn inwards, to look at yourself and your life – have a sort of personal springcleaning. Perhaps you could write a book. But if you fill your time with something useful, you may be able to look back on this incident in a few years from now and see that it was, in fact, valuable.'

After Padre Spong had gone, a warder went through the noisy procedure of unlocking the access doors to my block, and an African hard labour prisoner followed at his heels, carrying a tray with my lunch. I had lost track of time, so I asked Mr Lowe. He looked at his watch. 'It's just after eleven,' he said.

'That's rather an early lunch,' I said. 'When do I get supper?'

'At about 3.30.'

'Why are the prison eating hours so strange?'

'An African prisoner cooks your food,' he replied. 'You're the only European in the jail, and he says he used to be a cook so he looks after you and prepares your food as part of his day's work. You get breakfast at about eight, and lunch now. And you have to have your supper at half-past three because lockup's at four.'

When Mr Lowe had gone, I lifted a coarse cloth from the tray, then took a tin lid cover off the tin plate, and looked at my lunch. There were two small cubes of meat, and they were yellow. There was a mush of unidentifiable vegetables and coagulated rice. The smell turned my stomach, but I thought – you have to get used to this food, so just eat it. I cut a piece of meat and put it in my mouth but immediately spat it back onto the fork. It was cold and it had coated my mouth with grease. There was a tin mug containing half-an-inch of milk, and a pot of tea on the tray, so I drank the milk to clean the yellow meat taste from my mouth. When the milk was finished, I left the food untouched, and went to my own food supply for something to eat.

Later in the afternoon, Mr Lowe opened my block to let in the African prisoner bringing supper.

'The man who cooks my food is obviously in jail for false pretences,' I said. 'He's never cooked a thing in his life before.'

Mr Lowe looked sympathetic. 'I know, I looked at it,' he said. 'It was pretty awful. The thing is, we didn't have advance warning that you were coming, so at the moment we don't have proper food for you. You're having to eat African rations. But we should start getting reasonable meat for you from tomorrow. We have a contract with a firm in Bulawayo, and it has to come up from there.'

I looked gloomy and said: 'Well, I've got enough fruit and biltong to last me.'

Poor Africans, I thought. I lifted the tin lid, looked briefly at what was supposed to be supper, and went to have a bath and prepare for lockup.

chapter 6

When my Scale 1 European diet meat began arriving at Gwelo Jail, there was a major improvement in my meals. I found I could eat some of the food providing I didn't watch what I was doing, but simultaneously read a book or a magazine to take my mind off the look and the smell of what lay in my plate.

Yet there were compensations in this midlands prison. After a few days, I was allowed to have my radio. Supt Durand made representations on my behalf to the man with the furious face, who himself came stalking into my cell block to announce the news.

'I have decided to let you have your radio,' he snapped, 'providing you don't abuse the privilege.'

'I wonder if you could tell me what you mean by that,' I said. 'Perhaps you could lay down some groundrules.'

I thought I might be forbidden to listen to foreign radio stations, but he looked taken aback, as if he hadn't really considered how one might abuse a transistor radio.

Finally he said: 'Well, don't have it blaring at two in the morning.' I promised I would not, and he strode angrily away. I got the impression that he was actually in some pain, and was disguising this by his abrupt manner.

I found the Gwelo prison officials to be personally very pleasant and helpful. Supt Durand himself was new to Gwelo Jail, having been transferred there with his family only a day or so before my arrival, and they too were having trouble sleeping at night because of the Rhodesia Railways trains thundering and whistling their way past the prison and its adjoining staff quarters. Durand had been in the prison service for more than twenty years: a well-built and kind man who – in my case at least – actually practised the humanitarianism to which some other senior prison officials paid

C*

lip service. According to Padre Spong, Supt Durand also had a good reputation among African convicts and detainees.

Certainly, to Nonie and myself, Durand was courteous and sympathetic. He told Nonie that she could visit me for at least an hour every day if she liked, and I could write and receive as many letters as I wanted. In the early days of my arrest, with the collapse of my business, there was much for Nonie and me to discuss, and we met in Durand's office to sort out the mess. Durand gave us tea, and sat unobtrusively behind his desk during our meetings. Other Gwelo officials followed his lead, and my adjustment to prison life was eased.

Yet I was still in solitary confinement, and despite the kindness of officials, I hated the thought of Nonie having to drive for four hours to visit me, and then drive home again. I wondered about the condition of the car tyres, and felt the beginnings of fears for her safety which would grow as my imprisonment continued.

The prison system is designed to take all responsibility from the prisoner, but what it does, particularly in the case of detainees, is to render a man helpless to aid his family, while taking over none of his suddenly-abandoned obligations. Breadwinners disappear without warning, and wives and children are left to fend for themselves. If they apply to the social welfare department, it is unlikely they will be left to starve, but they will not be given money. There is no system of unemployment benefits in Rhodesia and social welfare assistance tends to run to food parcels. A detainee can spend hours, days, weeks, wondering how his wife and children are really making out, because short visits are usually taken up with both sides putting on brave faces, pretending it's not too bad in prison, and it's fine at home, with no problems to speak of, and each knowing the other is lying through his teeth.

Back in the cells, waiting for another visiting hour to come round, a detainee begins the debilitating process of wondering 'what if?' What if she's sick, or has an accident? I couldn't even go to her side. What if she dies, will I be able to go to her funeral, and will I be in handcuffs? What if Desmond Lardner-Burke takes it into his head to detain her as well? What if some sick-minded white Rhodesian throws a brick or a petrol bomb into her house?

Detention without trial is a rather refined process of mental torture, but to hear the Rhodesian Government talk about it, it's a reasonable step for a civilised administration to take when confronted with an unusual security situation. The fact that in many

66

cases, people have been detained for ten years or more does not dilute the inherent justice of the system, so the argument runs, and anyone who thinks otherwise must be on the side of thugs and Communists.

At the beginning of 1972, Premier Smith spoke of his attitude to detention. At the time, the Pearce Commission was in Rhodesia testing public opinion on the Independence settlement proposals, and there was rioting in African townships throughout the country, as black men and women underlined their opposition to the terms. At a Press Conference which I attended, Smith blamed the African National Council (ANC) for staging the riots, being responsible for arson and looting, and having direct links with outlawed black nationalist groups.

Mr Smith said his Government had prepared a confidential dossier on intimidation, which contained evidence of this, and had handed it to the Pearce Commission. (When the dossier was finally published, it largely comprised Press cuttings.) I stood up to ask a question: 'If this is so, sir, why is it that these individuals have not been brought to court, and do you not believe that an open court case would carry far more weight as far as the allegations of intimidation from your side are concerned, than the secret dossier handed in secret to the Pearce Commission, and not disclosed to the world?'

Mr Smith replied: 'The answer to your question is that a few hundred of them have already been brought to courts, and have been convicted . . . so we are very happy to do this . . . this is the best way of carrying out this exercise . . . we accept this.

'On the other hand, anybody who knows anything about Rhodesia, and who understands the African psychology must admit that he [the African] is very susceptible to intimidation. They themselves make this point. We have numerous examples. It is incredible to myself and maybe to the majority of you how susceptible to intimidation they are. If somebody came to my house one night and said "Don't you go to any meetings for the next few weeks . . . don't you vote "yes" . . . even if I was going to vote "no" I would go and vote "yes" the next day, just to prove my point, and I think this applies to the majority of you.

'Regrettably, the African reacts in the very reverse manner. We've known this for years. And this has been generally accepted. And this is why we have to resort to this system which has been accepted by all and sundry, even by the British Government, a system of detention and restriction.

'This is part and parcel of the new set-up which was agreed to by the British [the settlement proposals], with the proviso that we have an impartial Tribunal to look into and assess these cases. And this is something we've had for a few years now, and which we intend to preserve.'

Niesewand: 'Don't you believe Prime Minister . . .'

David Williams: 'Please stand up as you address the Prime Minister.'

Niesewand: ' . . . that Rhodesia may sometimes be guilty of rough justice in the cases of detention without trial?'

Smith: 'I am unaware of any such cases, and I would be happy if they were brought to my attention. You know, you have got to decide on whose side you're on in cases like this, have you not? Are you on the side of the decent, law-abiding man, woman and child in Rhodesia? Or are you on the side of the law-breaker, the mischief-maker, the intimidator? And when that question is put before me, I have no doubt in my mind, ladies and gentlemen, about whose side I'm on. I'm going to try to ensure that the decent, law-abiding citizen is given protection against intimidation, against thuggery. Don't tell me there's been none, that we haven't had cases of innocent people having their homes burnt, their motor cars burnt, who haven't been beaten up in the streets. This is there. I think it's a terrible thing. And I believe any responsible Government has a duty to try and prevent that sort of thing happening. And if we err at all, we err on the side of trying to help the person who is the law-abiding citizen, as opposed to the person who wishes to break the law. And I make no apologies for leaning in that direction.'

Sitting in my cell at Gwelo Jail, a year after that Press Conference, I wondered how Mr Smith had come to the conclusion that I was a law-breaker, a mischief-maker, or an intimidator, and I pondered on the corrupting effects of unfettered power.

I did not expect to be charged in court with any crime, and a few days after my detention, Mr Lardner-Burke himself said he knew of no action pending against me. Two senior British provincial journalists, who were visiting Rhodesia at the time as guests of the Ministry of Information, called personally at Mr Lardner-Burke's office to protest against my arrest. The Minister gave them no details of the case, but compared the situation in Rhodesia with that in Northern Ireland.

The journalists asked if I had been detained because of my activities as a newspaperman, and Mr Lardner-Burke replied: 'We do not disclose the reasons for any action taken ... where we have a security set-up, we feel these people must be put out of circulation ... I think he may be in prison. He is confined. He is taken away out of circulation.' Asked whether I was being held in Gwelo Jail, Mr Lardner-Burke said: 'Well, I think so. I am not certain. I think the one I signed said Gwelo.'

The journalists asked if I had been charged with any crime, and the Minister replied: 'Not to my knowledge.'

The Rhodesian Guild of Journalists, headed by Scots-born writer and sub-editor Bill McLean, expressed concern over my detention and said that if it had been ordered because of my professional activities, the Government should state what could and what could not be printed and published about Rhodesian affairs. The Guild also sent a deputation to see Mr Lardner-Burke, but again the Minister proved unhelpful. He would not say why I had been detained, but denied it was for criticism of the Government.

Mr Lardner-Burke told the Guild: 'Criticism does not mean detention. The Government does not detain its opponents.' He also said he did not know of any criminal charges pending against me.

After the meeting, a Guild statement said: 'Mr Lardner-Burke declined to give assurances repeatedly sought by the delegation that the freedom of expression of journalists in Rhodesia was not in jeopardy.' It is perhaps not surprising that Mr Lardner-Burke refused to give assurances on Press freedom, as all evidence points to the fact that general intimidation of journalists was one of the main reasons for my imprisonment.

I do not believe that, initially, the Rhodesian Government planned holding me for any length of time. Less than a week after my imprisonment, Ian Colvin, a senior correspondent for the London *Daily Telegraph*, reported 'informed circles' in Salisbury as saying that a move to deprive me of my Rhodesian citizenship might be pending. Mr Colvin had previously shown himself to have access to valuable and accurate sources within the administration, and from Mr Smith's point of view, deprivation of citizenship would have made sense. All it needed was for the Minister of Internal Affairs, Mr Lance Smith, to declare that I had shown myself to be 'disloyal to Rhodesia'.

Why did the Government instead embark upon an Official Secrets Prosecution, when the case against me was extremely flimsy? Why did they insist on the trial being held in secret, and the charges being kept from the public, despite the international uproar they must

69

have known would follow? A possible explanation is that Mr Smith was deliberately misadvised by a group of influential civil servants who actually welcomed the adverse publicity.

The *Daily Telegraph* reported, the day after my arrest, that the original detention move 'may have been advised by diehard groups hostile to a settlement with Britain.' If this assessment was correct, the anti-settlement diehards could well have persuaded the Government, in the face of mounting international pressure, to try and justify itself by taking further action against me – effectively plunging them deeper and deeper into controversy, and making it ever more difficult to call a halt without losing considerable face. Mr Smith, with his apparently consuming dislike of me, might easily be manipulated by senior officials. He is an ambitious and ruthless man, but in my view, not a clever one. He had already disregarded the advice of the Special Branch by ordering my detention. Could a combination of an anti-settlement faction with ready access to his office, and yes-men in the Attorney-General's Department, combine to steer him onto an ever more foolish course?

Every move the Rhodesians made was the wrong one. It is difficult to believe that such a relentless flow of mistakes was not deliberately planned.

During Nonie's first visit to me in Gwelo Jail, we discussed what treatment we might expect from the Government and from the media. I said we should work on my being held in solitary confinement for about eight weeks, and then allowed out on condition I left the country immediately and did not return. We could also expect to receive publicity for about a week, before we became unfashionable and the public's attention turned to other things. From then on, I thought we would just have to sit it out. Although the theory behind my assessment was reasonable enough, the practice turned out to be very different. We both realised that publicity was our only defence, but I knew that, however strongly newspapers and radio stations felt about my detention, they could not work in a vacuum. If I was simply sitting in solitary confinement, this would only be news for the first few days, to be then forgotten and resurrected, perhaps, on anniversaries or other special occasions. There has to be a news 'peg' for any Press report to hang on, or there's no story.

In my assessment of our publicity prospects, I did not count on such a volume of assistance from Mr Smith's Government. Whenever interest appeared to be flagging, the Rhodesians could be relied upon to take some action which would revive the story. But I had also not taken into account the masterly fight waged by Nonie to secure my release. She realised instinctively that one of the reasons so many Africans had vanished into detention without trace was that no one had fought publicly for them.

Their wives and families had remained fearful and silent, and had accepted without public protest the unjustness, unkindness and occasional viciousness of the authorities. It is, of course, both safer and easier for a European to stand up against the authorities in Rhodesia, but quiescence enables a Government to do as it pleases with people's lives, secure in the knowledge that hardly anyone knows, or cares.

Another example of a lack of fight can be seen in the case of Gerald Hawkesworth, a young white Land Inspector, employed by the Internal Affairs Ministry, who was kidnapped in January 1973 by a party of ZANU guerillas in the Mount Darwin district, and force-marched through Rhodesia into Mozambique. After some months, Mr Hawkesworth's mother – hearing reports that her son was then being held captive in Dar-es-Salaam – wrote to Rhodesian Minister of Information, Mr P. K. van der Byl, asking him to do something about securing Gerald's release. She was brushed off by Mr van der Byl and fell silent. If Nonie had been Mrs Hawkesworth, she would immediately have issued a series of Press statements, given radio and television interviews, rallied friends to stand with placards outside Mr van der Byl's office, written letters to the newspaper, and if necessary thrown an egg at Mr Smith's head – anything to keep alive public interest and maintain pressure on the authorities, not only in Rhodesia, but in Britain and Tanzania.

Nonie would have flown to Dar-es-Salaam to plead with the Tanzanian Government, even if she knew she'd be turned back at the airport. She'd have gone to London to lobby MPs in the House of Commons, or to New York to demonstrate at the United Nations. If you don't fight, you usually lose.

In my case, the combination of the Rhodesian Government and my wife proved a potent publicity mixture – and with the addition of strong protests from the National Union of Journalists in Britain, and journalistic organisations in many other parts of the world, the story gathered momentum as it went along.

But it was not only other journalists and politicians who cared. Nonie received hundreds of letters of support and encouragement from total strangers all over the world, an indication that the case had struck a chord among many ordinary people, particularly in

Britain. In my echoing isolation block at Gwelo Jail, I knew little of the growing protests. During her visits, Nonie outlined the situation to me, but it seemed too remote to take much notice of.

With my radio now allowed in my cell, and no restriction on the stations to which I could listen, I stopped singing and humming to myself, and tuned in to what was happening elsewhere in the world. On Thursday, 1 March – ten days after my arrest – I lay on my bed at sundown, listening to the BBC World Service transmissions from London. My cell was growing dark, but I felt I was settling into the routine of solitary confinement.

I was structuring my days more evenly – the toothbrushing, shaving, clothes washing, bathing, reading, radio listening and card playing periods were stretched over the eight hours between 'unlock' and 'lockup', and time did not seem quite as unyielding. Nonie had bought a month's supply of milk coupons and had left them in the prison administrative offices, so each morning I was given a pint of milk with my porridge. I was losing weight fairly fast, and although they said nothing to me at the time, Nonie and my family were worried. It wasn't only the prison diet: even on days when I couldn't face the food – and these were becoming less frequent as my standards dropped – there were always packets of grapes, oranges, biltong or chocolate sent from home. I kept outwardly calm, but in doing so, burnt up reserves of nervous energy and my weight dropped.

Still, I began to feel fairly pleased with the way I was coping with solitary confinement. Unlike Salisbury prison later, I experienced no unkindness from the staff, or officers at Gwelo Jail. There were the odd lapses in receiving newspapers or milk, but they were neither serious nor deliberate.

The officers at Gwelo were kept busy with other prisoners and, because I gave no trouble, they occasionally tended to forget I was there. I always got my food, however – again unlike Salisbury Jail, where sometimes it was left on the other side of a locked door – but two or three days might pass without me seeing a European warder. The African warders who locked me in and let me out, and opened the main doors so that my meals could be brought to me, came and went with hardly a word, whereas I could usually count on a thirty-second conversation with a white warder, and once I stretched this out to two or three minutes.

When they remembered, the officers let me have newspapers. At first, these were censored, and reports about me, or about the

Left to right: Peter Niesewand and Harvey Ward (Rhodesia Broadcasting
Corporation Head of News) interviewing the Rhodesian Prime Minister
Ian Smith for television, chaired by Bernard Gilbert. Interviews with
Mr Smith ceased in 1972 after a public clash between Peter Niesewand
and the Prime Minister

Niesewand arriving for the first day of the trial at the Regional Court

Niesewand looks out of the courtroom window during the trial

Defence lawyer Anthony Eastwood escorts Nonie Niesewand to the
Magistrates Court for the formal remand before sentencing

About fifty Rhodesians – black and white – demonstrated outside the
Magistrates Court during the sentencing of Peter Niesewand. Special
branch men walked openly among them taking photographs of the
demonstrators. All will now have files with the Security police

Nonie Niesewand talks to newsmen outside the Regional Magistrates Court after a sentence of two years was passed on her husband

Below left Isaac Maissels QC, who led the successful Appeal

Below right Peter Niesewand in London after his release

Rhodesian security situation, were carefully cut out. Later they just handed over the complete paper, and if it contained a mention of my case, they'd say 'You're on page five today,' or whatever it was, and I'd turn to it immediately.

I was still not allowed out of the isolation cell block and into the grassy exercise area, although Supt Durand said he had put in a request to his superiors for this facility. I had brought into prison with me a couple of packets of small cigars, with twenty in each box, and I smoked one a night as I lay in the gloom of my cell and listened to the radio. In this way, I marked off the days – one box of cigars finished meant twenty days had passed.

I was tuned in to the BBC, and smoking my cigar for the tenth day of my detention, when the news reader mentioned my name, and that I was to be charged under the Official Secrets Act, and my heart suddenly began pounding and I could feel my pulse pumping in my stomach. In solitary confinement, when you become dependent on a routine and fill the day by making a major production out of something simple like washing a shirt, any sudden and unexpected incident takes on threatening proportions. The longer you are in solitary, the smaller the incidents necessary to throw your equilibrium. According to a Rhodesian High Court judge, one month in solitary confinement is equivalent to a year's ordinary hard labour, and I believe him.

So I sat on the edge of my bed listening to my heart, then I prowled up and down the darkened cell with my mind racing and my thoughts disordered. First I was frightened, then angry. Why should I have to hear over the BBC news what was going to happen to me? When I calmed down, I knew I was being unreasonable. I was in jail a four-hour drive from Salisbury, and it was not easy for Anthony Eastwood simply to abandon other clients, hop in a car and drive down to Gwelo, thus losing a complete day, just to tell me I was to be charged under the Official Secrets Act. Nonie had taken a temporary job ot bring in some money, until her pregnancy was too far advanced. It was her first day at work and she couldn't drop everything and drive off. The BBC report had said no details of the charges had been given to my lawyer, so there was nothing constructive to be discussed. I knew Anthony would write to me, and as I expected, a letter arrived at Gwelo two days later, notifying me formally of the Government move. In fact, the defence team was only told the sections of the Official Secrets Act under which I would be charged after the news had been leaked to the Press, and we did not see the detailed charges for more than a week. The Director of Public Prosecutions, Brendan Treacy QC, handed them to the defence half an hour before I appeared before the Regional Court in Salisbury for a formal remand.

The stated reason for the delay was interesting. The Public Prosecutor's office said the charge sheet could not be prepared until the dockets had been received from the CID. The 'dockets' included the telex copies of my reports on the Mozambique war which the police had seized from my office in November, and had forwarded to the Director of Public Prosecutions for a decision on whether to charge me. Yet the Director had returned them to the CID.

There can be only one reason for this: at some stage, it had been decided that there were not sufficient grounds for a prosecution, and the suspect articles and other documents were therefore not retained by the Public Prosecutor's Department. This is normal practice. But suddenly, in the face of international criticism over my detention, and calls on the Rhodesian Government to either bring me to court or release me, there was an official change of mind, and it was decided to go ahead with a prosecution and link it, by implication, to the detention – although the two matters were totally separate.

Judge Harry Davies, the chairman of the Review Tribunal which holds secret investigations into the cases of detainees, said in a report to Parliament in 1971: 'Detention is not to be regarded as a punishment for what a detainee has done in the past, but as an administrative expedient designed to prevent him from doing anything in the future which would imperil the safety and order of the State.'

The Official Secrets prosecution was clearly based on a past act of mine, and it could not even be argued by the Government that my detention was a necessary preliminary to the court case. I was never interrogated on the Mozambique reports during my solitary confinement, except when I gave evidence in court. Had the authorities considered the case to be sufficiently serious, I could quite easily have been arrested by the police, immediately charged, and held in the Salisbury Jail as a remand prisoner, with the state opposing bail. Again, this is normal practice.

Yet nearly three months went by before even the decision to charge me was taken, and the delay made later official submissions about the gravity of the alleged offence, and the damage caused to the national security by my publication of Top Secret information, sound, to my ears, a little hollow.

I heard of my impending court case on a Thursday night, and on the following Saturday, Nonie drove up to Gwelo Jail to see me. I had by then adjusted to the new situation, but she did not know if I had yet been told. Mr Lowe came to my isolation block in the morning to escort me round to the main administrative offices where Nonie was waiting. She was, as usual, calm and composed, intent on giving me as much strength as possible.

After a few minutes, she said casually: 'They've decided to prosecute you under the Official Secrets Act, and a remand hearing has been set down for next Friday in Salisbury.'

I said: 'Do you think they'll send me to jail?'

She laughed. Knowing the substance of the reports, we did not feel that the matter was serious, and in any case, as I was already in solitary confinement, there seemed little I could lose.

During her visit, Supt Durand handed me the letter from Anthony Eastwood telling me officially of the Government's intention, and I took it back to my cell to study it. No details of the charges were yet available, Anthony said, but he let me have the wording of the relevant sections of the Act. The main allegation against me carried a maximum penalty of twenty-five years' imprisonment without the option of a fine. It alleged that I 'did wrongfully, unlawfully, and for a purpose prejudicial to the safety or interests of Rhodesia, obtain or collect . . . publish or communicate to a person, information which is calculated to be, or which might be useful, directly or indirectly, to an enemy.'

The alternative allegation carried a maximum jail sentence of twenty-five years, or a fine of $20,000, and its wording was similar to the first charge, except that it started from the premise that I had not specifically gone out to collect the information objected to by the Government, but already had in my possession or under my control information which 'related to a military matter', and that I had committed an offence by publishing it for a purpose prejudicial to the safety or interests of my country. It sounded very grand, but knowing what the military information was, and how widely it had been published previously, I found it difficult to believe the charges were much more than a face-saving tactic by the Government to try and justify my solitary confinement, as well as being an extension of the attempt to intimidate journalists into self-censorship.

My main worry was over being transferred to Salisbury Prison. Although I was glad Nonie would no longer have to drive a round trip of 360 miles every time she wanted to see me, I had a feeling that solitary confinement in the capital would be more unpleasant than in Gwelo.

I wrote of my fears to Nonie: 'We start again from scratch at Salisbury Jail,' I told her. 'For this reason I attach the letters I have received here, for you to add to the pile which we will one day go through together. . . . I fear they might simply be confiscated by a new régime, and I'd rather like to keep them together.

'When you come to see me in Salisbury Jail, I think it's best if you bank on us peering at each other through a window and shouting down a telephone. Maybe it won't be like that, and so it will be a nice surprise. I'm sorry this isn't a very jokey letter, because I actually feel fine.'

We did not have to endure visits in Salisbury Prison separated by a glass panel and forbidden physical contact, but leaving Gwelo meant the beginning of a new phase of my solitary confinement, including brushes with officials in which the dividing line between thoughtlessness and vindictiveness was so thin as to be invisible to the naked eye.

I was due to appear in the Salisbury Regional Court at 10 a.m. on Friday, 9 February, and it was therefore no secret that I would have to be moved from Gwelo. On the Thursday morning, Nonie telephoned the Prison Headquarters in Salisbury to find out when I was being moved, and she asked to speak to the Director, Mr Frank Patch. She was put through to his secretary, a woman with a permanent note of complaint in her voice.

'Mrs Niesewand,' said the secretary severely, 'Mr Patch is far too busy to deal with you. You'll have to speak to Mr Duncan, the Assistant Director.'

Nonie phoned prison headquarters again.

'Can I speak to Mr Duncan please?'

'Yes,' said the woman on the switchboard. 'Hold on.'

There was a click and a pause, then the woman came back to her. 'Who is calling please?'

'Mrs Niesewand.'

'Oh. Well, I'm sorry Mr Duncan isn't available.'

'When will he be available?'

'He's tied up in meetings all this morning.'

Nevertheless, Nonie phoned the prison headquarters every hour throughout the morning. When the switchboard operator asked who was calling and heard that it was her, Mr Duncan was not available. He had gone out, the woman said.

At two o'clock, after the civil service lunch break, Nonie phoned again.

'Can I speak to Mr Duncan please,' she asked.

'I'll put you through,' said the operator. 'Is that the Portuguese Consulate?'

'No, it isn't,' said Nonie.

There was a pause and the woman said suspiciously: 'Is that Mrs Niesewand?'

'Yes.'

'Mrs Niesewand, Mr Duncan is out.'

Nonie had had enough. 'We seem to be playing some kind of silly game on the telephone,' she said. 'I'm told that Mr Patch won't speak to me, and Mr Duncan is not in to me, but I will speak to somebody, and I will give you until four o'clock to find someone who will take my call.'

But she phoned again at 3 p.m.

'I want to speak to Mr Patch,' Nonie said.

The switchboard operator surrendered. 'I'll put you through to his secretary,' she said wearily.

Mr Patch's secretary was not pleased, and the complaint in her voice became more pronounced. 'Mrs Niesewand, we have told you before to ask for Mr Duncan,' she said.

'I've been trying to speak to Mr Duncan all day, but he is never available to me,' Nonie replied. 'He must have the busiest diary in the entire civil service.'

The secretary sighed, and said she would connect Mr Patch.

The Director of Prison's voice came on the line, the guarded, measured tones of a man who writes many of the regulations himself, and then hides behind them, pleading impotence.

'Mrs Niesewand?' said Mr Patch.

'Yes,' said Nonie.

'What's the problem?'

'I'm merely trying to find out whether my husband is in Salisbury now, or if he's still in Gwelo, and when he will be moved.'

Patch said: 'I am forbidden by the Emergency Regulations to tell you anything about the whereabouts of your husband.'

'Rubbish,' said Nonie. 'You must know where he is, and all I want to know is whether he's in Gwelo or in Salisbury Prison, and if he is still in Gwelo I want to know when he will be moved. He has to appear in the Regional Court at ten o'clock tomorrow morning, so it's no secret he'll have to leave Gwelo.'

Patch paused. Then he said: 'We'll tell you at 9 a.m. tomorrow.'

'But he's due to appear in court at ten.'

'Well, the only thing I can say,' said Patch, importantly, 'is that we may have some good news for you.'

Nonie put down the phone, feeling exultant. So that was the reason for the curious behaviour of senior officials at the prison headquarters. They obviously knew something important was going to happen, and Patch's 'good news' could only mean that I was to be allowed home under a house arrest order.

Nonie rushed home from her temporary job in a Salisbury Public Relations office, planning my homecoming. She bought some beef to roast, and my favourite vegetables, and her mother – who had moved in to stay with her as soon as I was detained – made arrangements to stay with friends for the weekend so that Nonie and I could be alone.

At nine o'clock on Friday morning, the telephone rang in Nonie's office, just as Mr Patch had promised.

'Mrs Niesewand?' said a voice. 'It's prison headquarters here. Your husband is being moved from Gwelo and he will appear in court at ten o'clock.'

'Yes I know,' said Nonie. 'But what about the good news? Mr Patch said there may be some good news for me.'

'Oh,' said the voice. 'Your husband is going to be detained at Salisbury Prison. You won't have to drive up to Gwelo any more. That's good news.'

chapter 7

On the Friday at 4.30 a.m., 18 days after my detention I was awakened by Mr Lowe who had obviously just got out of bed, and his bare legs showed beneath his official-issue greatcoat.

'I overslept a bit,' he said apologetically. 'We'll have to get a move on if we're going to be in Salisbury at nine. They want you at Prison Headquarters at that time.'

I had packed most of my belongings the night before, and had laid out my suit and other clothes to be worn in court.

'I'll be with you in half an hour,' I said.

'Fine,' said Mr Lowe, and went away, locking the main door behind him.

I got out of bed and went through to the bathroom. It was less than an hour until dawn, and the air was chill. For the first time since my detention, I carried toothbrush, toothpaste, hair brush, and shaving kit all at the same time. For today at least, it was not necessary to take my time.

I was just finishing dressing when Mr Lowe returned. He brought with him two African warders to help carry my suitcases, typewriter and radio to the car which had been driven along the gap between the outside prison walls and the first barbed-wire topped security fence. It was a tight squeeze.

Mr Lowe had organised hot tea in the guardroom and when we finished it, we reversed carefully out along the perimeter walls towards the front gate, where a guard let us pass. Then we drove out through the main entrance barrier, and turned into the town of Gwelo.

I sat in front of the small prison Renault – another sanctions-busting Rhodesian-assembled vehicle – and Mr Lowe drove. Behind us an African warder slumped in silence. Dawn broke as we headed along the open, deserted road towards Salisbury, and I saw again the grand vastness of veld and twisted trees which, more than anything, meant Rhodesia to me.

Mr Lowe and I talked most of the way. He showed me a copy of the *Gwelo Times* with a front-page photograph of schoolchildren being visited by the Minister of Education, Mr A. P. Smith, and pointed out his young son in the group. We discussed children, and schools, and he told me of an unsuccessful farming venture in which he had recently been involved, and of a road accident in which his face had been badly cut, explaining the scar which ran down his chin from his lip.

At about 7 a.m. we pulled into a layby, and he produced a thermos flask of coffee, a tin of sandwiches and small grilled sausages which his wife had prepared for my breakfast. It was a kind gesture, typical of the Gwelo officials. It would have been much easier for Mr Lowe to have ordered an African hard labour prisoner to prepare a few hunks of bread and margarine for me, and put a piece of dry cheese in with it. I was hardly in a position to complain.

We entered Salisbury just before 9 a.m. and drove up Jameson Avenue, past the Prime Minister's offices in Milton Buildings, and the High Court across the road where detainees' Review Tribunals are held, and finally turned into a car park next to the Prison Head-quarters. We left my luggage in the car, with the African warder looking after it, and walked to the single-storey administrative offices. Mr Lowe knocked on the open door of the office of the Chaplain-General.

'Hello Padre,' he said, 'can I leave Niesewand here with you for a moment while I go and check him in?'

'Yes of course,' said a voice from inside, and I was ushered through.

Father Clark, the Chaplain-General, had a shock of white hair, dark brown eyes set in a wrinkled, weathered face, and a gruff manner. He got to his feet, his eyes blazing. 'You're only a boy!' he cried in disbelief. 'Just a child! I thought you'd be much older. Come and sit down. What have you been up to?'

I sat down and looked around his office, with its carpet, and bookshelves and coffee table, and I smiled politely at another prison-uniformed, dog-collared man who smiled back.

'That's Padre Waugh,' said Father Clark. 'A good man. He's Free Church, but don't let that put you off. Do you want some coffee?'

'Yes please.'

'What's this all about?'

'I wish I knew,' I said. 'I'm not a particularly political person. . . .'

'Everything's political. Everyone's political. That's a stupid thing to say,' said Father Clark tetchily.

'I don't agree,' I said. 'I've never taken an active part in politics, or even joined a political organisation, and in fact I don't like politics very much. I've no idea why I've been detained. No one has ever told me, but I think it's an attempt to intimidate the Press.'

Father Clark poured boiling water onto a teaspoon of instant coffee in a cup, added milk and handed it to me with a bowl of sugar.

'What about this Official Secrets thing?' he said.

'Well,' I replied, 'I wrote some articles about the security situation in Mozambique. I said that Frelimo guerillas had attacked the Tete railway line, and Rhodesians were very worried about the way the war was going. I said Rhodesia feared that the road and rail links to Beira and Lourenço Marques may soon be cut by guerillas. . . .'

'That was a stupid thing to say,' Father Clark burst out. 'I've no time for people who stir up trouble.'

'I don't think it was stupid at all,' I said. 'Let me give you an example. More than a year ago, the *Rhodesia Herald* received a story that the road from Rhodesia to Malawi – which passes through Mozambique – was being mined by guerillas. The story was written by a reliable journalist, and his sources were trustworthy. But the *Herald* refused to print it. The editor said he didn't believe it, although he had no apparent reason to be disbelieving. Perhaps he thought, like you, that it would make people nervous, or embarrass the Portuguese, or stir up trouble. Anyway, the story was not printed. A week later, a carload of Rhodesians travelled down that road, and hit a landmine. An Asian man was killed, and others were injured. Now my point is that if the *Herald* had printed the landmine story in the first place, it's unlikely the Rhodesians would have used the road, and that man might still be alive today. It's not stupid to tell people what's happening. They've got a right to know.'

Father Clark said grudgingly: 'I suppose you're right.'

We talked for a while longer, then Mr Lowe returned.

'Mr Duncan wants to see Niesewand,' he said.

'All right, all right, I'll take him along in a moment,' said Father Clark, and he did. On the way, Clark thumbed through his diary and said he would be out of town for about ten days touring outlying prisons, but would see me when he returned. Then he ushered me into Duncan's office.

Harry Duncan, Assistant Director of Prisons, showed me a perfect set of matching porcelain teeth, and I, agreeably, showed him mine. He sat behind a large desk, with an armchair in front of it, and a small upright chair at the side, flush against the wall. His manner was so outwardly friendly that I was surprised he did not rise to greet me, and offer his hand, as he had at a previous meeting some years earlier. At that time, there had been criticism in the local Press of conditions at Salisbury Jail, and at its height, a party of journalists had been invited to tour the prison – the first, and last, time this had happened. We assembled in Mr Duncan's office and the humanitarianism of the official policy was explained to us. I remembered that, half in jest, we had left instructions with our offices to check on our whereabouts if we had not returned after two hours, and if necessary to telex off stories about how we had been tricked into entering Salisbury Jail, only to find the doors clanging permanently shut behind us.

I remembered too being shown a nicely furnished cell in the jail, with photographs on the wall, and a small carpet – 'a home from home', our guide had called it – and we had walked through the dining room as the prisoners sat down to a lunch of steak and chips. One of them said rather loudly: 'Steak! I've been here five years and I've never had steak before!' and we all went Ho ho, thinking he was joking.

Now that I was about to experience the real thing, I said to Duncan: 'I've been in Salisbury Prison before.'

He looked interested. 'Have you?' he smiled.

'Yes,' I said, 'I was in the Press party which was taken on a tour of the jail after there had been complaints about conditions there.'

'I remember,' he said, his teeth still shining at me, but his eyes now a little watchful.

'It was quite impressive,' I said. 'I'm looking forward to discovering it was not a put-up job.'

'Ha, ha,' said Duncan without conviction. 'Sit down,' and he motioned me away from the armchair and into the straightbacked chair against the side wall, lest I forget my place as a prisoner. After that, I lost interest in talking to him.

But he obviously had a job to do, and he chatted on for a while. 'We don't like detention without trial,' he said in a confiding voice. 'None of us do. But there's nothing we can do about it. It's a Government decision and we're just civil servants, and we've got to carry out official policy. People criticise us for this, but we can't even reply to them. Do you know, even if I'm personally attacked by a newspaper, I can't reply? But we don't like detention.'

He paused and looked speculatively at me, his teeth catching the light and glinting whitely.

'I've often thought what I'd do if I was detained,' he said, watching me carefully. 'I think I'd be a model prisoner, do all the right things, go to the Review Tribunal and say the right things, and then when I got out I'd leave the country and blow the whole lot sky high – tell everything.'

The silence began to stretch a little uncomfortably, so I said: 'Would you? I think I'd probably just like to get out and forget the whole thing.'

Duncan looked disappointed, but he said: 'Don't tell anyone I said that, will you?'

'No,' I said. 'I won't.'

Just before ten o'clock, I was driven from Prison Headquarters to the Regional Court. At that time, it was sitting in an office block across the road from the old Magistrates' Court, although, together with these lower courts, it was preparing to move to a newly-designed hexagonal building on the outskirts of town, a nightmare of corridors and staircases so arranged that the prisoners, magistrates and the public can come and go, without any of their paths ever crossing, except in the actual courtrooms. I was accompanied by three prison officers – two in the front, one beside me. One of them said: 'We're going to take you in the back way. There will probably be some Press people around, but you're a detainee, and you're not allowed to have your photograph taken. We've had strict instructions. Anyone who takes your photograph will be in worse trouble than you are.'

'Well,' I said, 'I'm not really in a position to stop anyone taking my photograph. But perhaps I could put a blanket over my head.'

No one laughed, and one officer said thoughtfully, 'Actually I could hold my cap in front of your face.'

'Yes,' I said, 'that would make a very nice picture.'

We turned into a sanitary alley which ran behind the Regional Court, and the officers jumped out. There were no journalists to be seen.

'Quickly,' said an officer. 'Up those stairs.'

'I don't think I like going up fire escapes,' I replied, but I went like a lamb, with the others crowding behind me.

We came out onto a balcony, and went in through french windows leading to the Reception area. On previous occasions when I had come to court to report important cases, I had spoken to the woman behind the desk, so I said cheerfully 'Good morning,' but this time she didn't even look in my direction. I had forgotten I had become invisible.

The warders led me into the first-floor courtroom, where Anthony Eastwood was reading through the detailed charge sheet which he had only just been handed.

'Hello Peter,' he said. 'Have you seen Nonie?'

'No,' I looked around. 'Where is she?'

'Oh,' he said, 'she was waiting for you at the front with a lot of journalists.'

'Ah. Well I was smuggled in through the back entrance.'

Someone went to call Nonie, and she came into court with my sister Wendy. I hugged them both, and sat on the public benches for a few minutes talking to them. About a dozen friendly journalistic faces crowded round, and I said hello. Apart from being there to cover the case, there was a fair amount of obvious professional support, for which I was grateful.

Someone said with concern: 'You've lost such a lot of weight. I can't get over it.'

'Have I?' I said in surprise. 'It's probably the porridge.'

'What's the food like?'

'Slop,' I said.

A court official motioned me into the dock, and I took my place on the wooden bench. The dock was set along the side of the court, forming a T with the desks for the Defence, with, further away, the table for the Prosecution where Brendan Treacy avoided my eye. I noticed that his face was sweating quite heavily, and I was surprised because it was not a very hot day. I thought he might be ill. Perspiration ran from his brow, down his slightly-overweight, once-handsome face, and he looked grim.

Three knocks on the door, we all rose, a voice called 'Silence in court,' and the magistrate and assessor entered, bowed, and sat down. Anthony handed me a copy of the charges, but my mind was not sufficiently keen at that stage to take in what I was reading, so I put it to one side.

Treacy stood up. 'May it please your worship,' he said. 'The charges which have been brought against the accused will be under the Official Secrets Act . . . the purpose of the accused's appearance in court today is twofold. In the first instance, it is to remand him for trial on Monday, 19th March next, and secondly, the State wishes now to apply for an order in terms of Section 403A of the Criminal Procedure and Evidence Act (Chapter 31) that the trial be held *in camera*.'

It was the first suggestion we had heard that the Government wanted to stage a secret trial.

Treacy said he had prepared an indictment which set out both the charges and the particulars of the offences alleged, but because the defence had not yet had an opportunity of examining and studying the details, he did not propose calling upon me yet to plead Guilty or Not Guilty.

Treacy then canvassed the sections of the Official Secrets Act under which I was charged, and read the relevant portions to the court.

'It is, of course, of fundamental importance as a matter of public policy that justice is not only done, but that it is manifestly seen to be done,' Treacy said. 'There must, therefore, be cogent reasons before the court will exercise the powers conferred by Section 403A. The State submits that in this case, such reasons do exist.'

On the bench, the Regional Magistrate, J. E. T. Hamilton, frowned down at the indictment. He was a big man, about 6 feet 4 inches tall, with large hands and black hair – in his forties, I guessed. Nonie said she thought he looked like a giant turtle. Beside him on his right sat the much smaller, neat-featured assessor, Mr R. Coleman, who was about twenty years his senior.

I had watched Hamilton in action on previous occasions, and he had mannerisms unusual in a magistrate. I had seen him act out little charades in court, yawning ostentatiously if he did not believe a person's evidence, opening his eyes wide and assuming an expression of mock alarm as he put a question to a witness and made it clear he expected to hear a lie in reply, or simply laughing in someone's face. You tended to know the verdict long before the end of the trial, just by watching Mr Hamilton's behaviour. It wasn't necessary to hear all the evidence. In my case, I knew before five minutes were up that I had lost. The unknown factor was the sentence Hamilton would impose, and the Defence fought the Magistrates' Court case mainly to get facts on record in preparation for the appeal. The higher up in the Rhodesian judicial system you go, the more likely you are to receive justice. But in the few moments of open court, Mr Hamilton – conscious no doubt of the publicity the case was attracting – was serious-faced and earnest. He felt able to relax into his normal manner later.

Treacy referred Hamilton to the Schedules attached to the Indictment – these comprised copies of the Mozambique report I had sent to the *Guardian* and the two versions I had telexed to the BBC, one for use in the programme 'Focus on Africa', the other for Radio Newsreel and news bulletins.

Treacy drew the court's attention to specific paragraphs in the Schedule which referred to 'Rhodesian military sources' and 'intelligence reports'.

'If your worship would peruse paragraph 6 on the first page of the Schedule,' Treacy said. 'Also I would refer your worship to page 2 of the same Schedule, paragraph 2 . . .'

Treacy avoided mentioning that the Schedules were Press reports, sent openly overseas, and published openly under my name, and he did not quote from them. For all any spectator in court knew, they could have been photostats of vital military documents which I had stolen and sold to the Russians, but that, it appeared, was what the Government hoped people would think.

Then Treacy added the clincher, which made me sit up. 'At the trial,' he said, his lips pressing grimly together between phrases, 'the evidence for the State will be that this information was, and still is, classified in the "Top Secret" category.'

I looked into the body of the court, at where Nonie was sitting, and raised my eyebrows at her in surprise as Treacy went on to read a little lecture: 'State security is of paramount importance at all times,' he said. 'In the interests of State security and because of the secret information which is alleged to be involved in this case, it is absolutely essential in my submission that the trial be held *in camera*.'

It may be, Treacy said, that the restriction could be relaxed at certain stages of the proceedings, but not – as he saw it – while witnesses were giving evidence.

The State therefore sought an order that the trial be heard *in camera*, that all unauthorised persons be excluded from the proceedings, that information revealing, or likely to reveal, any place or locality concerned or mentioned in the proceedings, should not be published, and that the whole of the proceedings – with limited exceptions granted by the Magistrate – should be kept secret.

Treacy sat down, still sweating. On the bench, Hamilton frowned down at the indictment and looked grave. After a moment, Anthony Eastwood rose.

'The Defence has only received a copy of the indictment shortly before the court commenced this morning,' he said, 'and I have hardly had time to peruse it. I have only had time to glance through it.

'At this stage, I can do little more than reserve my client's rights to ask your worship to reconsider any order your worship may be disposed to make at this stage.'

He then tried to take the sting out of Treacy's observations on the 'secret information' involved. 'With respect,' Eastwood said, 'although there may be parts of the Schedules which do support what my learned friend has said, they do appear to be documents of a public sort of nature which have been published generally.'

Turning to the particulars of the indictment Eastwood said he did not see why these should be kept secret. 'They simply describe the charge without giving any technical details, so to speak . . . my client has every interest in having his trial quite open and for the public to know what charges he is facing, and to counteract any ill-founded rumours which may otherwise circulate.

'I am not in a position to take my argument any further at this stage,' Eastwood said, 'but I do reserve my rights to do so at a later stage.'

On the bench, Hamilton shuffled his papers gloomily and stared down at Anthony Eastwood.

'The Court naturally abhors holding proceedings *in camera*,' Hamilton replied solemnly, 'but it is quite clear from the Schedule to the charge that the particulars refer to defence matters. We have the statement of the Director of Public Prosecutions that some of those matters are classified as Top Secret, therefore on the face of it, it does appear that it is in the interests of the defence of the country that the proceedings be held *in camera*. Further, the Director of Public Prosecutions has applied that all persons other than officers of the court and other persons whose presence is necessary in connection with the trial be excluded from the proceedings. Also that information revealing, or likely to reveal any place or locality concerned or mentioned in the proceedings shall not be published, and the whole of the proceedings, with limited exceptions, shall not be published.

'It is, on the face of it,' Hamilton declared, 'in the interests of defence that the Court direct accordingly.'

So I was remanded until 19 March, without even the charges against me being published, and in terms of my Detention Order, I was returned to solitary confinement. When the court rose, I walked over to say goodbye to Nonie, and remarked to journalists gathered around: 'That sounded much more exciting than it really was.'

Prison officers tapped me on the shoulder, and I was escorted to the back of the building, down the fire escape and through a narrow alleyway to the sanitary lane where the prison car stood. A small group of Press photographers waited there, and the officers held a hurried consultation. Then they walked ahead of me, holding their hands aggressively towards the cameramen and saying 'No photographs . . . you're forbidden to take photographs. . . .' The group lowered their cameras obediently, and I walked out.

'Hello gentlemen,' I said to my colleagues, and they chorused a muted reply.

We sped away to Salisbury prison.

The maximum security jail is on the left as you drive out of the capital along the Enterprise Road in the direction of the Mozambique border – acres of high walls, barbed wire and watchtowers, with a newly-built four-storey cell block stretching above the walls and visible from the road, its windows barred and covered with thick steel mesh. On the top floor are cells for African detainees. The prison adjoins a large area of open land running parallel to the main road where, behind fences, African hard labour convicts plant vegetables and tend the land.

We turned in to a dirt road where a sign said 'Salisbury Prison – Remand and Holding Section', and at the perimeter security fence, African guards opened a high wire gate, then lifted a boom, and we drove through to the main door. A smell of open drains, or perhaps sewerage, hangs around the prison, musty and unpleasant. One of the officers lifted the highly-polished brass knocker and dropped it with a sharp bang, and after a second, the peephole opened and an eye peered through at us. Inside a voice called 'Gate!' and there was a rattle as a key came down a metal chute a few yards away to be retrieved by the guard on duty. Like other prisons, Salisbury has two large and heavy wooden double doors, and inset into the right-hand door is a small wicket gate. You have to stoop and step over a foot high section of wood at the base of the main door to climb through, which we did when the panel was unlocked.

I stood for a moment inside the prison, looking around. I was in a fairly large, covered-over area, a bit like a garage with a window at one end and a sign for visitors saying 'Please leave your car keys here.' A passage ran off to the left to the offices of the Prison Superintendent, Brian Ruff, and his second-in-command, and at the end, there was a visitors' room just big enough for a small table and three upright chairs. To my right were more administrative offices and a sign saying 'Reception'. The sign warned that all money, valuables, passports and drivers' licences had to be handed in, and failure by prisoners to comply would lead to immediate confiscation of unauthorised goods.

I was led through to the Reception office, where everyone ignored me for a few minutes. It must be a prison rule. Then I saw Mr Lowe, who had brought my bags and property from the prison headquarters. He handed over to the Salisbury authorities the bag containing my rings and wristwatch, and the $1.67 that had been taken off me at Gwelo Jail, together with a list of my property. This was entered into the Salisbury Jail 'valuables book' and I signed it.

Mr Lowe turned to me and held out his hand. 'Well, goodbye,' he said, speaking more loudly than usual so that the others would have no trouble hearing. 'Good luck. Behave yourself here as well as you did in Gwelo and you'll have no trouble.'

I grinned at him and shook his hand firmly. 'Goodbye Mr Lowe,' I said. 'You've been very kind.'

When he'd gone, the three officers behind the desk in Reception apparently again forgot my existence, and I stood around for nearly half an hour. Finally a warder came through and said: 'Niesewand, Mr Ruff wants to see you now.'

I followed him down the passage, across the entrance area, up two steps into another passage and along the concrete floor to the office of the Superintendent of Salisbury Remand and Holding Prison.

The officer knocked twice and said: 'Niesewand, sir.' He stood aside as I went in, and then positioned himself behind me near the door. Supt Brian Ruff looked up from his desk, a pile of mail in front of him – including two letters addressed to me – and stared with cold eyes. He was well-built and flat-voiced, a man in his thirties with dark hair cropped short. His mouth was thin and slightly reptilian, and the overall impression was of someone making a conscious effort to keep himself in check. His voice was too soft and mechanical, his face and body too deliberately relaxed, his pauses too long, and his eyes, which just missed being 'quiet', had settled somewhere between coldness and hostility. He slowly twiddled a thin metal dagger-shaped letter opener. I stood in front of him and waited.

He shifted his gaze to the letter opener, and addressed most of his remarks to it, only occasionally staring up at me.

'You're a detainee, but that doesn't mean you don't have to submit to prison discipline,' said Ruff. 'You might think that you're being held in solitary confinement, and in a way you'll be correct. You will be kept in an isolation block, and you are forbidden to have contact with any other prisoners. They will be mostly remand prisoners awaiting trial, and you're in detention and there are security factors in your case. Do you understand?'

'Yes.'

'You will be allowed to send and receive one letter a week, and you will be allowed one visit a week lasting half an hour.'

I said: 'Won't it be possible for you to authorise more frequent visits? In Gwelo, I was allowed a visit every day.'

Ruff looked at me. 'I don't know what they did in Gwelo, but the rule here is one visit a week. I take it you'll want the visit to be from your wife?'

'Yes, please.'

'And you'd also want your weekly letter to be from your wife? If she sends one?'

'Yes.'

'All your visits will be conducted within sight and sound of a prison official.'

'Even visits from my lawyer, when we're preparing the Official Secrets defence?' I asked.

Ruff paused and examined the letter opener closely. 'I don't know about that,' he said. 'As a detainee, you're only allowed private visits from your lawyer if you're laying a charge of some sort against myself or against any member of the prisons' staff. Then it would be improper for us to be present.'

There was a long silence. I said: 'When I appeared in court this morning for remand, I was given a copy of the charges against me. And I've also brought with me some letters and some photographs of my wife and son which I received in Gwelo, and which were passed by the prison authorities there. I'd like to keep them.'

Ruff held out his hand, and I gave him the small pile of mail – all of it from Nonie – together with the photographs and the indictment.

'I'll look through them later,' said Ruff, putting them to one side.

'I'd also like permission to keep my typewriter and my radio in my cell.'

'I'll consider it. But I don't think you'll be allowed the radio. Did you have it in Gwelo?'

'Yes, I was allowed to keep everything with me. I'd also like to keep and wear my own clothes, and I've got a cardboard box of fruit and chocolate and so on which I brought from Gwelo.'

Ruff nodded assent, and there was another silence as he fiddled with the thin silver knife.

He looked straight at me. 'What's happening about the Official Secrets charge?' he asked.

'I've been remanded until 19 March for trial.'

'Do you think you're going to be found guilty?'

'I've no idea. I'll cross that bridge when I come to it.'

'A very wise attitude,' Ruff said evenly. 'In any case, as a detainee, you don't know how long you're going to remain in prison, so it's best if you don't get yourself worked up.'

'I think you'll find,' I said, 'that I will be no trouble.'

Ruff stared up at me. 'All detainees who come in here start off with the best intentions. But frustration breaks some of them.'

I was escorted out, along the passage and into the entrance area. A warder shouted 'Inside!' and the keys to the inside gates, a trellis of metal separating casual visitors and lawyers from the prison proper, came rattling down the chute and were taken by an African warder who opened a padlock and pulled the gates partly open to let us pass through.

We walked through a tarmac enclosure to a row of storerooms, where I was handed three blankets, a pillow, a pair of large flannel pyjamas without a cord for the pants in case I hanged myself, two sheets and a pillow slip also of flannel. I was given a rough green towel, and a khaki shirt and trousers. I would get a change of clothes and sheets once a week.

The officer pulled a large cardboard box from a shelf and dropped it onto the floor. 'Put your civilian clothes in there,' he said. 'You're only allowed to keep your underwear, socks and shoes.'

'I thought Mr Ruff said I could keep my own clothes,' I said.

He hesitated. 'I don't know,' he said. 'I'll check. Meanwhile, you'd better take these.'

I stripped and packed my suit, shirt and tie into the cardboard box, taking some sweets and chewing gum out of a pocket. The warder said: 'What's that?'

I showed him. 'You're not allowed gum,' he said.

'Why ever not?' I asked.

'In case you saw through the bars and use the gum to hide the marks.'

'Oh really,' I said, interested. 'What am I going to use to saw through the bars?'

He shrugged. 'I've no idea.'

I put the gum back into the suit pocket, and pulled on the khaki prison dress. 'It's not exactly from the Pierre Cardin spring collection, is it?' I said, and he rewarded me with a thin smile.

'What are you in for?' the warder asked.

'I'm a detainee, and I'm also being charged under the Official Secrets Act, but they're not connected.'

Noncommittal: 'Oh.'

We walked off in silence, through another door and into the European and coloured (mixed blood) remand section. We were in about a quarter of an acre of carefully-tended green grass and flowers, bounded by high walled compounds, each housing five or more prisoners. The entrance to some of the compounds was through six-foot-high doors built of metal bars, and on the far side of small concrete courtyards stood the thick wooden doors of individual cells. It was a bit like a badly planned zoo. Some white prisoners sat on the concrete with their khaki shirts off, catching the sun. A group of half-caste men hung on the bars of their compound gate shouting 'White trash', and 'Hullo jailbird', and 'Have you got a cigarette?' and I smiled at them.

We stopped at an administrative office while the warder balanced a tiny tube of toothpaste, a new toothbrush, a razor, brush, blades and shaving soap, and a cake of cheap soap for washing, on top of the pile I was carrying. In one corner of the prison garden was the entrance to Block D, and we walked towards it. The warder turned the key in the brass lock, then pulled a handle which moved with a loud bang, and the wooden door swung open.

I stepped into a concrete courtyard, surrounded by twelve-foot-high walls. At the entrance, I looked straight into the doorless ablution block with its lavatory, bath and basin. Barbed wire was strung above the courtyard to form a sort of ceiling – a barrier between me and the sky.

The warder went to the far cell and the door opened with a crash. I walked across, laden with prison bedding and equipment and looked with a sinking heart into my 'home from home'.

'Gracious,' I said tonelessly.

'We call it the Bridal Suite,' said the warder, and went away, locking the main door after him.

chapter 8

The cell was small and gloomy, with a reinforced concrete ceiling, and two small high windows covered by bars and heavy steel mesh. Most of the space was taken up by an iron bed, whose covering wire strands sank dramatically in the middle, and were only half attached to one side. On top was a filthy coir mattress which looked as if it had been dragged through mud at some stage in its long history. There was nothing else in the cell, except a long piece of paper fastened onto the back of the door with a drawing pin, and headed 'PRISON OFFENCES'. It began with mutiny, and went on to include wilfully refusing to eat the food provided, escaping, and suicide. The original list had been extended, and a quarto sheet of paper had been glued to the bottom of a foolscap one, to cope with the overflow. It made dispiriting reading.

I thought I had better do something about the mattress first, so I covered it with one of the prison blankets, and immediately the cell looked more pleasant. Then I made up the bed, and went exploring. The cement-floored cell itself was eight feet long and six feet wide. The exercise yard, with its barbed wire ceiling, was perhaps twice this size and with the outside door locked, was completely shut off from the rest of the Remand Section. The bathroom looked clean enough, and I ran the tap marked 'Hot' to see if it was. Warm water came out, and also a worm, about two inches long and dead.

I heard a key turn in the lock and I hurried back to my cell so I wouldn't be seen waiting near the door for someone to come. I was sitting safely on the bed by the time the door crashed open and a voice shouted 'Scoff!' I went out and took from an African prisoner a tin plate of food and a knife, fork and spoon. 'Thanks very much,' I said, and returned to my cell to find out what meals were like at Salisbury prison. It was the first time I had ever eaten fish which tasted solely of grit and peanut butter, and after two mouthfuls, I

93

gagged on the taste and the smell, and ran for the bathroom for a drink of water. Mindful of the dead worm, I sucked the liquid through my teeth, then leaned against a wall, panting.

After a few minutes, I felt better, and returned to the cell holding my breath against the smell of the food, to get the fish plate out and into the exercise yard. I did not know if I was allowed to leave the meal, or whether it would be considered a Prison Offence, so after some thought I scraped it into the lavatory bowl and flushed it away. It vanished without trace.

I did not know what time it was, but I imagined it to be nearly midday. Anthony Eastwood had said he would be visiting me in the afternoon to discuss the Official Secrets charges, but of course, I no longer had the indictment: Supt Ruff had taken it away for inspection. So I lay on my back, stared at the ceiling and waited.

Outside the prison gates, Nonie was beginning to fight her first major battles with the prison authorities: campaigns I only heard about in detail after my release. The first issue was that of visits. Prison Headquarters advised Nonie to contact Supt Ruff to make arrangements for seeing me, and she phoned him at 2 p.m. that Friday.

'Good afternoon, Superintendent Ruff,' she said. 'It's Mrs Niesewand here. I understand you are holding my husband as a detainee.'

'Yes, that's correct,' Ruff replied.

'Well, I've been told to phone you at this time to find out when I can visit him.'

'You can visit him any weekday between nine and eleven thirty, and two and three thirty. Visits are only permitted between those hours, but not during weekends.'

It sounded virtually the same as the arrangements at Gwelo Jail, and Nonie was relieved that conditions wouldn't be as bad as I had feared. She would be able to see me virtually every day, without having to drive a round trip of 360 miles.

'Oh that's great,' she said. 'So I can come any time during the week?'

'As long as you only stay for half an hour,' Ruff said.

'Half an hour?' asked Nonie. 'Oh you mean I can see him for half an hour every day during the visiting times?'

Ruff's voice had an edge to it: 'No,' he said. 'Detainees receive one half-hour visit a week.'

'This is ridiculous. I can't get only half an hour a week. I've got too

94

many business problems. I desperately need to clear them up with Peter and also from the humanitarian aspect, I have got to see him more often.'

'No form of business may be conducted from a prison,' replied Ruff, and Nonie, who had begun to cry, hung up.

She sat in her Salisbury office, weeping for the first time since the day I was detained. Her bosses were kind and sympathetic. They organised a cup of strong coffee, and poured a slug of brandy into it.

When she had collected herself, Nonie phoned Ruff again.

'Superintendent Ruff, it's Mrs Niesewand,' she said.

'Ah,' he said.

'I would like to find out from you whether you have permitted Peter to have his radio and his typewriter.'

'I have taken away his radio and his typewriter.'

'Why?'

'It's a matter of prison security. He will not be allowed a radio in prison. It's prison policy. Mr Patch says so.'

'This is nonsense. It's not prison policy because he had a radio for three weeks in Gwelo Jail.'

'Well he won't have one here.'

'Can you explain why he was allowed to have a radio in Gwelo, and isn't allowed to have one here?'

'Possibly Gwelo slipped up.'

'Well,' said Nonie, 'our lawyer will look into the matter of both the typewriter and the radio being returned to him.'

'I don't think your lawyer will get away with that one,' Ruff replied.

Anthony Eastwood arrived at the prison that afternoon to take my instructions on the Official Secrets prosecution, and I was escorted to the visitors' room to meet him.

'I haven't been able to think about this very much,' I said, 'because Mr Ruff has taken away the indictment, and I haven't had a chance to read it.'

'Why did he take it away?' asked Anthony, surprised.

'I've no idea,' I said. 'I think he wanted to read it himself.'

Anthony let me see his copy of the charges, and we discussed the situation as best we could, but we were handicapped by the fact that I hadn't had an opportunity to consider the detailed indictment. The weekend was coming up, and Anthony would not be able to see me again until the Monday. We had only ten days in which to prepare our defence, and we had already lost three of them because of Mr Ruff's action.

'If we're not ready, we could always ask for a postponement,' Anthony said.

'Oh no,' I said. 'Please don't. It just means I have to sit in solitary confinement longer, because I doubt if the Government will release me from detention until after the court case.'

I was worried about the question of timing. The Review Tribunal had notified Anthony they would consider my detention on the following Wednesday morning. Armed with nothing more than the knowledge of my innocence, I hoped to be able to persuade them that the order made against me was unjust. If I managed to do this, or at least convince them to recommend my release from solitary confinement, and my detention under house arrest, it would be helpful to have the Official Secrets case out of the way. It would tend to clear the decks for the authorities. The Minister of Law and Order is not obliged to accept the recommendations of the Tribunal, although, in practice, he usually does. I wanted to make it easier for him – and therefore for me.

Anthony said he would do his best to have the Defence case ready, despite the latest handicap. He also had some good news: Michael May, QC, one of the best legal minds in Rhodesia, had agreed to lead the Defence team in the Regional Court, and Anthony would sit in with him as an adviser. Mr May had previous experience with Official Secrets cases which would be very useful.

Then Anthony left and I was returned to my cell. It was just after three o'clock, and another tin plate of fish was awaiting me. I flushed it away without even trying to eat.

It was a busy afternoon. Ruff and a prison warder came to my cell, and stood looking in, Ruff lightly tapping a leather-covered swagger stick into the palm of one hand.

He glanced around my cell and said mechanically: 'I'll bet you didn't expect such luxury.'

'No,' I said. 'I don't know if I'll ever be able to tear myself away, although I'll certainly try.'

He gave me a watery smile.

'Your wife is a bit upset because you are only allowed one visit a week. I've told her that it's the regulations.'

'Well,' I said, 'Probably the reason she's upset is that she was allowed to visit me whenever she liked in Gwelo, and so were my family. It's not easy adjusting from a liberal regime to a less liberal one.'

'Extra visits can only be granted on humanitarian grounds,' he replied.

'Superintendent Durand at Gwelo thought that the fact that I was detained in solitary confinement, and Nonie was pregnant, and my business had collapsed, and she was trying to sort it out, were enough to justify daily visits.'

Ruff swung his swagger stick casually by his side and took his time. Finally he said: 'Well it isn't enough for me. Extra visits are the exception, not the rule.'

There wasn't any point in pushing the matter further, and I was certainly not going to plead with him.

'Anything else?' he said.

'Yes, I wonder if I could have the box of fruit and sweets which I brought from Gwelo and my clothes.'

Ruff looked at the warder who said: 'I haven't had a chance to go through it yet and make a list, sir.'

'Wasn't there a list from Gwelo?' Ruff asked.

'Yes sir, there was.'

'Well, it will all be on there. You can just hand them over to him.'

They went away, and within half an hour, I had a suitcase, a holdall and some food, and the Bridal Suite began to look a little brighter.

Lockup was at 4.30, and when the door banged shut, the cell darkened suddenly and seemed to close in. I shut my eyes and lay back on the bed, wondering how I'd manage to sleep in the bottom of the dip on such a lumpy mattress. Then I heard the high whine of a mosquito, then another, and a third, and the prospect of sleep seemed almost as remote as the prospect of release from jail. I folded the trousers of the prison pyjamas into a crude swatter, and tried to follow the progress of the mosquitoes but they were impossible to see in the gloom. I had an aerosol can of insect killer in the cardboard box, but as there was so little ventilation in the cell, I wondered if it would be a good idea to spray. I compromised by giving a couple of short bursts from the can in the direction of the insects' whine, and there was silence for a short time.

At about sundown, I heard footsteps coming along the concrete path through the prison garden, and the key in the outside lock, then the crash of the door opening, and more footsteps, and more rattling in my cell keyhole, while the light clicked on and an eye looked at me through a peephole. I felt an urgent need to go into a song and dance routine, but settled on just glaring back. The door opened and a warder came in, peered under my bed and behind the door.

'What are you looking for?' I asked.

The warder flushed slightly. 'You never know,' he said. Then: 'Are you all right?'

'Yes thank you. I'm fine.'

'Goodnight.'

'Can you leave the light off please?'

'Why?'

'Because I want to go to sleep now and because if it's on, the cell's going to fill up with even more mosquitoes than are here already.'

'Oh all right. Goodnight.'

'Goodnight.'

The door slammed shut, the light switched off and the cell was suddenly very dark. A few minutes later, a light in the exercise yard came on, to burn the whole night and shed a glow through one of the barred and meshed windows. A light also shone through the window on the opposite wall – reflections of the floodlight which illuminated the distance between my cell and the main prison wall, with its barbed wire top. I was perhaps ten yards from a watch tower, and this was another disadvantage of the Bridal Suite. I lay awake over many nights, listening to jolly conversations, and one loud argument, between the African on watchtower duty and the man guarding the main perimeter fence entrance. Guard duty at night is no doubt very boring, but so is enforced listening to shouts and laughter.

That first night was one of the worst. I lay for an hour, swatting at the mosquitoes as they whined their way towards my face and arms, until I heard the crashing opening of the compound entrance door, boots over concrete. My light flicked on and someone peered through the magnifying peephole at me.

'You OK?'

I screwed up my eyes against the harsh light. 'Yes, I'm fine,' I said, and the cell was plunged again into darkness. When the boots had gone and the compound door had crashed shut, I got out of bed and again felt in the cardboard box for the aerosol spray. It would be worth spending the night in a cell filled with pyrethrum spray just to get rid of the infuriating mosquito noise. The hiss of the spray sounded loud in the small cell, and I directed the jet around the window sills, into the air, under the bed and around the door. When I had finished, the smell of insecticide was heavy around me and tickled in the back of my nose. I stood very still listening, but there was no sound from the mosquitoes.

I climbed back into bed, and pulled the sheet over my face to try and filter out some of the spray, but the flannel was too thick to let in much air. Half an hour later, my ears caught the high-pitched whine of a mosquito, and then another, and I lay with my sinuses blocking in an aerosol-spray-filled room while mosquitoes flew imperviously around me, making low passes over my face, with the occasional sudden silence indicating one had landed. I swatted hard at my face from time to time, but finally just lay trying to control my rising temper, and trying, without success, to give some hard thought to the forthcoming Review Tribunal and the Official Secrets trial. I dropped off to sleep for an hour or two around midnight, and then lay motionless on my back with my eyes closed, waiting for dawn. The mosquitoes had fallen silent: they were presumably filled with my blood, and content.

Just after dawn, I heard the low rumble of a hundred voices as African prisoners were escorted from their cells to go out in work gangs, and a few minutes later, my cell block was opened by a short, fair-haired warder who stood aggressively in the door. He was about eighteen years old and had grown a spiky moustache in an attempt to look more imposing. His voice was hard and threatening, modelled perhaps on some Regimental Sergeant Major. If he hadn't been so young, I should have found him extremely disagreeable. Perhaps in years to come, prisoners in Rhodesia will find cause to hate this man heartily.

'Good morning,' I said, but he ignored the greeting.

'Do you want BREAKFAST?' he demanded, and I was surprised at his ability to make this simple question sound like a military order.

'Yes please.'

'THEN GET UP AND FETCH IT.'

So I did. I put on a white towelling dressing gown from my suit-case and padded out into the concrete exercise yard to the main door, where two African prisoners stood, one holding a plate of mealie meal porridge, and the other a pot of tea. I said thank you to the Africans, and gave the young white warder a friendly smile. He looked away, his pale blue eyes hostile. At barred gates nearby, white prisoners stood silently, porridge plates in hand, watching me with interest. 'Good morning gentlemen,' I said, and they replied at once. No hostility there.

I re-entered my compound and the warder slammed the door shut behind me. The porridge was at least hot – an improvement on Gwelo – and I ate around the splash of milk until there was no more to dilute the mealie meal, then I flushed the rest away. I swept out my cell, the exercise yard and the ablution block, made my bed, and sorted through the cardboard box of provisions. The warder had obviously not checked through it, as several packets of chewing gum lay at the bottom. I wondered whether to turn them over to the warder in case of a later search, and disciplinary action, but in the end I hid them and ate my way secretly through the stock.

A slight movement caught my eye: a mosquito. I had nearly forgotten about them. Around the ceiling, they stood bloated and the one that had been flying moved sluggishly. I reached for the prison pyjama pants and began swatting. I killed seventeen mosquitoes in my cell that morning, and in the days following, the after-breakfast kill rate was at least five.

Later I sat cross-legged on my bed and played solitaire for most of the day. Lunch at 11.30 was a vast improvement on Friday's fish and the Gwelo meals – there was a piece of low-grade meat, highly peppered, with mashed potato and dry butter beans, and I ate hungrily. In the afternoon, a warder brought me a food parcel which Nonie had just delivered to the prison, including a hot bowl of a delicious babutie – a Cape Malay dish of meat, egg and spices, which a few minutes before had been cooking at my home. I was delighted to have it, but special kindnesses like that cut deep, and I ate the babutie sitting on the edge of my bed feeling more desolate than at any time before.

After lockup, I lay looking into the darkness and wondering if I would ever be free. I thought about the prison authorities taking away the cord of my pyjama trousers in case I hanged myself, yet providing me with a kitchen knife to keep in my cell with a fork and spoon, and a packet of razor blades. I thought briefly about cutting my wrists, and long about cutting other people's throats. If anything happens to Nonie because of my detention, I thought, I will dedicate my life to revenge. I will hire assassins to kill members of the Lardner-Burke family, and the Smiths, starting with their children and ending with the politician fathers. In the unreal world of prison, and detention without trial, melodramatic thoughts of murder and revenge seem perfectly reasonable. The politicians had suddenly and unjustly plunged my family and myself into an ordeal, which had no scheduled end, and it was an easy matter to decide that the nightmare should be turned back on them.

It was ridiculous: I had been in solitary confinement for less than four weeks. What, I wondered, was the state of mind of African detainees – the future political leaders of Rhodesia – who had been in prison without ever being charged or brought to court (even before a secret court) for ten years and longer? Whose young children were now adult strangers, and whose wives had become used to effective widowhood, and an overriding fear of the white authorities. It is an easy matter for Mr Lardner-Burke to sign a Detention Order without paying much attention to it ('I think he may be in prison . . . I think the one I signed said Gwelo . . . He is confined, he is taken away out of circulation') but it is not easy for those directly concerned to live with the consequences of his action.

The following day, I no longer wanted to revenge myself on the Rhodesian Government, but I could not shake the feeling of desolation and hopelessness.

On Monday, Nonie resumed the fight on my behalf, with two targets – getting me my radio and typewriter, and improving the visiting arrangements. She telephoned the Special Branch to ask if they had any objection to my having a radio. No, they said, none at all. The radio had not been taken away on their instructions, but when pressed to write a letter to the prison authorities saying so, they declined to do this on the basis that they could not interfere with the operations of another department.

Nonie then sat down and wrote a letter to Frank Patch, the Director of Prisons. She said she understood from Supt Ruff that she could only visit me for half an hour a week, and when she had explained she had to see me more often for business reasons, she was told that no business could be conducted from a prison. Nonie said: 'I must explain to you a little of what this detention without trial has meant to us both. I will ignore any reference to the pain that this separation has caused – that is a private matter Peter and I have to face alone. But the break-down of Peter's business through his detention is a matter that does involve the Government authorities, as they are making it so difficult for me to operate the business.

'The Government has deprived my husband of his livelihood but not of his financial commitments. Aside from my job taken to help support the family, I am running Peter's office. With ten clients – all of whom have individual book-keeping systems and complicated paying procedures (all earnings come in as foreign exchange) – you can perhaps appreciate some of the problems I face.

'I have taken on the services of a journalist and a book-keeper to relieve some of the pressure. Obviously, their services have to be paid for – I am selling our recently-purchased house to raise money. I have also had to foreclose on Peter's insurance policies and pension schemes for the same reason.

'All these matters need to be referred to Peter, and his advice taken.

'I also need advice on some of the administrative snags we run into. I stress that these problems do not, in any way, involve the sending out of Press reports from Peter's office. They are purely administrative.'

Nonie said that Supt Durand at Gwelo prison would be able to confirm that our hourly visits every second day were taken up almost entirely with business matters.

'I would be most grateful,' she wrote, 'if you could grant me permission to see Peter more often – it would help somewhat to relieve the almost intolerable burden I am carrying.'

It took ten days for her to receive a brief reply – from Assistant Director Harry Duncan, not from Patch – who said that requests for extra visits should be made to Mr Ruff, and added: 'I would, however, point out that extra visits are the exception and not the rule.'

It was not the prison regulations, nor the authorities' alleged dislike of detention without trial, nor even their concern with humanitarianism, that finally effected a change in the arrangements. What it took was some string-pulling by Nonie with Desmond Lardner-Burke. After a word from the Minister, extra visits for me suddenly became the rule, not the exception, and Patch, Duncan and Ruff began to jump about. However, this took almost a month to arrange. For African detainees, whose wives did not grow up as neighbours of the Lardner-Burkes, it could take forever.

Nonie achieved quicker results in her campaign to get me a radio and my typewriter. On the Tuesday after my arrival at Salisbury Jail, Ruff – during a telephone conversation – agreed that he would let me have the typewriter and a radio which could not pick up foreign stations, but only transmissions from the Rhodesia Broadcasting Corporation. Nonie immediately went to my office to fetch a small transistor desk radio which could only receive medium-wave signals, and she dropped it in at Salisbury Jail. A day or so later, Mr Ruff asked a member of his staff to pass it on to me.

With my own clothes, food parcels from home and from friends, a radio, typewriter and books – and a trestle table which a friendly warder organised for me – the Bridal Suite looked less gloomy. A white officer looked around my cell one day. 'It looks like you've got everything,' he said.

'Yes,' I replied. 'Except freedom.'

'That's true,' he said seriously. 'That means a lot.'

With my Review Tribunal coming up on the Wednesday morning, I lay on my bed preparing myself mentally for it, rehearsing what I would say to Judge Davies and his two 'assessors', and puzzling over what allegations the Government had made. I could not expect to be told the charges against me, but if I guessed correctly, I stood a good chance of winning my freedom. I was fairly confident that – if I just talked on and on about settlement, security, the Ministry of Information, my life as a journalist, and sanctions – I would cover most of the suspect areas, and I hoped the Tribunal would throw in a question or two to indicate whether I was close to the heart of the matter or not.

On the Tuesday night, I managed to get some sleep, and woke feeling calm and prepared. I ate my breakfast porridge, then dressed and shaved. Just after 7 a.m. the young warder with the spiky moustache came to my cell.

'Are you expecting to go to the Tribunal today?'

'Yes,' I said. 'They're hearing my case at ten o'clock.'

'They're not. It's been postponed.' He turned to leave.

'Well why? What's happened.'

'I don't know.'

'Are you sure about this, because they formally notified my lawyer that it was due to sit this morning at ten? There must be some mistake. Does my lawyer know?'

'I suppose so. I've just had a telephone call saying it's off.'

'Who phoned? Do you know?'

'I think it was your lawyer. I forget the name.'

'Eastwood?'

'It may have been Eastwood.'

'Well, why has it been postponed?'

'I don't know.'

'When will it be held now?'

'Next week. It's been postponed until next week.'

When he had gone, I lay in my cell and tried to stop trembling. Having prepared myself mentally for this new ordeal, I found the sudden disappointment incredibly hard to take, but I thought: they're trying to break me, and I knew it was important to get quickly back onto a more even level – to switch from alertness back to the empty world of solitary confinement. Yet I felt rage building up in me, and I could not control it. I wanted desperately to smash my fist into somebody's face, but I knew I would be in real trouble if I attacked a warder. I picked up a suitcase and crashed it into the wall, but it did little to relieve my feelings, so at last I began to hit myself, smacking my hand across my face hard and often, until the stinging and the rush of blood to my cheeks made me stop. Then I lay on my face on the bed.

Anthony Eastwood came to the jail the following afternoon with Michael May to discuss the Official Secrets trial. It was the first time I had met May, and it was very important to discuss my defence, but I first had to know about the Tribunal. Anthony had not been informed of the postponement until the last moment. He had been told that the Tribunal did not want to consider my case until after the trial was over, a decision I found extremely difficult to understand as the two matters were not linked. Detention is an administrative expedient ostensibly designed to prevent me committing crimes in the future: the trial was considering an action committed in the past. Anthony was not able to clarify the matter – his information from the authorities had been both late and sketchy. Judge Davies, who was on record as considering that a month of solitary confinement was equivalent to a year's hard labour, was content to leave me in detention for as long as it took the Official Secrets matter to be decided. There is often a considerable difference between what Rhodesian officials say, and what they actually do, and it was being brought home to me in a most unpleasant way.

Anthony, Michael May and I sat in the small visitors' room, and when I had finished asking about the curious workings of the Review Tribunal, we turned to the Official Secrets trial and defence tactics. I had suggested to Anthony that it might be better if I did not give evidence at all, but instead made an unsworn statement from the dock which meant that I could not be questioned at all. I knew I would be cross-examined on my source of information, and I could not answer the court's questions – a refusal which, I thought, might anger the Magistrate unnecessarily. May advised me not to adopt this course of action. He thought that the favourable points I could make during my evidence would outweigh any possible damage caused by protecting my sources, and I agreed to take the stand.

Back in my compound, I began the psychological buildup to the trial – to suddenly being taken from solitary confinement, put on a witness stand, and bombarded with questions by an able and aggressive Director of Public Prosecutions. I needed to be articulate and quick-witted. As I ran a bath in the ablution block, I went through an imaginary cross-examination in my mind, and I wondered what the listed Prosecution witnesses would have to say, and particularly the Secretary for Law and Order, John Fleming, who was obviously going to be the State's star witness, around whose evidence was going to be built the case that I had published Top Secret information, useful to an enemy.

My train of thought was interrupted by the sight of five white worms floating in my bath water, and I scooped them out with my hand and threw them into the lavatory. There was obviously a worm colony somewhere in the water tank above the door leading into my compound – a tank which, when the sun was shining sufficiently brightly, heated up by the afternoon to provide warm water. I supposed I could complain: but decided if I did, they might simply withdraw the warm water supply. I'd sooner fish out worms.

chapter 9

The trial began on Monday morning, 19 March. I awoke at 6 a.m. to the sound of the African hard labour gangs leaving the prison. After morning porridge, I dressed quickly, cleaned my cell and settled down to wait. The court was due to begin sitting at 9 a.m., and I expected to be taken from the prison about an hour earlier. I listened to the 8 a.m. news relayed from Radio South Africa which told me I was going to court that day, and then a musical request programme, but still no one came to get me. At 9 a.m. I began wondering if the case had been suddenly postponed, and no one had bothered to let me know. Almost half an hour later, the main compound door opened and John Edmondson, a European warder, looked in.

'Are you supposed to be in court today?' he asked.

'Yes,' I said. 'At nine o'clock.'

'We'd better get a move on then. There was no record at Reception that you were due up today, and we've just had a telephone call from the Magistrates' Court asking where you were.'

We hurried out of the Remand block, and waited at Reception for a few minutes while transport was arranged. Then Mr Edmondson and I climbed into the front of a truck and an African driver took us quickly into the city.

For about three weeks of my stay at Salisbury Prison, John Edmondson was in charge of the section which included my compound. He was about my own age – twenty-eight – and I found him pleasant, and within the confines of the system, kind. He was also more intelligent than many of his colleagues in the Rhodesian prison service. We did not drive down the sanitary lane behind the Regional Court, but stopped in the street at the front, and Mr Edmondson and I walked across to the entrance where about a dozen journalists and photographers waited. No prison officials held up their hands to try and stop my photograph being taken, and I exchanged greetings with my colleagues before walking up to the first-floor courtroom.

As the Defence was to make submissions on the case being held in open court – and as we had a reasonable expectation that later at least part of the actual case would be in public session – the court was crowded. Some journalists had flown into Salisbury from Britain and South Africa, but at the time – unaware of the growing international furore – it did not occur to me that they had come specifically to cover my trial.

I sat with Nonie in the public benches for a few moments, until officials indicated that the magistrate and assessor were ready to begin, then I took my place in the dock. Hamilton and Coleman entered, and bowed to the court. Hamilton looked at the packed public benches.

'The proceedings are *in camera*,' he said.

Michael May rose immediately. 'Before that is formally decided or continued, may I make a submission?' he asked.

Hamilton did not wish to listen. 'The position is that the order has been made that the proceedings are *in camera*,' he said. 'I think we should start from there.'

Michael May persisted: 'I understand that the position is that the Defence's position was reserved to make further submissions, and I would at least ask that our submissions should be, as the State's submissions were, made in public.'

Hamilton refused to budge. We would not be permitted time in open court to reply to the Prosecution's claim that the information objected to was Top Secret, and vitally affected national security, nor would we be able publicly to state that the alleged offences had been published Press reports, and that I had not been spying for a foreign power.

Mr Hamilton was content to close the matter to the public after hearing only the Prosecution's side of the argument. In these circumstances, rumours could – and did – flourish, and as I expected, an official smear campaign was launched. My wife and family were left to fend these off as best they could.

'I think we must start from where we left,' Mr Hamilton ordered. 'The proceedings are *in camera*, and will continue as such.'

The court was then cleared, and the doors closed.

Michael May began his argument to have the trial, or at least part of it, open to the public. He said that the *in camera* order was made by the Magistrate without receiving a certificate signed by Desmond Lardner-Burke in his capacity as Minister of Justice. He went on:

'It is submitted that without a Minister's certificate, one cannot simply accept the say-so of the State that there will be prejudice to public safety or defence, but the matter must be considered. It cannot simply be said that something is Top Secret, and therefore the matter should be *in camera*.'

Hamilton was not impressed.

May argued that while the State might be able to make out – either generally or *ad hoc* when each witness was called – a case for that particular piece of evidence to be held *in camera*, there was no justification for the charge itsel, and the three published Press reports on which the allegations were based, not being published.

'It is the accused's ordinary right to be tried in public,' May said, 'and certainly at least his ordinary right is to have published what is alleged against him.'

In fact, May pointed out, it was part of the charge that what was alleged against me had, in fact, already been published in the *Guardian* and over the BBC.

He said: 'The Defence's case will be not only that what has been published is not prejudicial to Rhodesia, and is not useful to an enemy, but that the only part of it – the one part of it which might be argued to be in some degree prejudicial – cannot be prejudicial because it has been denied as being the truth by the Prime Minister, and it can hardly be said that the publication of a fact which is not a fact is prejudicial.

'In all the circumstances,' May went on, 'I would submit that the accused should be accorded his ordinary rights of at least having the nature of the charge in full which is brought against him made public, and that it will rest with the State to establish a case for any particular piece of evidence, or even possibly the whole of the evidence being heard *in camera*, or not being published. I apply accordingly.'

Brendan Treacy, the Director of Public Prosecutions, rose to reply. I was glad to see that he was not sweating that morning, but looked freshly scrubbed. The State's attitude, he told the Magistrate, was the same as it had been at the formal remand ten days earlier.

'I indicated then that the evidence will be that the information regarding the deployment of Rhodesian troops in Mozambique is Top Secret,' Treacy said. 'The evidence will be it is not generally known, and the re-publication of this will not only embarrass the Government in its relationship with the Portuguese Government, but also it is prejudicial to the interests of the State.

'As regards the publication of the charges, in my submission that again cannot be done, because the charge alleges 15th November. It alleges publication in the *Manchester Guardian*, and that by itself would necessitate that information becoming known again by a person who merely purchased a back copy of the *Manchester Guardian*. In my submission, there are cogent reasons why the evidence should be heard *in camera*, and I ask accordingly.'

May rose to challenge Treacy's argument on keeping the charge secret. 'The only point he made about the charge was that it puts the date when something was published in the *Manchester Guardian*,' May told the court. 'With respect, that difficulty, if indeed it is a difficulty, can easily be overcome. The order can be that the charge be published without the date. Then there can be no objection. Alternatively, even if that is not done, I submit that at the very least, the charge alone, with or without the date, should, without annexures, be published. Otherwise I submit that there is a very serious incursion into the accused's ordinary right to be charged and tried in public.'

Hamilton did not pause for thought. 'Mr May, as I think I said last time, the courts are never very sympathetic to proceedings being held *in camera*,' he said, his face set in an expression of concern for human rights. 'In fact, they are strongly opposed to it. But we have this statement from the Director of Public Prosecutions that the proceedings will relate to matters described as Top Secret: that is, matters that inevitably must be very important to the country. I think even if your application is granted and the charge is published, there is a danger that top secret matter could be identified, and it is obviously not in the interests of the country, not in the interests of the defence of the country, that that should be. For that reason, I think the application should be refused, and the proceedings continue *in camera* as previously ordered. If at a later date in the course of the proceedings, the court has reason to change its mind, then I will be the first to do so.'

So before the first witness was heard, we knew where we stood. Magistrate Hamilton had accepted the state's contention that my published reports contained Top Secret information which 'inevitably' had to be very important to the country. There is an old journalistic maxim which Mr Hamilton would do well to frame and hang above his bed: The only thing that is inevitable is death. My acquittal in the Appeal Court underlined this.

As for the court being 'strongly opposed' to secret trials, with the magistrate determined to be the first to let the public in if, during the course of proceedings, 'national security' was no longer at stake, this claim sounded rather hollow at a three-minute formal remand hearing later in the month when Mr Hamilton ordered the court cleared merely so that he could announce the date for the judgment.

The argument on the *in camera* hearing completed, and the assessor formally sworn in, I was asked to plead to the charges.

'Not guilty,' I said, and the state began to present its case against me.

The first prosecution witness, Assistant Commissioner Ronald Eames – who had led the November raid on my office and home – gave me a wintry police smile as he took the stand. I had heard that he did not like the Press, but he had been personally pleasant to me, and his face often smiled even if his eyes did not. Mr Eames gave evidence firmly and professionally about the search of my office, and the handing over of telex copies of the *Guardian* and BBC reports.

Treacy asked: 'Did you ask the accused for his source of information at all?'

'I did,' said Eames, 'on several occasions whilst I was in his office. I asked the accused to disclose his source of information, but he declined to do so.'

'Later on the same day did you take a warned and cautioned statement from the accused?'

'That is correct.'

'Did you record his reply, read it back to him and did he adhere to it?'

'That is correct.'

This warned and cautioned statement was then read to the court and put in as an exhibit. It said: 'As a journalist, I can say nothing which would tend to reveal my source on any matter.'

Treacy then led Eames off at a tangent with a series of questions indicating it would be the state's intention to try and prove that my reports had contributed towards the deteriorating security situation, and guerilla attacks, in the north-east. It was a curious thought, but it showed how serious the Government was in its attempt to convict me, justify the detention and frighten the Press.

Treacy said: 'You are the Provincial Criminal Investigation Officer for Mashonaland, is that right?'

'Salisbury and Mashonaland,' Eames replied.

'Can you say when the most recent incursions into this country by terrorists occurred last year? When was the first attack?'

'The first incident that was logged was on 21st December of last year.'

'Whereabouts was that?'

'That was an attack on Altena farm in the Centenary area.'

'Have there been any other attacks since then?' Treacy asked.

'There have. Up until the 15th of this month, in excess of two hundred incidents have been logged.'

Treacy did not pursue the matter further, and sat down. Michael May looked through his notes. 'When you went to the accused's office in Robinson House,' May said, 'I gather from your evidence that he was co-operative.'

'Very co-operative and friendly,' said Eames.

'Also that he did not attempt to conceal from you any of his documents, files or anything?'

'Not at all. He assisted us in this search.'

Eames left the witness stand, giving me another wintry smile, and I gathered he wished me no ill.

The next two prosecution witnesses gave evidence that the reports had in fact been published. William Crossan, who although in plain clothes appeared to be a policeman – he had been allowed to remain in court when the public were ordered to leave, and while the other witnesses were kept waiting in a nearby room – said that he bought a copy of the *Guardian* of 16 November 1972 while on leave in the United Kingdom, and it was handed in as an exhibit.

The second witness, Supt Michael Eddon of CID Headquarters said that it was often his responsibility to listen in to BBC broadcasts from London.

'On the evening of 15th November 1972, did you listen to a broadcast programme called "Focus on Africa"?' Treacy asked.

'That is correct,' said Eddon, and produced a transcript of the broadcast, which became Exhibit 5.

Michael May rose to cross-examine Eddon: 'How frequently do you listen to the BBC?'

'On selected occasions.'

'Do you frequently listen for "Focus on Africa"?'

'Again on a selected basis.'

'Can't you give us any better idea than that?'

'Well, let me say this,' Eddon explained. 'I myself will listen to this particular programme infrequently, but members of my staff will listen to it all the time.'

'Have you heard previous broadcasts by the BBC on the activities of FRELIMO terrorists in Mozambique?'

'I have.'

'Frequently?'

'Yes.'

'In other words, from your listening to the BBC, the activities of FRELIMO terrorists in Mozambique is something which would be well known?' May asked.

'That is correct.'

'A little more specifically, it would be well known that they made the road from Rhodesia to Malawi unsafe for travelling?'

'It has been stated, yes.'

'Before 15th November 1972, this had been publicly stated?'

'On the BBC, yes.'

'And on the RBC [Rhodesia Broadcasting Corporation]?'

'No, I can't comment there. I would say it would be reasonable to suppose it had been commented on elsewhere.'

'From your experience as a Rhodesian, reading Rhodesian newspapers, presumably, would it not be correct to say that it has been published locally?'

'That what has been published locally?' asked Supt Eddon. 'That the road is unsafe?'

'Yes,' said May.

Supt Eddon looked impassive. 'I can't comment on that,' he said.

The state then called an official of the Posts and Telecommunications Corporation, Desmond Dormer, to give evidence that the published reports had in fact been telexed from my office to London. I had known Des Dormer for years. He had helped me on several occasions with communications problems, and had always been friendly and co-operative. That morning in court, he looked hunched and uncomfortable, and refused to meet my eye. He produced Post Office monitor copies of all transmissions through the international exchange that day, and marked the ones sent from my office.

Michael May asked him: 'Would it be known to most subscribers to your service that there is always a print-out in your custody?'

'I think it is known insofar as people know when they query the duration of a call, or whether the call has actually gone through, that we would have to have some means of being able to answer the query,' Mr Dormer said.

'So it would be known to the subscriber that sending anything through your overseas service would mean that the content of the message was not secret?'

'I wouldn't like to say that it is known, insofar as it is not a feature of the service which is advertised by the Posts and Telecommunications Corporation.'

May asked: 'In fact, the content of any message sent through your overseas service is not secret, it is available to you or to anybody through you at any time?'

'It is secret insofar as any traffic which the Posts and Telecommunications Corporation handle for the public is confidential,' Mr Dormer said.

'Confidential in that sense,' Michael May persisted, 'but it is available to you?'

'Yes.'

'And it is available to anybody like the police who might have powers to demand it from you?'

'Yes.'

A middle-aged woman took the stand, neatly dressed with gloves, a hat and a necklace of pearls, looking efficient and trustworthy and extremely nervous. Joan Goodacre gave evidence that, as a secretary employed by the Ministry of Information, Immigration and Tourism, she had listened in on a telephone extension as David Williams, the Director of Information, asked me to disclose my source of information for the Mozambique reports. She said she made shorthand notes of the conversation, but had not taken a verbatim note, and she later transcribed it. The transcript was read to the court, and put in as an exhibit. Joan Goodacre thankfully stepped down and was replaced by the Director.

'I asked Mrs Goodacre to take a note because of the possibility of Mr Niesewand dictating what he had written to me on the telephone,' David Williams said.

Treacy asked: 'You expected him to dictate something?'

'Yes, there was a chance he might do that.'

'The publication in the newspaper, the *Manchester Guardian*, and the broadcast over the BBC – we have evidence before the court that it related to the deployment of Rhodesian troops in Mozambique. To your knowledge, had this ever been published before?'

'To my knowledge, no.'

With Mr Williams on the stand, the Defence at last had something to get its teeth into, and Michael May rested his fingertips lightly on a file of newspaper cuttings.

'You have known Mr Niesewand for some time, have you?' he asked.

'Many years, yes,' said Mr Williams.

'Have you found him, in his dealings with the Ministry of Information, to be reasonable and responsible in his attitude?'

'Yes.'

'Have you found him to be prepared, for instance, to refrain from publishing anything if you suggested to him it was undesirable?'

'I can't recall having had occasion to request him to refrain from publishing anything.'

'Have you had him ask you whether it was desirable to publish something, and on your saying that you did not think so, or did not know, he has refrained?'

'I can't honestly say that that is so,' David Williams said, colouring slightly.

'Would it surprise you if there was an occasion like that?' Michael May asked.

'It would surprise me, yes, if in fact he had asked me.'

'You can't remember an incident when there was a story about atrocities having been committed by troops in Rhodesia which he . . .'

'Oh yes, I beg your pardon,' said David Williams, as my eyes widened. 'I do recall that.'

I didn't. The atrocities reports – alleging that white troops had raped African women in the Chiweshe district – had been submitted for comment to the Ministry of Information, but no reply had ever been received by me, and I certainly was not asked by Mr Williams to refrain from publishing it. I did not send off the reports, simply because they were not substantiated. If they had been substantiated, I would have filed them. My defence counsel had misunderstood a comment of mine during an earlier meeting, and now Mr Williams had reinforced the misunderstanding with a mistaken recollection. In the context of the court case and my detention, it was too good an opportunity for me to pass up, and I never corrected the error, but accepted it gratefully.

Michael May asked Mr Williams again if I had referred the atrocity reports to him. 'Yes, I do recall that,' the Director of Information said.

'And did you indicate you felt it was undesirable to publish it?'

'Yes.'

'Because it was unreliable information?'

'Yes.'

'And did he refrain from publishing it?'

'Yes.'

Mr Williams was turning out to be a good defence witness and Brendan Treacy sat staring stonily at a piece of paper in front of him. From the bench, Hamilton looked down, an expression of virtuous surprise on his face.

Mr May pressed on. David Williams had said in his evidence-in-chief that the information relating to the deployment of Rhodesian troops in Mozambique had not previously been published 'to his knowledge' and the Defence was anxious to know how far his knowledge extended.

Under cross-examination, Mr Williams said that the Information Ministry received most of the Press cuttings published in the United Kingdom, and these were 'subject to rigorous examination by us'.

The Ministry of Information also received South African newspapers, and cut from them reports relevant to Rhodesia which were then passed to him.

May asked: 'In November of last year, was the situation in Mozambique and on the border of Mozambique, so far as you know, already such that it was well known that Rhodesian troops were operating in Rhodesia, but on the borders of Mozambique?'

'I would say inside Rhodesia, Mr May.'

'But on the borders of Mozambique?'

'In that area I would say, yes.'

'There had been frequent previous publications of that, had there not?'

'Yes.'

'Was the situation such that it was already known that troops might go across in certain circumstances?'

'I wouldn't like to say that.'

'Would you like to say that it was not?'

'To my knowledge, it certainly was not.'

'As far as you know, it was not?'

'Yes.'

'You had not heard previous reports of troops, Rhodesian troops, operating in Mozambique?'

'I had,' said David Williams, 'but not by means of newspaper publications.'

May had set him up, and was ready to move in. He selected a newspaper cutting from his file and turned to the Director of Information.

'Can I put to you a report in the *Rhodesia Herald* of the 5th April, 1972? I think the easiest thing is if I read it out. The headline is:

"Silence on army aid to PEA". "The Government was not prepared to comment yesterday on the report published in France claiming that Rhodesian officers had been advising Portuguese troops in Mozambique. Writing in the weekly *L'Express*, the French journalist, Mr Pierre Doublet, said a dozen Rhodesian army officers had served with the Portuguese army in Mozambique as advisers. A Ministry of Information spokesman said: 'We never divulge information of this nature. Therefore we have no idea where Mr Doublet got his information.' The writer also claimed that the South African and Portuguese air forces each day fly over the frontier regions ready to give the alert'".

The report went on to discuss the strengthening links between the countries of 'the white south' of the African continent, but Mr May had made his point: information similar to that contained in my despatches had been published within Rhodesia seven months prior to November 1972.

He put down the cutting and looked across at Mr Williams, who had stood silently, listening.

'Do you remember that report?' he asked.

'Yes.'

'So there had been previously a report about Rhodesian troops operating in Mozambique?'

'Yes, there had been.'

'It was a report which your Department denied, or didn't actually deny, but you expressed puzzlement at it because you didn't know where he could have got his information?'

'Yes.'

Michael May paused for a moment, then said: 'There had been other reports, had there not, of co-operation at the border between Rhodesian forces and authorities, and Portuguese forces and authorities?'

'Yes, there had been reports,' said Mr Williams in a low voice.

'So it was a situation in which it was very likely that circumstances might arise in which Rhodesian troops would find it necessary to go across?'

'I am not qualified to answer that.'

'Are you aware that it had already been widely reported by word of mouth within Rhodesia that Rhodesian forces did operate in Mozambique?'

'Yes,' said David Williams. 'Such rumours had come to my attention.'

'These rumours were widespread?'

'I wouldn't know how widespread they were.'

'You had heard them on a number of occasions?'

'Yes, certainly.'

'In fact, there had been published incidents of Rhodesian troops going across the border, not for operational purposes, but for purposes of visiting their Portuguese counterparts?'

'Yes.'

'In fact, three young men were blown up by a mine in 1971 doing that.'

'Yes.'

'So there had been crossings of the border?'

'Yes.'

'I take it it is not within your knowledge whether or not Rhodesian troops, by the middle of November 1972, had operated in Mozambique?'

'No,' said David Williams, and Michael May sat down to indicate the cross-examination was over. Brendan Treacy, still staring gloomily at a piece of paper, had no further questions, and the Director was excused.

As he left the courtroom, he saw Nonie standing waiting in the corridor outside, and said 'Hello Nonie.' She replied icily: 'Good morning Mr Williams,' but she would have been more cordial had she known how helpful he had been to the Defence's appeal preparation. He had been extremely fair in his evidence – and at one point because of a Defence misunderstanding and a lapse of memory, more than fair.

Inside the court, Brendan Treacy said: 'Call Mr Fleming,' and the State brought out its principal witness – the man on whom their case was to depend. John Andrew Cameron Fleming, the Secretary for Law and Order, bustled in, grim-lipped and self-important. He was slightly overweight, and his complexion gave the impression that recently he had been lightly boiled. He told the court that he was a member of the Rhodesian Government Security Council, which was chaired by the Prime Minister. Other council members, he said, were the Minister of Law and Order, the Minister of Defence, the Minister of Internal Affairs, the Chief of the Army, the Chief of the Air Force, the Commissioner of Police, and the Secretaries of those Ministries.

Treacy asked: 'What about the Director of Central Intelligence?'

'He is also a member,' said Fleming.

'In your capacity as Secretary for Law and Order, and as a member of the Government Security Council, have you visited the border areas between Kariba and Kanyemba?' [most of Rhodesia's northern frontier].

'I have.'

'Have you also visited the joint operations command in the north-eastern area of Rhodesia?'

'I have, at Centenary.'

'Prior to November 1972, had terrorists infiltrated into Rhodesia?'

'They had.'

'Where had they come from?'

'From Zambia, via Mozambique.'

'FRELIMO, I understand, is an organisation operating in Mozambique?' said Treacy.

'That is correct.'

'It is a terrorist organisation?'

'Yes.'

'ZANU – is that also a terrorist organisation?'

'A Rhodesian one, yes.'

'Do you know who was responsible for the recent attacks on Rhodesian farms in the north-eastern area of Rhodesia?'

'ZANU,' said Fleming.

Treacy then referred him to the reports I had sent to the *Guardian* and the BBC, and to the references to FRELIMO guerilla activities – including one saying 'Guerillas are operating from bases in Malawi.'

Treacy said: 'I just want to know if reports of this nature were received by the Government?'

'They were.'

'Can you vouch for the accuracy of these reports?'

'No,' replied Fleming.

'All you can say is that these reports were, in fact, received?'

'Yes.'

'Looking at the first Schedule [the *Guardian* report], if you look at the sixth paragraph which reads as follows: "Military sources said the Rhodesians are already taking an unofficial part in the Mozambique guerilla war" . . . '

'Unofficially, yes,' said Fleming.

'Including supplying aircraft of the Rhodesian Air Force for specific tasks in the neighbouring territory, and sending patrols of soldiers across on request?'

'Yes.'

118

Treacy continued to read from the *Guardian* report: ' "In August, Rhodesia's Minister of Defence, Mr Jack Howman, said that if the Portuguese military authorities asked Rhodesia for help to fight terrorists in the Tete area, this would be granted.... Military sources say that although the Rhodesian Government is reluctant to officially admit its forces are already taking an active part in the Mozambique war, the true position is that security forces from this country have been involved for most of this year." Is that information regarding the deployment of Rhodesian troops in Mozambique true or not?' Treacy asked.

'Correct. It is true,' said Fleming.

'Including the supplying of aircraft of the Rhodesian Air Force?'

'As far as I know, yes.'

'How is such information classified?'

'As far as the Rhodesian Government is concerned, do you mean?'

'Yes.'

'Top Secret.' Fleming looked defiant.

'Was it the policy of your Government it should be published or released?'

'No.'

Treacy asked again: 'Were Rhodesian troops actively engaged in Mozambique for most of the year 1972?'

'Off and on, yes,' Fleming said.

'Has publication of this information caused any concern at all to Government?'

'Yes, great concern, because it was Top Secret.'

'To your knowledge, had it been published previously in Rhodesia?' Fleming shifted his gaze to stare at me.

'No,' he said, 'and it still hasn't.' I smiled back at him, remembering the *Herald* cutting in Michael May's cardboard folder.

Treacy clamped his lips together, held his hands behind his back and stared into space. 'Apart from FRELIMO and ZANU, are there any other organisations hostile to Rhodesia?'

'ZAPU, FROLIZI, which is the Front for the Liberation of Zimbabwe, the Organisation of African Unity, the United Nations.'

'What about Zambia and Tanzania? Would you classify them as hostile to Rhodesia?'

'The countries themselves, yes.'

Treacy referred his witness to my reports, and the references to Rhodesian intelligence reports, Rhodesian military sources, and security sources.

'Now,' he said, 'do you know what sources are referred to there?'

'No,' said Fleming. 'Not official ones.'

'Would such information have been released officially by any of the sources mentioned?'

'No.'

'This continuous reference to the information emanating from Rhodesian security sources, Rhodesian military sources and so on – what impression did that give you?'

'That it was emanating from some sort of authoritative Rhodesian source, which it was not.'

'Is there any question of embarrassment to the Portuguese Government?' Treacy asked.

'Yes, as far as I know,' said Fleming. 'Certainly to the Rhodesian Government.'

Treacy sat down, and his principal witness was in the hands of Michael May, who proceeded – quietly at first, then ruthlessly – to demolish Mr Fleming's evidence. I sat in the dock, fascinated. It was better than television.

chapter 10

Michael May is a quiet-voiced, trim man who at first gives the impression of diffidence. He is unfailingly polite and never aggressive in the loud, tight-lipped, barking manner of Brendan Treacy: yet when circumstances warrant it, his voice develops an icy edge and he cross-examines with an academic ruthlessness. I was glad to have him on my side.

Michael May picked up the three reports I had written and looked across at John Fleming, who looked defiantly back at him.

'You have studied these Schedules, I take it?' May asked.

'I have not learnt them off by heart, or anything,' Fleming shot back. May was unmoved.

'No,' he said, 'but you know the substance of them?'

'Yes.'

'In going through them before hearing your evidence,' May continued, leafing through the Schedules and peering at jottings he had made, 'it struck me that there were, in substance, five points that you might be complaining of. I would like to check whether or not you do complain about all of them.' He shot a sympathetic glance at Mr Fleming to put him at his ease.

May said: 'I shall use the first Schedule, because I think there is nothing in substance in the other two which does not appear in the first Schedule. Firstly it says: "FRELIMO guerillas in neighbouring Mozambique have launched a major new offensive on the railway line which runs from the port of Beira to Tete, site of the giant Cabora-Bassa hydro-electric scheme. According to Rhodesian intelligence reports, FRELIMO bands crossed the border from Malawi last Saturday and laid landmines at about twenty points on the Tete line." '

May paused and looked at the witness. 'Is there anything there that you complain about?' he asked.

'No,' replied Fleming. 'All I said is that we have had those reports, but I can't say whether they are correct or not.'

'You are not suggesting it is prejudicial to Rhodesia to publicise the fact that FRELIMO guerillas have made a new attack, or that they are using Malawi as a base?'

'No.'

'Secondly, in the fourth paragraph, it says: "The Rhodesians are watching the security situation in Mozambique with growing concern." Do you take exception to that?'

'No. I would say that is correct. We were watching it with concern.'

'Thirdly it says: "For months now, the road from Rhodesia to Malawi – which runs through Tete – has been officially considered unsafe." Do you take any exception to that? There had in fact, been . . .'

Fleming cut in: '. . . numerous reports about what was going on on that road.'

'Convoys going at a slow pace, a young Salisbury Indian being killed and so on?'

'Yes.'

'Fourthly: "The Rhodesians fear that their vital supply routes to the ports of Beira and Lourenço Marques may soon be threatened." Do you take exception to that?'

'No, because that is what was happening.'

'But it must be an obvious concern?'

'Yes.'

'So then,' said May, 'there comes the passage: "Military sources said the Rhodesians are already taking an unofficial part in the Mozambique guerilla war – including supplying aircraft of the Rhodesian Air Force for specific tasks in the neighbouring territory, and sending patrols of soldiers across on request." That is the passage, or one of the passages, to which you take exception?'

'That is right.'

'And the other is over the page: "Military sources say that although the Rhodesian Government is reluctant to officially admit its forces are already taking an active part in the Mozambique war, the true position is that security forces from this country have been involved for most of this year." So in substance, those two things are the same.' May looked across at Fleming again, and held up the three reports. 'Is there anything else in this Schedule, or in either of the other two, which I have not mentioned, to which you take exception?'

'Do you want me to go through it all again?' asked Fleming, aggrieved.

'I just want to know whether I have covered everything. I have tried to suggest everything that seems a possibility.'

'That was basically correct,' Fleming admitted.

'There is nothing else you can point to?'

'No.'

May had prepared the ground, and was ready to move in.

He said: 'I take it in November 1972, the situation was such that it was well known that Rhodesian troops were operating on the Mozambique border within Rhodesia?'

'Yes,' said Fleming. Then he said: 'I don't know about that. I would say it was well known we were operating, because there were terrorists in Rhodesia.'

'But near the Mozambique border?' May persisted.

'Probably, yes.'

'It was a relatively new development that it was the Mozambique border as well as the Zambian border that we were concerned with?'

'Yes.'

'But it was well known . . . ?'

'I don't think it was mentioned in the Rhodesian Press that Rhodesian troops were operating in the border area with Mozambique. It might have been Zambia.'

'I'm not saying *in* Mozambique, I am saying in Rhodesia, near the Mozambique border.'

'I don't think it was ever mentioned there until after December some time, when they kept referring to the north-eastern border. Then it was obvious it was Mozambique,' Fleming said.

May reached for his cardboard folder of Press cuttings. 'Can I put to you a cutting from the *Rhodesia Herald* of 29th April, 1971? A report from a *Herald* reporter that three soldiers of the Rhodesian Light Infantry died after an army vehicle struck a terrorist land mine inside Mozambique, and a fourth was in Salisbury Central Hospital, seriously wounded. They were reported to have gone across for what is called "friendly contact with Portuguese border authorities . . ." Do you remember that incident?'

Fleming furrowed his brow. 'I think I do, yes; as I said, troops were going backwards and forwards in hot pursuit into Mozambique.'

'So it was known troops were going backwards and forwards in hot pursuit?'

'Well, I don't know. I don't think that' – pointing at the *Herald* cutting – 'indicates that we were operating in there.'

'That doesn't indicate it. I thought your answer did. I thought your answer was: "It was well known troops were going backwards and forwards in hot pursuit."'

'No.'

'What did you say?'

'That they were – well – we never admitted that our Rhodesian troops were actually in Mozambique.'

'Let's go back to this news article,' May said. 'This news article makes it plain, does it not, that firstly Rhodesian troops must be operating, or were stationed, in Rhodesia near the Portuguese border?'

'That report there?' asked Fleming, with a disdainful inclination of his head.

'Yes,' said May.

'Yes.'

'And that not for operational purposes, but for other purposes?'

'Friendly contact.'

'They had crossed the border?'

'So it would appear, yes.'

It had taken some time to extract the admission from the Secretary for Law and Order, but it was worth underlining it, so May picked up another Press cutting.

'Can I refer you to another report from the *Rhodesia Herald* of 29th September 1971, referring to the stepping-up, as they call it, of the Tete convoys on the Nyamapanda-Malawi road. You remember reports to that effect in the local newspapers?'

'About convoys, yes.'

'In that, there is a passage which reads: "The increased terrorist activity in Portuguese territory on Rhodesia's north-east frontier was involving Rhodesian security forces in the coverage of larger areas, Mr G. J. Ginsman, counsellor at the Rhodesian Diplomatic Mission in Pretoria, said in Germiston on Monday night." Do you remember that report?'

'No.'

'Do you remember it being publicised at that time, that is, towards the end of 1971, that Rhodesian troops were operating in Rhodesia, but covering the Portuguese border?'

'I can remember that security forces were, and there was a report, it probably was that one, that the security forces were being extended to that extent.'

'And were covering the Portuguese border?'

'Yes.'

'Do you remember a report by a French journalist, Mr Pierre Doublet?'

'No.'

'You don't remember it?' asked May. 'It was published in the *Rhodesia Herald* on 5th April, 1972. I will put this to you. The headline is: "Silence on army aid to PEA". It reads: "The Government was not prepared to comment yesterday on the report published in France claiming that Rhodesian officers had been advising Portuguese troops in Mozambique. Writing in the weekly *L'Express*, the French journalist, Mr Pierre Doublet, said a dozen Rhodesian army officers had served with the Portuguese army in Mozambique as advisers. A Ministry of Information spokesman said: 'We never divulge information of this nature. Therefore we have no idea where Mr Doublet got his information' " . . . Don't you remember that report?'

'No I don't,' said Fleming. 'Could I have a look at it.'

'Yes, please do,' replied May, and a court official handed the cutting up to the Secretary for Law and Order, who stared accusingly at it.

At length Michael May said: 'It is obviously a genuine *Herald* report.'

'Yes.'

'So at that stage in April of last year, nearly a year ago, there were reports being made of Rhodesian troop activity in Mozambique.'

'That is so, yes,' said Fleming. May handed in the cutting as Exhibit 9, then turned back to his folder of clippings.

'Do you remember reports of a meeting on the border between Rhodesian and Portuguese forces, and Government authorities – co-operation between them?'

'No,' said Fleming, but looked apprehensive.

'I have here . . .' May began.

'I do remember one lot that was embarrassing to us about Special Branch people meeting. I don't know how that got out. That was South Africa, Portuguese and Rhodesian.'

'A report in the *Herald*, was it?' asked May, interested, as this was one cutting we did not have in our folder.

'I can't remember,' said Fleming, sorry he had raised the matter.

'In a local newspaper?'

'I can't remember where it was.'

May let it drop, and selected another cutting. 'I have a report here from the *Herald* of 23rd June, 1972, which is a fairly long one, so I won't read out all of it. It concerns mainly the dangers of the Nyamapanda-Tete road, and refers to co-operation between forces at the border. For instance, there is a passage reading: "A bevy of Rhodesian police officers arrives and with much tortuous translation, begins an hour-long conference with the Portuguese brass which the barefoot Transvaalers beerily try to join ... a Rhodesian spotter plane cruises low overhead." That sort of passage, indicating a meeting together at the border of Rhodesian and Portuguese forces or authorities. You don't remember reports of that nature?'

'I don't really remember it. I wouldn't know whether it was true or not either.'

'No,' said May, 'I am just suggesting there had been previous reports of this nature.'

'There were quite a few which were embarrassing to us.'

'Quite a few of what?'

'Of these reports of our activities in that part of the world.'

'Of what nature?'

'Like this.'

'Meeting Portuguese authorities?'

'That we were operating in Mozambique.'

'There were quite a few reports that you were operating in Mozambique?' asked May, unable to believe his luck.

'You have read out two already now.'

'Are you confirming there were quite a few reports that the Rhodesian forces were operating in Mozambique?'

'There probably were. You have read two out now.'

The magistrate came to the rescue. 'Operating in Mozambique, or at the border?' Mr Hamilton asked.

'At the border,' Fleming said, but Michael May would not be dissuaded.

'You said just now: "In Mozambique",' he pointed out. 'Which do you mean?'

'We were operating in Mozambique, and we didn't want it to be known that we were,' Fleming was defensive.

May's voice had a cutting edge: 'I am not for the moment concerned with what was actually happening, or with what your desires were.'

Fleming capitulated: 'There were other reports, definitely.'

'There were definitely reports before November 1972 that Rhodesian forces had been operating in Mozambique?'

'Yes. Probably a little bit of thumb-sucking going on. I don't know.'

'But there had been reports in the newspapers, I take it?'

'You have read two of them out to me now.'

'Are you saying there had been others?'

'I am not sure.'

From the bench, Hamilton interjected, waving his hand disparagingly towards the newspaper cuttings.

'Well, those don't say actually operating in Mozambique, but only at the border,' he said.

'This one does,' said Michael May, indicating the report on the Nyamapanda to Tete road.

'And the French one?' asked Hamilton.

'That one says in Mozambique.'

'That is the twelve liaison officers?'

'Yes.'

'Not quite the same thing, is it?' said Hamilton. 'However.'

'No,' said Michael May, 'it is not quite the same thing.' He turned back to Fleming. 'I want to get back to this, Mr Fleming. As I understood you, you were saying that there had been reports that Rhodesian forces were operating in Mozambique?'

'No,' said Fleming.

'You are not saying that?' asked May, surprised.

'There were some,' said Fleming. 'You are getting me confused now, Mr May. I am saying that Rhodesian forces were there, but we were embarrassed by reports saying that they were there.'

'That does mean you are saying there were such reports,' May pointed out. 'If you remember this embarrassment, it must mean that there were such reports.'

'From the accused and others,' said Fleming.

'I am talking about before November 1972, as I said earlier. Are you saying there were reports by the accused before November 1972?'

'I am not sure about that.'

'You are saying there were reports by others before November 1972?'

'You have just read out two.'

'Is that the only reason you are saying it? I want to get this quite clear, because as I understood you just now, you said that there were reports we were operating in Mozambique, we didn't want it to be known, and we were embarrassed by reports that it was happening.

'Yes,' said the Secretary for Law and Order.

'Is that your evidence?' asked Michael May.

Fleming looked uncomprehending. 'Would you just say that again?'

May's voice was patient: 'We were operating in Mozambique, we didn't want it known, and we were embarrassed by reports we were receiving.'

'That is possibly correct,' Fleming conceded.

'That was your evidence?'

'Because neither Rhodesians nor the Portuguese wanted it to be known,' Fleming said rather lamely.

'If that is your evidence,' May replied, 'I must suggest to you that you must necessarily be saying that there were reports which you knew of that we were operating in Mozambique.'

'No.'

'Surely it necessarily follows?'

'No, I don't think it does.'

'How could you be embarrassed by reports if they didn't exist?'

'I was talking about ones the accused produced on this particular day.'

The magistrate cut in. 'No,' he said to Mr Fleming. 'Mr May is talking about prior to November 1972. Had there been any reports, to your knowledge, not of operating at the border, but positively in Mozambique?'

'No, I don't think so,' Fleming said. 'I don't remember this one from this French correspondent.'

Michael May decided to approach the same point from a different angle. He pulled from his folder a telex despatch I had sent to the BBC the previous August. 'I don't know whether you will have any knowledge of it, but I must put to you certain earlier despatches sent by Mr Niesewand. I have here a despatch dated 31st August 1972 from Mr Niesewand to "Focus on Africa" – that is a BBC programme. This is not really about penetration into Mozambique, but it includes a passage about security forces fighting a battle with a FRELIMO band which crossed from Mozambique in August last year. Seven FRELIMO guerillas were killed. Do you remember the incident?'

The magistrate asked: 'In 1972? Are you saying that was from the accused?'

'At the moment I am just asking if he remembers that incident,' May said.

'Oh, the incident,' replied Hamilton.

Fleming was handed a copy of the telex despatch, and looked through it. 'The incident was referring to some time in 1972,' he said.

'Yes,' agreed May. 'Referring to August 1972, and FRELIMO guerillas crossing from Mozambique into Rhodesia and fighting the Rhodesian troops here.'

'No,' said Fleming. 'I don't really remember that. Did that appear in the *Rhodesia Herald*?'

I was surprised at his faulty memory. The clash between FRELIMO and the Rhodesian forces had indeed appeared in the local Press, having been contained in a Press Statement issued by the Ministry of Information. Mr May, however, did not have the original statement.

'Well, at the moment all I have here is a despatch,' he said. 'It was despatched. I am asking you whether you remember the incident, and whether you remember the publication of the incident?'

'No,' said Fleming. 'I don't really.'

'Do you remember any publication of Rhodesian forces fighting against FRELIMO, not in Mozambique but in Rhodesia?'

'No. As far as I know, FRELIMO haven't been into Rhodesia.'

'Was there not an official Government statement concerning that at the time?'

'I honestly can't remember. That was back in 1972, was it?'

'Yes, it refers back to August 1972.'

'I can't honestly remember that.'

Hamilton asked: 'That was an attack inside Rhodesia?'

'This was a fight inside Rhodesia, yes,' May said. 'I am just at the moment putting it that there had been an engagement between Rhodesian forces and FRELIMO.'

Hamilton looked confused, and Fleming looked blank. The grey-haired assessor looked benevolent and made a note.

May returned to the attack. 'In 1972, before November 1972, when the despatches with which we are concerned were sent, were you aware that it was commonly being said that Rhodesian troops were operating in Mozambique against terrorists?'

'No,' said Fleming, firmly.

'You were not aware of that?'

The Secretary for Law and Order began to backtrack. 'I understood that there were various soldiers and people talking back here in Salisbury, but officially it was not being said. You can't stop soldiers and people talking,' he said.

'You can't stop soldiers talking, and you can't stop people living in the border areas from talking,' May continued.

'That is true.'

'Would you agree that as a result, it was widely known that Rhodesian forces were operating in Mozambique?'

'No,' said Fleming, 'I don't think so.'

'Mr Fleming,' said Michael May wearily. 'Our evidence will be that it was widely being discussed.'

'Here in Salisbury, do you mean?'

'In Rhodesia,' said May.

'I would say not,' replied Fleming.

Hamilton leaned forward and asked May: 'Would you like to say amongst what sort of circles? People generally?'

'Among people generally,' May confirmed.

'No, I would say not.'

'And particularly, it was widely believed to be so among journalists.'

'That could well be,' said Fleming. 'I don't know.'

'You have agreed that it was, in fact, happening, and that you can't stop people from talking.'

'That is true.'

'So isn't it a probability that a large number of people knew it was happening?'

'Yes,' agreed Fleming. 'Quite a few people. Obviously, if you have people talking there, and coming back and talking in Salisbury.'

May said: 'I want to put to you one or two other despatches by Mr Niesewand. There is one dated 20th October 1972 from Mr Niesewand to the BBC. That includes this passage: "It is believed the South Africans and Rhodesians are very anxious about the security situation in neighbouring Mozambique, and they are trying to consolidate their ideas on defence. This may include taking a more active part in the Mozambique guerilla war." Do you remember that being published by the BBC? I can't put it to you that it definitely was, but I am suggesting to you it probably was.'

'I don't listen to the BBC, shall I put it that way.'

'In a despatch of 24th October, 1972, from Peter Niesewand after discussing the dangers in Mozambique generally, there is this passage: "But Rhodesia's defences have now been extended to the areas bordering both Zambia and Mozambique, and sources in Salisbury say that Rhodesian contingency plans include moving the country's defensive link deep into Mozambique to protect the road and rail supply lines from the ports of Beira and Lourenço Marques. Security sources in Rhodesia say that on a number of occasions, Rhodesian troops and police have taken part in manoeuvres across the Mozambique border." Do you remember anything like that?'

'No.'

'You wouldn't dispute that it was published?'

'No, I wouldn't.'

'And a despatch dated 26th October, 1972, from Niesewand in Salisbury to the *Guardian* in England dealing with discussions between the South African Defence Minister, Mr P .W. Botha, and Commandant-General Admiral H. H. Biermann, with their counterparts here. Do you remember that in October?'

'Yes.'

'After dealing with discussions generally,' said Mr May, 'this passage appears: "The talks are understood to have concentrated on white Southern Africa's future defence strategy. Political and security sources have hinted that Rhodesia may soon be forced to involve itself more directly in the guerilla war in neighbouring Mozambique." Do you remember publication of that in October?'

'I think I do, yes.'

'So that is publication . . .'

'Is that after Mr Botha came to Rhodesia?' asked Mr Fleming.

'Immediately after, yes,' Michael May replied.

'I think I do remember it.'

'Rhodesia might have to involve itself more directly in guerilla warfare in neighbouring Mozambique?'

'I seem to remember that.'

Michael May pushed the folder of Press cuttings away from him with the tips of his fingers. 'It would appear that there had been, partly in the form of newspaper reports, and partly in the form of word-of-mouth inside Rhodesia, fairly widespread publication of the fact that Rhodesian forces were taking part in guerilla warfare in Mozambique. If that is the situation, how can one further report to that effect create any prejudice?'

Fleming burst out: 'It was most embarrassing to the Rhodesian Government because, as you have indicated, it was nibble, nibble, nibble.'

May's voice had an edge to it again. 'We get to the stage in the middle of November where a large number of mouthfuls have already been taken as a result of the nibble, nibble, nibble, and it is public knowledge.'

'I wouldn't say that,' said Mr Fleming.

'Well, it is known to a large number of people, both inside and outside Rhodesia, that Rhodesian forces operate in Mozambique.'

'Mainly outside, by the accused.'

'No,' said Mr May. 'Not mainly outside.'

Mr Hamilton looked down from the bench at the Secretary for Law and Order: 'This is prior to November 1972?' he asked.

'Yes,' said Mr Fleming.

May again: 'It is known, both inside and outside, that Rhodesian forces have been and are operating in Mozambique; how can one more report to this effect create any prejudice?'

Fleming began to bluster. 'As I say, it has been going on for a long time. I presume the Portuguese certainly were embarrassed, and so were we, otherwise we would have made it public knowledge.'

'In what way does it prejudice Rhodesia?'

'Mainly, I should imagine, because we had offered to help the Portuguese, and I presume the Portuguese are too proud to admit that they want help, or need help. In fact, for our own security, we had offered to come in there and operate in Portuguese territory.'

'How,' asked May once more, 'is one more report of something which is already widely known going . . .'

'I don't say it is widely known,' said Fleming wildly, 'because we were trying to keep it quiet. Journalists were queering the pitch, and still are.'

'The only prejudice that you have pointed to, the only prejudice to Rhodesia, is that it might queer your pitch with the Portuguese?'

'And with the terrorists.'

'All right,' said Mr May. 'Let's take those one at a time. It might prejudice you because it would queer your pitch with the Portuguese.'

'Yes.'

'Are you suggesting that it was not known to the Portuguese authorities that it had been reported that Rhodesian troops were operating in Mozambique?'

'Yes.'

'Are you suggesting that?'

Fleming was flustered. 'That it was known to the Portuguese?' he asked.

'That it was not known to them,' said May.

'It *was* known to them,' Fleming conceded.

'It was known to them?'

'Yes.'

'So what difference on that score would one more report make?'

'That I wouldn't know.'

'Well, can I suggest that the obvious answer is that you do know, and it is nothing?' That edge to May's voice again: I listened in admiration. 'It can't make any difference.'

'We have been keeping it secret all along, and still are,' Fleming insisted.

'But that is not the point.'

'The point is,' said Fleming aggressively, 'that we didn't want all and sundry to know we were operating in Portuguese territory.'

'With respect,' said May, almost with a sigh, 'that is not the point. The point is that *vis-à-vis* the Portuguese, what difference can it make to their attitude if, instead of two dozen reports, there are two dozen-and-one reports?'

'It just makes one more cross,' replied Fleming.

'It is going to make no substantial difference, isn't that so?'

'No, I don't think so,' Fleming, defiant again.

'Can you point to any reason to support your statement that you don't think so?'

'I think it was going on and on and on, undermining what we were trying to do.'

'We are not dealing with going on, and on, and on,' said May.

Hamilton was not entirely happy with the way things were going, and he interrupted with a question to the Defence: 'Is this not an objective test?'

'Test of what?' asked May.

'Whether it is prejudicial or not,' said the magistrate.

'Yes, it is an objective test, but objective tests are still based on facts, and I am trying to elicit the facts.'

'All right,' said Hamilton, and sat back in his chair.

May turned to Fleming. 'We are not concerned, Mr Fleming, with going on, and on, and on. We are concerned with charges which relate to actions which took place on the 15th and 16th of November 1972 only, two or three despatches on the 15th, published on the 16th. That is all we are concerned with. I am suggesting to you that you have put forward no reason to show that there is any fact supporting this statement that there is any prejudice to Rhodesia in this one additional report.'

'I would say yes,' said Fleming, 'because we have all sorts of authoritative ... the accused says Rhodesian military sources, intelligence sources, security sources – all these sort of people are giving him his information and they were not. This is detrimental to Rhodesia. I don't know where the other people got their information from.'

'Obviously, it would have to be in the same way, wouldn't it? When you mentioned just now, soldiers will talk, obviously it would be military sources.'

'Do you think so?' asked Fleming, scornfully.

'Well, wouldn't it?'

'I would have thought a journalist would get better information than just an ordinary soldier talking if he is going to broadcast it all over the world.'

'Inevitably soldiers talking would, in fact, be military sources?'

'I don't agree.'

'You don't?'

'No.'

'What would you call soldiers talking?'

'Bar chat,' said Fleming.

'Regardless of the seniority of the soldier?'

'Yes. If he is a senior soldier, he certainly wouldn't be talking.'

It seemed to be a fruitless line of questioning, so May said: 'Anyway, the other form of embarrassment you said was in relation to the terrorists?'

'Yes.'

'What was the embarrassment caused by these particular reports in relation to terrorists?'

'I won't say it was embarrassment, but it could quite easily. If I was a FRELIMO strategist sitting in Lusaka, or Dar-es-Salaam, and I read of these reports emanating from Rhodesia, which is the ones they are aiming at, I would be able to put two and two together and say: "Well now, they have their forces stretched out there. I will strike in the west, or through Kazengula, or Botswana" or something like that.'

'Are you saying FRELIMO?' asked the magistrate, interested.

'Any one of the FRELIMO – or terrorist organisations who are aiming at Rhodesia,' said Fleming. 'The more information they can get of this nature, the better, presumably.'

Michael May was also interested in the reply. He said: 'You referred in starting that answer to "all these reports". What I would submit we are concerned with here is not all these reports, but the reports with which the charge deals.' He held up the Schedules. 'What would that add to the useful knowledge of anybody?'

There was a long silence, as Fleming paged through the three reports, looking for something to back up his views. The court waited for perhaps two minutes. Then he said: 'The only one I can think of straight off is this paragraph 5 of the first Schedule. "The guerillas are staging hit-and-run raids on lines of communication in the area, and the Rhodesians fear that their vital supply routes to the ports of Beira and Lourenço Marques may soon be threatened." I think a passage like that could well inspire a FRELIMO terrorist to realise that their strategy is working, and to have another crack at it, and hammer it home. Things were happening according to their plans and now is the time to get cracking on it.' He did not sound convincing.

'Let's try to get this quite clear,' said May. 'I put that same passage to you at the beginning of your cross-examination and you had no complaint concerning it.'

'But it has come round now to why the terrorists might have a look at this.'

'I put it to you whether you had any complaint concerning it, and you said no.'

'Well, we were worried about it, and still are.'

'Let's get down to the details of this,' said May, patiently. ' "The guerillas are staging hit-and-run raids on the lines of communication in the area." Is publication of that fact going to be useful to a terrorist?'

'Maybe, I don't know.'

'Come, Mr Fleming,' said May. 'Obviously not. If that is true, he knows it, doesn't he? So it is not going to be. You go on: "And the Rhodesians fear that their vital supply routes to the ports of Beira and Lourenço Marques may soon be threatened." Surely, as you said earlier, the position there is that it is quite obvious that the Rhodesians must be concerned about this. It is self-obvious. So with respect, I would suggest to you that it is as you originally said, there is nothing in that passage with which you could have any complaint.'

The Secretary turned his head away from Michael May, and stared towards the ceiling. He did not answer. Brendan Treacy looked gloomier than ever, and a notebook was rapidly filling with jottings of points he hoped later to retrieve.

Finally Mr Hamilton said: 'What is your answer?'

Fleming said: 'My answer is that everything that came out in these despatches does not help Rhodesia. It helps those who are opposing us.'

'This,' said May, 'is a generalisation which would justify saying there shall be no publication of any news at all whatsoever about that.'

'No.'

'Surely you must be a little more specific about that?'

Fleming looked across at him, his face pink and angry. 'Can I ask you a question then, Mr May? How come this sort of thing has not appeared in the *Rhodesia Herald*, which presumably has been more responsible in their reporting?'

'I don't think that is a particularly helpful question,' Michael May replied.

Fleming shrugged his shoulders. 'All right,' he said.

'Because,' May went on, 'we are concerned with whether or not these despatches are prejudicial and are useful to an enemy.'

'I would say they are.'

'I know you would say that. What I want to know is why you would say that?'

'I am trying to explain.'

'Yes? Go on?'

'They *are* helpful to an enemy,' said Fleming, a note of finality in his voice.

'How can this . . . ?'

'The fact Rhodesian troops are operating in Mozambique. It would be most helpful to them, I would say.'

'It is not the first time this information is being published. How can it be useful to an enemy?'

'I presume people go on and on doing it, and you are practically at war. It can be helpful to an enemy. It must be.'

'The enemies you have mentioned have been the various African nationalist bodies, FRELIMO, Zambia and Tanzania?'

'And ZAPU and ZANU.'

'The African nationalist bodies, and Zambia and Tanzania. Can it be seriously suggested any or all of these enemies or potential enemies of Rhodesia would be unaware Rhodesian troops were operating in Mozambique?'

'Could be, until such time as they get their intelligence back on the ground.'

'Surely they know Rhodesian troops have been operating against them there for some time?'

'I wouldn't know if they do.'

'They do, in fact, operate against those three African nationalist bodies and their guerilla fighters?'

'Who?'

'The Rhodesian troops.'

'Mainly ZANU,' said Fleming.

'ZANU?'

'In Mozambique.'

'ZANU would know, would they not?' asked May.

'I suppose they would, yes.'

'And FRELIMO would know?'

'FRELIMO would know.'

'If ZANU and FRELIMO knew, wouldn't it be almost a dead certainty Tanzania and Zambia . . . ?'

'The message would get back in the end.'

'It would have got back long before November 1972.'

'I am not sure of that.'

'How long have they been operating for? The Rhodesian troops in Mozambique?'

'I think mainly off and on, in 1972.'

'So it is many months?'

'They weren't there for a long period. They would go in and then come back.'

'Surely,' asked May, 'it must be taken as almost a certainty that all the potential enemies you have mentioned would know that they were attacking from time to time?'

'In the end, yes.'

'By November 1972?'

'I wouldn't say even by then.'

'Why not?'

'Because it takes a long time for anything to get back to Dar-es-Salaam, for instance,' Fleming said.

'When you say a long time, do you mean months?'

'I don't know how the African mind works. They certainly haven't publicised it.'

May looked down at his fingers. 'You have mentioned such bases of prejudice or usefulness as you have been able to put up. Isn't there one counter-factor? Wouldn't the fact that Rhodesian troops were operating in Mozambique tend to make terrorists, particularly FRELIMO, rather more careful on the borders of Rhodesia, and not feel they could get away with things so easily?'

137

'I suppose that could be said.'

'That would not be prejudicial. It would be anything but prejudicial.'

'Well, that could help them. They could come from Botswana, or somewhere else.'

'But they would know that in one particular place at any rate, it was policed?'

'Yes.'

'It would be helpful in that aspect to Rhodesia?'

'The main thing was, we didn't want it known that we were being extended by the terrorists.'

'Surely this does not indicate that you are being extended?'

'It does, if the war is spreading right over the north-east and eastern parts of Rhodesia.'

'Now Mr Fleming,' May being patient again. 'It was a well-known fact, as you have agreed, it was known the war had spread to the north-eastern part of Rhodesia.'

'Yes.'

'The fact that you are also operating in Mozambique rather, I would suggest, would indicate that you are not extended rather than that you are extended.'

'You mean the Portuguese are containing them?'

'No,' said May. 'You are not only able to cope with your own borders, but you are able to cope outside your own borders.'

'I wouldn't say that,' said Fleming.

'There is no suggestion, I put it to you, in any of these despatches, that Rhodesian forces are being extended. Quite the opposite, I would suggest to you.'

'All right,' said Fleming, looking long-suffering. 'Have it your own way.'

'No, don't answer like that, Mr Fleming. What do you point at in these despatches which indicates that Rhodesian forces are being extended?'

Another long silence as Fleming stared blankly at the three Schedules. Finally he said: 'I can't really point to anything, but I think it could be said that our forces have been extended by this part here saying "including supplying aircraft of the Rhodesian Air Force for specific tasks in the neighbouring territory, and sending patrols of soldiers across on request." That indicates we are operating on the north-east border.'

'And you are able to do it.'

'We have to do it!'

'Which indicates just the opposite of being extended.'

'It could indicate they are extended on this border, and somebody can come in on the western border.'

'You have said that, in fact, Rhodesian troops have been operating throughout 1972?'

The magistrate to the rescue again. 'In and out,' he said to Michael May.

May inclined his head towards the Bench. 'From time to time in Mozambique?'

'Yes,' said Fleming.

'I just want to know, what is the source of your knowledge? I will explain to you why. It is because I have a transcript, or rough note, of an interview which the Prime Minister gave in December 1972, in which he said that it had not happened. So what is the source of your knowledge?'

'My membership of the Security Council of the Rhodesian Government.'

'Of which the Prime Minister is chairman?'

'That's right.'

'Are you aware that the Prime Minister said in December that this had not happened?'

'I don't remember that, but he probably did. I don't deny that he did, but I am not a politician.'

'When you say the source of your knowledge is being on the Security Council, what does that mean? That means you are on the Council which receives reports?'

'That's right.'

'Another member of the Council as a result of receiving reports, has said the opposite to what you say.'

Fleming looked blank. 'I don't get you,' he said.

May explained: 'You received reports, as a result of which you believe that our troops do operate in Mozambique.'

'Yes.'

'And you have said so in evidence.'

'Yes.'

'The Prime Minister receives reports as a result of which, apparently, he believes our troops do not operate in Mozambique, as a result of which he said so.'

Michael May had lost the magistrate, too. 'Which he said what?' asked Mr Hamilton.

'I am putting the question: "as a result of which he apparently believes our troops do not operate in Mozambique," and he said this at a conference publicly.' Then, to Fleming again: 'In one case, what was said either by you or by the Prime Minister is opposed to what you were told by other people?'

'I presume so.'

'You have no knowledge of your own whether or not our troops operate in Mozambique?'

'Oh yes,' said the Secretary. 'I have been to the Headquarters at Centenary, and I knew they are. I haven't been into Portuguese territory with them.'

'So that you have been told in the Council, and also at Headquarters in Centenary?' asked May.

'Yes.'

'Everything is based on what you have been told?'

'Yes.'

'Just as everything the Prime Minister says is based on what he has been told?'

'Yes.'

Michael May did not pursue this line of questioning further, but in his summing up to the magistrate, he pointed out that Mr Fleming's evidence on Rhodesian involvement in Mozambique was based on hearsay, and was therefore inadmissible. May said he could have applied then and there for the Secretary's evidence to be stricken from the record, but that as the court had gone so far with the witness, it seemed reasonable to leave the matter until the summing-up stage. Hamilton looked thoughtful, but later accepted Mr Fleming's evidence in its entirety.

May cross-examined Mr Fleming on the Top Secret classification the State alleged had been given to the information contained in my report.

'You said in your evidence-in-chief that the fact our troops – assuming for the moment it is a fact – are attacking in Mozambique was classified as Top Secret. What do you mean? Is this in terms of any legislation, or what?'

'No,' said Fleming. 'All Government departments have this classification of Top Secret, Secret, Confidential, Restricted. Top Secret is stuff that you don't want to go out which concerns the country as a whole.'

'I am just wanting to know the source of this,' said May. 'It is purely, as I understand you now, an internal, departmental, administrative classification?'

'I would say probably, yes.'

'It is not something which derives its authority from the Official Secrets Act?'

'I don't know at all.'

'Have any warnings been put out to journalists that this is Top Secret?'

'Not that I know of.'

'Can you point to anything which would make any journalist aware that the information about troops operating in Mozambique is Top Secret?'

'Unless they are warned by the Ministry of Information, or something like that,' said the Secretary. 'It is not my portfolio.'

May persisted: 'Can you point to anything which would make a journalist aware, without warning, that publication of a report would be likely to prejudice Rhodesia?'

Fleming glared balefully across at me. 'If he were a Rhodesian and knew what was going on in the country, I would say that he should know instinctively.'

'Why?' asked Michael May.

'Well, you don't go telling your enemies exactly what is going on in your own country, do you?'

'Well, if the matter is already common knowledge?'

'I don't say it is common knowledge.'

'What do you point to as meaning, or saying, that a journalist should appreciate that publication of this fact would be prejudicial unless he had been given any warning?'

'I suppose it depends on the journalist himself.'

'Yes,' said May. 'You can conceive then, can you, in certain cases of a journalist, perfectly *bona fide*, believing that publication of this fact would not be prejudicial?'

'Yes,' replied Fleming. 'On the other hand, some journalists have been hung for this sort of thing, I should imagine.'

'In civilised countries?' asked May, eyebrows raised.

'Lord Haw-Haw.'

'Well, that was hardly the same thing, was it?' said May, ice in his voice again.

Fleming was virtuous: 'I don't say the accused is a traitor to his country, but sometimes when you don't know where to stop, that is what might happen to you, is it not?'

May asked Fleming if he knew of any system of warnings – such as the British 'D' notices – which were given to journalists in Rhodesia when the State wanted a security matter kept confidential, but the Secretary did not. When the Defence had finished with his star witness, Brendan Treacy rose to pick up some of the pieces.

He dealt first with the Prime Minister's denial that Rhodesian troops had been operating in Mozambique.

'What is the official line on this matter?' Treacy asked.

'The same as the Prime Minister's,' said Fleming.

'Denial?'

'Yes.'

'Now, my learned friend has asked you about warnings given to Press journalists regarding this sort of secret information. Are you aware of the provisions of the Emergency Powers Regulations?'

'Yes.'

'Which is part of our law. Is there a penalty there for "any person who, without leave of such authority as the Minister may appoint, publishes any information with respect to the movement or dispositions of troops"? Were you aware of that provision?'

'Yes.'

'It makes it an offence for any information regarding the movement of troops – this is information published in Rhodesia. It doesn't refer to outside Rhodesia. Now would you have presumed journalists would make themselves aware of the law of the land?'

'I presume so.'

'Which would you consider more serious?' Treacy asked, pursing his lips. 'The publication of information regarding movement of our troops outside Rhodesia, or inside Rhodesia? For example publication in the *Rhodesia Herald*, as against publication over the BBC?'

'That is a difficult one,' said Fleming. 'I would say, if you ask my opinion, probably the one overseas.'

Treacy sat down, and the court had a question. Mr Hamilton asked: 'Would the accused have any lawful authority to publish the information in these Schedules quoting the alleged sources?'

'No,' said Fleming.

The assessor, Mr Coleman, asked: 'Are troops regarded as intelligence sources at all?'

'I suppose so,' the Secretary replied. 'When it all comes up to the top, maybe yes, because the Director of the Central Intelligence Organisation gets his information from all sources.'

'Thank you,' said Hamilton. 'You may be excused, Mr Fleming,' and the witness stepped down and hurried from the courtroom, intent on matters of state. It had not been a good day for him, and it was only lunchtime. The court adjourned for two hours.

chapter 11

John Edmondson had escorted me from Salisbury Prison to the Regional court the first morning of the trial, and was then replaced by another white prison officer – a short, stocky young man in his early twenties – who sat in the courtroom looking tired and bored. A packet of sandwiches was sent up to us from the nearby Magistrates' Court, and Anthony Eastwood went out to buy some pies and soft drinks. With the court in secret session in the morning, Nonie had returned to her office, but when we adjourned for lunch, she was told I would be kept in the court for two hours and she could come up and see me. While I waited for her to arrive, I prowled up and down the empty courtroom, and after a while, the prison officer went to a nearby phone to call his mother or girlfriend – from the tone of the conversation, I wasn't sure which. I wandered casually over to the windows looking onto the street, and saw below a number of photographers. I had a feeling that restrictions on photographs would soon be back in force, so I leaned out pretending not to notice they were there, while shutters clicked and cameras whirred, and a prison official across the road in the Magistrates' Court waved me frantically back. I pretended I could not see him.

The court resumed just after 2.00 p.m. and with the state case closed, the defence began to present its evidence.

Our first witness was Michael Keats, a thick-set no-nonsense Australian, who was manager for Southern and East Africa of United Press International – one of my clients. He had flown up from Johannesburg to give evidence: we mainly wanted a character testimonial.

Michael May asked: 'What has been your experience of Mr Niesewand's responsibility and objectivity as a journalist?'

Keats replied: 'I have nothing but the absolute utmost regard for Mr Niesewand's accuracy, his professional integrity as a journalist which I have known over eight years, both as a competitor and as a colleague working for the same firm. In the two-and-a-half years he has been associated with me, the fact that he has worked for other organisations has never hindered our service from him or anything else.'

'What are the standards to which UPI works in objectivity?'

'Oh put it this way,' said Keats. 'A news agency such as ours, we have a tremendous problem, because we serve clients everywhere in more than a hundred countries. The news that emanates from our London office to come to Africa goes through the Middle East, African countries, right down as far as South Africa so it has been read by people as far apart as Tel Aviv, Cairo, Nairobi, Salisbury and South Africa. In between you have Turkey and Greece. All these people read the same wire, which makes it essential, as far as we are concerned as an agency, to be totally unbiased, otherwise you have the Israelis saying we favour the Arabs, and the Arabs saying we favour the Israelis, we have the South Africans saying we favour Black Africa, and vice versa.'

'In your experience as a journalist for UPI, has the accused lived up to this standard?'

'I think one hundred per cent, because I read his reports as they come, as do clients in Rhodesia and South Africa. I have never had any complaint from anyone.'

May then questioned Keats about his knowledge of guerilla activity in Mozambique. Keats said he knew the guerilla war had escalated, and he had heard and read a number of reports of Rhodesian troops operating in Mozambique. 'I think it is fairly common knowledge to any newsman,' Keats said.

'Speaking for yourself as a journalist,' May said, 'if you had received information that Rhodesian troops were operating in Mozambique, what would your attitude to that have been?'

'I think it depends on the circumstances,' replied Keats. 'I wouldn't, for instance, be reporting a fact that the Rhodesian Light Infantry was moving from Salisbury up to the border. However, if after an engagement, it was known there was an engagement and the thing had happened, and it was finished, and they were involved in that engagement, I see nothing wrong with publishing this information.'

'What of the statement that Rhodesian troops have operated or are operating in Mozambique?'

'That general statement, I see nothing wrong with that.'

144

Mr Hamilton asked: 'After the engagement?'

'Yes. I wouldn't like to say that they were moving to the north now.'

May said: 'As a general statement, without relating it to before or after: a general statement that troops have operated in Mozambique, or are operating in Mozambique?'

'I have no objection to that whatsoever.'

Treacy rose to cross-examine. 'How many times do you say that you read about Rhodesian troops being in Mozambique in a newspaper? Did you read it published?'

'Published,' said Keats. 'Well, do you mean the same story? I read a lot of newspapers.'

'Yes. Of Rhodesian forces in Mozambique?'

'I would say I have seen printed about five.'

'In your evidence-in-chief you referred to two.'

'I referred to two which stick in my mind. When I say five, two of those papers might have been about the same story with a follow-up. I wouldn't like to say exactly, but in my office I get the *Telegraph*, I get the South African papers, I get the *Mail*, the *Star*, plus associated ones. I read a lot. Some I absorb, some I don't. But I would say I have seen, at least in Afrikaans and English, five or six stories.'

'Are these newspapers still available?'

'If you have the files, yes, I should think so.'

'Do you have the files in Johannesburg?'

'In Johannesburg, yes.'

'Did you refresh your memory from those newspapers before you came up?'

'No I didn't unfortunately, because I had no idea what the charges were. If I had known, I would have been able to.'

Hamilton looked disapproving at the suggestion that his order, keeping the charges secret, could possibly have affected the Defence case, and Treacy fell silent for a moment.

Then he said: 'If you had been informed by some source that Rhodesian troops were operating in Mozambique, would you have published it without consulting somebody?'

'No,' said Keats, and added: 'It would depend on the source. A newsman has his sources in a vast and wide field. It could be an army major, which would be fine. He says: "I know, I have been in that area with five hundred of my troops, but don't quote me." That is an army major. You would then ask the Government for their attitude, if they wanted this, what was the comment. You had a report that there were five hundred troops there, what has the Government to say to that?'

'You would go and try to have it confirmed.'

'Oh yes.'

'If your source was an ordinary soldier, would you be wary about that?'

'No, if he had told me he had been in action, or he had been there. But again you would follow it up.'

When Treacy had finished, Michael May had a further question: 'Do you have experience of occasions when Governments will deny something publicly, but at the same time deliberately leak it privately, because they want it to be known, but they don't want it to be known that they are letting it be known?'

'Yes,' said Keats. 'I have had experience of this. I have also had experience of Governments who will give you information and say: "Don't quote us. This information is true, it will not be denied, but it will not be confirmed from us." Which includes this Government, I might add.'

The second Defence witness was Anthony Ryder, the Central African representative for the South African Morning Newspaper Group, and not a client of mine.

May asked: 'Have you heard any reports of operations by Rhodesian troops in Mozambique?'

'It was talk among journalists in Salisbury,' said Ryder.

'From when?'

'Rather early on in 1971. I remember reporting in March 1971 about the death of three Rhodesian security force members across the border, and the fact they were across the border occasioned no surprise to me and my colleagues.'

'Why was that?'

'We understood this was, in fact, happening – that Rhodesian troops were crossing the border.'

'They were crossing the border for what purpose?'

'Presumably for co-operation with the Portuguese security forces.'

'From whom did you receive these reports?'

'From colleagues.'

'Have you yourself ever sent a despatch including a report of Rhodesian troops operating in Mozambique?'

'Yes I have. The example I referred to in 1971. But I quoted the security force communiqué which said they had gone across for fraternisation, or social contact.'

146

'That is the only one?' asked May.

'That is the only direct reference to Rhodesian troops being across the border.'

'Have you ever had any warning from the Ministry of Information or any other Government source that this sort of information should not be passed on?'

'No.'

'Have you ever been in any way given to think there was anything wrong in it?'

'Not from Government sources, no.'

'Anything prejudicial to Rhodesia in doing so?'

'No.'

Treacy cross-examined well, if loudly. 'You heard of these reports of Rhodesian troops being in Mozambique from 1971, throughout 1972?'

'Yes,' said Ryder.

'Did you yourself ever write any article about these troops being in Mozambique? You never wrote an article about troops actually being deployed there?'

'No.'

'Why not, if you knew it?'

'Well, because I didn't feel at that stage I had its sources strongly enough to warrant. Had I had it strongly sourced, I would have used it.'

'Would you have tried to confirm it before using it?'

'Possibly I would have, yes.'

'You say that you heard these reports from your colleagues?'

'Yes.'

'Who are your colleagues?'

'Newspaper colleagues in Rhodesia and people on other newspapers who have visited Rhodesia from time to time, and in general talk among ourselves, as is the custom with newspapermen when they get together to talk shop. This was among the sort of items of information on the border war which emerged.'

'Did you know that Rhodesia was sending aircraft in there?' Treacy asked.

'I first became aware there was a possibility Rhodesian aircraft were going across the border only in – I think it was the end of last year.'

'Where did you hear this?'

'I heard it, in fact, from a member of the security forces.'

'Did you ever read any article in a newspaper about Rhodesian forces being in Mozambique?'

'I seem to have a recollection that a reporter on one of the Afrikaans newspapers had mentioned this, and I was trying to find the cutting over the weekend, but I couldn't, so I can't swear to it.'

'You never read it in an English-language newspaper?'

'No.'

'It is not widely publicised in newspapers?'

'No,' said Ryder.

When he had left the stand, Michael May said: 'I call the accused, Peter Niesewand,' and as I walked across, I hoped that six weeks of solitary confinement had not blunted my reactions too badly.

May said: 'I think you admit that you sent the despatches, the contents of which are alleged?'

'Yes I did,' I replied.

'Before 15th November 1972 had you previously sent any despatches concerning the operations of terrorists?'

'Yes, I had sent a number of such despatches.'

'Did that include the operations of FRELIMO in Mozambique?'

'Yes it would.'

'Apart from despatches which you had sent, had you seen reports published of such terrorist operations, both in Rhodesia and Mozambique, published in other newspapers?'

'Yes, I had. There were two or three references in Rhodesia some months before I sent the despatches in question, and these articles had never been categorically denied by the Ministry of Information. It had been said that the Ministry of Information would not confirm them, but there had never been a categorical denial.'

'What are you speaking of when you say these had not been denied?'

'I am talking about the use of Rhodesian troops across the border in Mozambique. I had also read this in other newspapers, and I think the *Guardian* carried a number of references to this by different people over the months. I was also aware, from my own contacts, that the situation was in fact taking place, and Rhodesian troops were being used across the border in Mozambique. . . . It was to my knowledge, very widely known.'

'You have heard reference this morning to a report by Mr Pierre Doublet that Rhodesian troops are operating in Mozambique. Were you aware of that report?'

'Yes I was. I had that in my files.'

May opened his file of Press cuttings. 'Were you aware of a report printed in the Sunday *Mail* in Salisbury on 13th August 1972, claiming that there had been a massacre by Rhodesian troops in Mozambique?'

'Yes,' I said. 'That was a report by a priest who had worked in Mozambique. He made the statement.'

'Is that the report?' May asked, and a court official handed it up to me.

'Yes, that is the report.' It was put in as Exhibit 10.

'I think, as appears from the Schedules to the charge, you were aware also that the Minister of Defence, Mr Howman, had said on at least one occasion that Rhodesian troops might have to be used in Mozambique?'

'That is correct.'

'Apart from these particular reports, where had you heard, as you have said, it was suggested by word of mouth that Rhodesian troops had been used in Mozambique?'

'I heard it from a number of sources, not only security forces inside Rhodesia, but it was widely known among ordinary people. A number of friends and contacts in the farming community, for example, and in the cities knew, and I had heard it from them. It was common knowledge.'

'Would they bring it up with a query whether Rhodesians were operating in Mozambique, or stating that they were?'

'Stating that they were.'

'In the three despatches which are the subject matter of the charge against you, what was the main point which you were reporting?'

'The main point I was reporting was the new FRELIMO assault. This was the only new information I had at my disposal, and I used it as the lead in all my reports. Because the situation of Rhodesian troops from time to time going across the border into Mozambique was, to my knowledge, well known, I simply used this as background. It did not form the meat of the despatch.'

May asked: 'You obtained this report concerning this new attack from a source which you had previously used, did you?'

'A source which I had previously used, and which I trusted.'

'Was that source an official source?'

'No,' I said. 'My source was not an official source. I must explain: I got a tip-off that the FRELIMO assault had taken place, and I went to my source which I had used on several previous occasions and asked him to check it up. He went to his military source, checked it up, came back and said: "It is true, this has happened, and these other factors are also relevant." '

'In reporting that Rhodesian troops were operating in Mozambique, did you rely upon your sources on this occasion, or on your previous knowledge?'

'On both. As far as Rhodesian troops were concerned, there was nothing new that I was told, but I was told it again, and therefore I included it.'

'After you had obtained the information, did you do anything to confirm it? That is, the information about the new FRELIMO attack?'

'Yes. I phoned a correspondent in Mozambique, but I gathered from his tone, although he knew about it he would rather not talk about it. They are under some pressure in Mozambique, and this source was not keen actually to confirm the information to me until he had an officially-censored despatch. But he made it clear in his turn he knew what I was talking about, and, in fact, the following day he did confirm it.'

May paused and shuffled his papers. 'What was your purpose in sending the despatches which are the subject of the charge?'

'There was first of all the news, which could have no bearing on the Rhodesian security situation in that it took place in Mozambique, on the Malawi border,' I said. 'The rest of the despatch was to show that the security situations in the two countries are very closely linked: that Rhodesia keeps a close watch on Mozambique, has been a bit disturbed about the deterioration of the situation there, because it does affect this country, and has plans in hand to deal with it and see it does not spread across to this country.'

'Did it occur to you, when you sent the despatches, that the publication of any of the matter in these three Schedules would be prejudicial to the interests or safety of Rhodesia?'

'I had no reason to suspect that this was so at all.'

'Or that it would in any way be useful to any enemy of Rhodesia?'

'No, on the contrary, I would think it would be the opposite. It would tend to make terrorists in Mozambique think again before believing they had a safe base in Mozambique from which to stage hit-and-run attacks on Rhodesia if they thought the Rhodesians were prepared to come in hot pursuit.'

'Did it occur to you some people might read into it there was some degree of official confirmation that Rhodesian troops were operating in Mozambique?'

'I think people would read into it that Rhodesian troops were taking an official part, and although the Rhodesian Government would not like officially to admit this was so, they were quite happy to have it known privately it was taking place. It helps people to get the situation in perspective. It makes them understand what Rhodesia is up against. It has been published before in Rhodesia on at least two occasions by the Rhodesian Press, and had not been categorically denied by the Government. Had it been categorically denied by the Government, I might have had reason to suspect they didn't want it known. But in fact, when asked about the story written by Mr Doublet, they simply said they didn't know where the information had been obtained. They didn't say it was untrue. From that it certainly looked like unofficial confirmation.'

May said: 'Have you had experience of occasions on which the Rhodesian Government has officially denied something, but at the same time, had quite clearly leaked the information by indirect routes?'

'Yes,' I said. 'This has happened on a number of occasions. It is a well-known technique of Governments. They use it all the time.'

'What is the purpose of operating in that manner?'

'Well, if you take the Mozambique situation as an example, the Portuguese tend to be very touchy about suggestions that the security situation in Mozambique is deteriorating. Rhodesia obviously does not want to say anything official to make the Portuguese authorities angry at them, but at the same time, it is in their interests, or it was certainly my impression that it was in their interests, to make it generally known what the situation was confronting Rhodesia, and what she was doing about it. In that way people in Rhodesia and elsewhere would know what the situation was. But she herself could not have a finger pointed at her to say "you have said this officially." Governments leak things like that all the time."

Brendan Treacy's turn, and I saw before him sheets of notes: it would be a lengthy cross-examination. It also turned out to be a high-pressure one, with Treacy scarcely bothering to disguise the hostility in his voice, and often shouting. I wonder if he would have shouted in open court.

'You say that you saw your source before 15th November, and that he gave you information regarding the use of Rhodesian troops in Mozambique which you already knew, or he repeated it to you. What did he tell you about that?' Treacy asked.

'That is correct,' I said. 'He told me about the use of Rhodesian troops.'

'Yes?'

'He told me substantially what appears in the annexures, that Rhodesian troops have been operating from time to time in Mozambique over the past year, and that Rhodesia is worried about the deteriorating situation there, but has plans to deal with it, and, in fact, has been taking a part in Mozambique.'

'You say this was widely known and widely published?'

'It was published in Rhodesia, certainly on two occasions.'

'Let's get down to these two occasions,' said Treacy. 'What were they?'

'The two occasions were the claim by the Portuguese missionary of a massacre in the Tete province, which mentioned that Rhodesian troops had been involved inside Mozambique. And there was a report by Mr Doublet, which has been quoted in court.'

'What did the report of Mr Doublet say, do you recall?'

'Yes. The report by Mr Doublet said that Rhodesian troops and planes had been operating inside Mozambique, and that the Mozambique security situation was deteriorating, and the reasons for it.'

'That is two. Any others?'

'I can't recall offhand. He said . . .'

'No. Any other newspaper reports about Rhodesian troops being used in Mozambique?'

'Yes, there were reports I have read in the *Guardian Weekly* and in *Le Monde*.'

'Who wrote that?'

'I don't recall, I'm afraid. The information was already known to me. It wasn't new information. It was simply recapitulation.'

'What else?'

'Well, there were some reports in South African newspapers. I think probably I had read myself between six and eight separate accounts of the fact that Rhodesians have been involved in Mozambique.'

'Did they say they were involved there for a whole year?'

'Yes sir. From – well, at that time, it wasn't a year. Reports indicated that involvement had been taking place for the preceding few months.'

'Did they say aircraft had been sent in?'

'Mr Doublet's report said aircraft had been sent in, and I believe I read another report saying this. There was this report from – I think it was the *Rhodesia Herald* – quoted in court today, talking about the Rhodesian spotter plane circling overhead. That was in the local press.'

'Over the border?' asked Treacy.

'A plane would be going over the border if it was on a spotting mission.'

'Altogether you say you have read these reports in about seven or eight newspapers?'

'Six or seven.'

'Did you think then, our enemies had this information already?'

'Yes I did.'

'How did you know that?'

'Because it was widely reported.'

'How did you know if they got these papers in Zambia or Dar-es-Salaam?'

'Because the report of Mr Doublet's article is a report which is carried on a news agency, I think it is Reuters which has contracts, I know, in Zambia, and it has contracts in Dar-es-Salaam, and all over the world, so all their subscribers would have received the story.'

'Does the BBC broadcast in Zambia?'

'It is received in Zambia.'

'Do your reports come over the BBC Zambian system?'

'There is no Zambian system of the BBC.'

' "Focus on Africa" – would that come across?'

'That would come across the BBC. It could be picked up in Zambia, but it is not transmitted by Zambia.'

'Is it picked up by Dar-es-Salaam?'

'It can be picked up anywhere in the world. "Focus on Africa" would be picked up mainly on the African continent.'

'So if people hadn't read those seven or eight newspapers previously, it would be news to them, wouldn't it?'

'I think with regard to the terrorist organisations, this would be very old news.'

Treacy's voice had a tone near to loathing in it. 'How do you know?' he asked. 'Have you contacts with terrorist organisations?'

'No, I don't.'

'How do you know? How can you say that?' He was shouting.

'Mr Doublet's story would be carried in Dar-es-Salaam and Zambia. . . .'

'Say they didn't read it?'

Michael May broke in with a low, warning 'Let him finish.'

I said: 'Because it was, in my view, widely known. Even if, assuming by some amazing possibility, over the course of the year, this information had not come to them, even though their bands had been just across the border in Mozambique, even though they could look up in the sky and see Rhodesian aircraft with Rhodesian markings, and even though they hadn't read the accounts of the various reports which had been inside Mozambique, even assuming all these things, I think the information could not be of assistance to them, but, in fact, would make them think again about using Mozambique as a base for hit-and-run attacks, as they have been using Zambia.'

'You say they had this information?'

'I believe they had.'

'You couldn't be certain about it?'

'I couldn't be certain. I have no links with terrorist organisations.'

'It might have been news to them,' Treacy insisted.

'Not useful,' I said.

'It might have been news to them.'

'There is a very faint possibility: a very faint possibility.'

'There is a possibility it might have been news to them?'

'Yes, there is.'

'If it was news to them, it would have been useful to them.'

'I think not. If I was a terrorist in Mozambique, I would like to think I have a safe refuge there. I would simply cross the Rhodesian border, strike with impunity, and then cross back and be safe. If I were a terrorist, I would certainly have second thoughts about being followed into what one might have considered to be a safe refuge.'

'This source of yours,' said Treacy, looking down at his notes. 'Did you request this source to obtain the information for you?'

'I requested him to confirm a piece of information which had reached me, but which was at that stage not sufficiently well sourced for me.'

'Was this your source in Mozambique?'

'No.'

'How many sources have you?'

'On this particular item?'

'Yes.'

'I had two sources; the source of the initial tip and the source who gave me the information.'

'The tip-off and the information source? I don't understand.'

'Well, I received a tip-off that there had been a major FRELIMO attack.'

'Yes?'

'I then contacted my source and asked this source to check it for me.'

'I see.'

'The source then came back and said: "It is true, this is what happened. The situation is that we are worried about Mozambique, and as you know, we've been attacking there for some months." He confirmed what I already knew.'

'Where did you meet, you and your source?'

'I could not say, because it would tend to identify the source.'

'The identity of your source is not known to the authorities?'

'No.'

'You are not prepared to disclose his name?'

'No. As a journalist, it would be totally against all journalistic ethics. One guarantees one's source secrecy.'

'You are aware you could be summoned before a magistrate and asked to disclose his name?' said Treacy.

'Yes.'

'Presumably it was an official source,' said the magistrate.

'No,' I replied, 'my source was not an official source.'

Treacy: 'Your source also might be contravening the Official Secrets Act.'

'If I am found guilty of this offence, then my source might have contravened the Official Secrets Act,' I agreed. 'But I had no reason at that stage to suspect that this was so at all.'

'Did you pay your source for the information received?'

'No. I have a number of journalistic sources who give me tip-offs and whom I pay, but I do not pay people who are not journalists to give me information.'

'How do you remunerate them for their kindness?'

'I do not remunerate them at all.'

'Do you do them other favours?'

'No.'

'Did you know it was an offence to publish information regarding the movement of troops in Rhodesia?'

'Yes,' I said, 'but in my mind I was not publishing information regarding the movement of troops in any detail which would be of any use to anyone at all. I was speaking in very, very broad and general terms. Even if I had the information, I wouldn't have given placenames, or dates, or times or anything of that sort.'

Hamilton went into a wide-eyed pantomime: 'Why not?' he asked, leaning forward, as if it would have been such an exciting thing to have done.

'Because that could well be taken to be of assistance,' I said. 'If for example, I knew troops were moving up to the border, I would never use it, because that could be of assistance to terrorists, knowing the disposition of troops in detail. As it was, they knew Rhodesian troops were along the border. Troops had been in hot pursuit of them on a number of occasions and so they knew this. There was nothing detailed, or nothing I could see which would be of any assistance to them in the report I gave.'

Hamilton leaned back in his chair, looking disbelieving.

Treacy picked up the Schedule: 'In your report you referred to an interview, or to what Mr Howman said.'

'Yes.'

' "In August, Rhodesia's Minister of Defence, Mr Jack Howman, said that Rhodesia would help if necessary." '

'Yes sir.'

'Is this one of these official leaks?'

'Mr Howman?'

'Yes.'

'Oh no. Mr Howman was speaking on television.'

'Is that what you mean when the Government denied information and then let it be leaked?'

'Yes, that is the sort of thing. Also the denial which accompanied Mr Doublet's story. That is another indication.'

'You think the Government wanted to publish that their forces were in Mozambique?' asked Treacy, his voice flat.

'I don't think the Government was at all embarrassed by the fact that it was known. They would have been embarrassed if it had been known officially. In fact I said: It has been officially denied.'

'In your report, you referred to official sources, didn't you?'

'No, I spoke of military sources.'

'You didn't say "private military sources", you said "official sources".' (Shouting again.)

'I don't think I ever used the word "official".'

'The inference was that they were official sources.'

'I don't think that necessarily follows.'

Hamilton leaned forward again. 'You did say military sources,' he said.

'I did say military sources, but it doesn't mean to say it was the Ministry of Defence.'

'What military sources were you referring to? Your informant?'

'The situation, if I can explain it, is this: my source was not an official source. My source had contact with a military source. He relayed back to me what the military source said. I had no direct contact with the military source.'

'It is not soldiers in bars?' asked Hamilton.

'I would not expect it to be soldiers in bars, because my immediate source is very well trusted. If it had been soldiers in bars, I should have known about it many years before, and I would never have used that source again.'

'The inference here,' said Mr Treacy, looking again at the Schedules, 'is that Mr Howman is not telling the truth when he says Rhodesian forces have not been invited or asked to go into Mozambique.'

'He was practising politics.'

'He wasn't telling the truth?'

'He wasn't telling the truth,' I agreed.

Hamilton's brow furrowed. 'Did you suppose that your contact's military source was a responsible one?'

'Yes sir.'

'Spoke with authority?' he asked incredulously.

'Yes sir.'

A smile: 'With the authority of whom did you think he spoke?'

'I imagined it was some official authority. It could come under the heading. . . .'

'What do you mean by "some official"?' asked Hamilton.

'Insofar as it would come under the heading of a leak. The Rhodesian Government would not be averse to the information about FRELIMO, or to a recapitulation of the security situation, but they did not want to say so by issuing a Press Statement.'

'So it was your view that this military source was speaking with authority?'

'It was my view that he was. . . .'

'Whether he was bringing about a leak by authority, or something else, he was a person speaking with authority?'

'Yes sir.'

Hamilton nodded, and Treacy asked: 'Did you check out his authority?'

'No, I don't know his identity, the military source.'

'How did you know it was reliable?'

'Because,' I said, 'my immediate source had links with the military source, and he was extremely reliable and trustworthy, and I have known him over a period of years. I trusted that his sources would be extremely good ones, and in fact, so it has turned out. If one has a source who gives incorrect information, one never uses that source again.'

'How can you establish if it is correct or not, if you don't know the derivation of the information?' asked Treacy.

'Because it becomes known over a period of time. In this particular instance, I got the information of the FRELIMO attack, and it was confirmed the following day.'

Hamilton rustled the pages of the Schedules. 'You say on page 2 of the first Schedule: "Military sources say that although the Rhodesian Government is reluctant to officially admit its forces are already taking an active part in the Mozambique war, the true position is that security forces from this country have been involved for most of this year." '

'Yes.'

'Did you get that information from your source?' he asked.

'The information was re-stated to me by my source.'

'Quite,' said Hamilton. 'In view of the source, or your knowing that the military source said "Government is reluctant", wouldn't that have put you on your guard?'

'No.'

'Or did you think this was an official leak?'

'I thought it was an official leak. I wasn't on my guard because of the official reply to Mr Doublet's article.'

Hamilton said: 'It was a denial.'

'No,' I replied. 'It wasn't a categorical denial.'

'No,' Hamilton agreed, 'but it was a negative one.'

'I think the spokesman said: "I don't know where he could have got his information from, he didn't get it from us." It left the question rather in the air.'

'But didn't those words put you on your guard?' Hamilton said, feigning astonishment.

'No, because it is something which is done so often by Government.'

Treacy came in again, his voice harsh: 'Did you check out this at all? Did you check this information?'

'No, I didn't.'

'Why didn't you?'

'Because it was well-known information. I had no reason to doubt it was true, and I had no reason to suspect that it would have been embarrassing in any way to the Government to have it re-stated.'

'You did not bother to check whether this information about the troops in Mozambique was embarrassing to Government, or whether it was true or not?'

'Well, I had my source, who had previously told me it was true. It had been widely published, and not categorically denied.'

Hamilton said in surprise: 'It had been widely published?'

'Widely published,' I said.

'Or do you mean widely rumoured?'

'No, it was published on two occasions at least inside Rhodesia, and also in newspapers outside. I had no reason to suspect the Rhodesian Government considered this information to be Top Secret. If it had considered it to be Top Secret, I would have expected, when it was first reported inside Rhodesia, it would have been categorically denied, and furthermore, word would have gone out to us that this would be very embarrassing to Rhodesians if this was known. But this was never done on any occasion.'

Treacy went into the attack again. 'Is it your attitude to publish regardless?'

'No. There is a lot of information on matters like sanctions busting which I do not publish, because it would be clearly harmful to the country.'

'Are your articles friendly towards Rhodesia?'

'I try to be as objective as I can in my ordinary news reporting, which makes up probably ninety-five per cent of my output. On a few occasions, I am asked for my opinion of a situation and I give my opinion, to the best of my ability. I am not a member of any political organisation, and I am professionally indifferent to whether the present Government, for example, stays in power for another twenty years, or forever. It is not my journalistic job to be anti-anyone. I write about Rhodesia.'

'Some of your articles are anti-Rhodesia,' said Treacy.

'Some of my articles are critical, some are not.'

'Some of your articles are harmful to Rhodesia.'

'I have never knowingly written anything which would be harmful to Rhodesia.'

'Do you not think this article was harmful to Rhodesia?'

'I have no reason to suspect it was. The only new information concerned Mozambique, and the other was recapitulation.'

'Suppose,' said Treacy 'there was a terrorist strategist in Zambia, and he hadn't read any information previously about Rhodesian troops in Portuguese East Africa. Say he heard this over the news on the night of the 15th November. Don't you think that would have been useful to him?'

'No. It was not specific. If in the highly unlikely event that he was a strategist and had never heard anything about the subject before, then what he would know would be – it is getting harder to attack Rhodesia, because the security forces are keeping a very close watch.'

'Would he not know that not all Rhodesian troops were concentrated on the northern border, but others were, in fact, fighting a war in Mozambique?'

'Well, if he were a guerilla strategist, he would certainly have known that before.'

'I am not asking you that,' Treacy shouted. 'I put the example: he had *never* known before – he heard for the first time.'

'I would think it would be useful in deterring him from entering Rhodesia.'

'Wouldn't he know now there are less troops on our northern borders because some are in Mozambique, and our northern borders would be more vulnerable to attack?'

'I don't think that follows from my reports at all.'

'Surely,' said Mr Hamilton, staring down at me from the bench, 'any troop disposition is of use to an enemy, even those that warn him?'

'Dispositions on a perfectly general basis, insofar as guerillas know that troops are along the border with Zambia, they knew they were along the border with Mozambique. If they knew specifically where they were, it would certainly be useful.'

'I see,' said Hamilton. 'All right.'

'But just knowing they were there, there is no implication, in my submission, that Rhodesian resources were strained in any way,' I said.

Treacy said: 'It would be logical to assume there were less on the northern borders because there were more troops in Mozambique?'

'No,' I replied, 'that would be an erroneous first assumption that all Rhodesia's forces were concentrated on the border with Zambia. I don't believe that to be true. Any terrorist tactician who made such an assumption would be making a grave error.'

'Might it not enourage the terrorists to attack Rhodesia again?'

'I don't think so for a second,' I said. 'I think it would deter them.'

'You published your news on the 16th of November.'

'Yes.'

'We had a terrorist attack on the 21st of December at Whistlefield Farm.'

'Yes.'

'I am not saying there is a direct link between the two, the publication of your news and the terrorist attack, but it is a coincidence.'

'No,' I said. 'The terrorists who attacked Whistlefield Farm, it has been officially said since then, had been in the country for about six months. In addition to that, before publication of my article, there had been, I think, on two occasions, terrorist attacks in Rhodesia launched across from Mozambique. There had been incidents. I cannot believe for a second it could have made an ounce of difference.'

'The point is,' said Mr Treacy, 'your news might have encouraged active terrorism in Rhodesia. It might urge terrorists in Zambia to penetrate, because now is the time to attack as some of Rhodesia's forces were in Mozambique.'

'No, I don't agree. I think what a terrorist would think is: it is becoming more and more difficult to attack, and it is becoming less and less worthwhile to attack, because Rhodesians are not only watchful on the Zambian border, but also on the Mozambique border, and they are not against going in hot pursuit of any attempt to attack Rhodesian farms, families, tribesmen or anything. I think it would be a deterrent.'

'Again from your article, would a terrorist strategist deduce that the FRELIMO successes in Mozambique would mean that as long as these successes continued, Rhodesian troops would continue to be deployed there?'

'I think it would be obvious that while Rhodesian terrorists are using Mozambique, and while FRELIMO forces have from time to time crossed into Rhodesia and have raided villages, that Rhodesia would be vigilant on her border until such danger was past. I think this would be obvious to anyone.'

'In other words,' Treacy persisted, 'the news disclosed that Rhodesia had opened up another front in Mozambique.'

'I don't think so. It was known that Rhodesia was guarding the Mozambique border. If my story had suggested Rhodesia was *not* guarding the Mozambique border, that would have been a different matter.'

'Didn't it disclose Rhodesia had opened up another front against FRELIMO?'

'No. Rhodesia is not concerned with FRELIMO. Rhodesia was only concerned with FRELIMO on the occasions FRELIMO actually came across the border and attacked a Rhodesian kraal.'

'Isn't it obvious from your article that Rhodesia was waging a war against FRELIMO?'

Hamilton broke in: 'Your words are "taking an unofficial part in the Mozambique guerilla war".'

'Have I not explained it this way,' I said. 'FRELIMO and ZANU and ZAPU, the Rhodesian terrorist organisations, have close links, and ZANU and ZAPU are, in fact, under the wing of FRELIMO in Mozambique. So an attack on terrorists inside Mozambique would be an attack not only necessarily on the band of Rhodesians who crossed back across the border, but if they got as far as the base camp, it would be an attack on FRELIMO itself. Rhodesian troops have been fighting FRELIMO in Mozambique, but that is not the prime object in Mozambique.'

Treacy said: 'What did you mean by "They are already taking an unofficial part in the Mozambique guerilla war"?'

'The fact that the terrorist organisations have banded together. They are co-operating with one another.'

'Just confine yourself, please, to this information I am putting to you, which is in the first Schedule. You say here: "Military sources said the Rhodesians are already taking an unofficial part in the Mozambique guerilla war, including supplying aircraft of the Rhodesian Air Force for specific tasks in the neighbouring territory, and sending patrols of soldiers across on request." Also you go on to say: "Military sources say that although the Rhodesian Government is reluctant to officially admit its forces are already taking an active part in the Mozambique war. . . ." That is understood, that they are fighting FRELIMO.'

'Not exclusively fighting FRELIMO.'

'You don't explain it very clearly,' said Treacy sourly.

'Perhaps I could have gone into more detail,' I said, but wondered what the court's reaction would have been had I done so.

Hamilton adjourned the trial until the following morning, and the prison officer escorted me downstairs to a waiting Landrover. More photographers stood outside, and again no one ordered them to stop doing their jobs.

The following morning, the *Rhodesia Herald* carried a front-page picture of me arriving for the first day of the trial. The prison authorities were angry that the photograph had been taken and published,

162

that I had been brought to court nearly an hour late, and that I was not in handcuffs.

I was taken from my cell at 7.00 a.m. – more than two hours before the court was due to resume for the second day of the hearing – and packed, with thirteen others, into the tiny middle section of a black prisons truck. Thick blinds covered the windows, to stop photographers seeing me. Most of those in the middle compartment were prison officers and warders. I looked through a dingy glass window into the cab of the truck, where two officers were reading the *Herald* and discussing it, and I could just make out the picture.

We arrived at court at about 7.30, and I was locked into a small bare first-floor room, with burglar bars at the painted-out windows. The prison officials went away, and I prowled around a little, then peered out through a small gap in the paint, and down into the street. I watched people walking past for several minutes, before I recognised a group of men from the BBC Television programme 'Panorama'. I moved across to the door and looked out through the spyglass, but the officials were not to be seen. I went back and opened the window to the street and looked out. BBC Reporter Richard Kershaw spotted me within twenty seconds, and a minute after that, the crew were assembled in the street, filming me staring down through the bars.

They had finished and gone away, when the officers came back into the room and closed the windows tightly.

'You're not to open it,' one said.

'It's very stuffy in here.'

'That's too bad. There are Press people outside.'

Nonie arrived at court half an hour before the resumption, and I was allowed to see her and some journalists in the corridor outside.

Then back into the witness stand.

'I remind you that you are still under oath,' said Brendan Treacy.

'Yes.'

'Did I gather from your evidence yesterday that before you sent this despatch on 15th November last year, that you personally were not in a position to say what information the enemy had regarding the disposition of Rhodesian forces?'

'All the information contained in the despatches was already available and had been available for some time to any enemy of Rhodesia,' I said, 'with the exception of the actual attack made by FRELIMO on the Tete railway line, which would not have been available, as it had only taken place some days previously.'

'I am not asking you about the attack by FRELIMO,' Treacy shouted. 'I am asking you about the disposition of Rhodesian forces, and what the enemy knew about that.'

'I would say all the banned nationalist organisations knew about that. Any other enemy who had read the news reports which had come out in the preceding months would have known about that.'

'Did you personally know that our enemies had this information?'

'I have no personal contact with the country's enemies.'

'So you don't know?'

'I was not absolutely one hundred per cent positive, but I could not conceive of a case where an enemy would not have known.'

'That is just conjecture on your part. You personally don't know what information they had.'

'I have no contact with them.'

'If they didn't have this information available, you took a risk in reporting it.'

'As far as I knew, I took no action which, in my view, could have damaged Rhodesia at all, or compromised her position at all. I was simply re-stating a well-known position.'

Treacy refused to give up. 'If the enemy didn't have this information, you took a risk in reporting it.'

'Even if the enemy didn't have this information,' I said, 'I would submit that the fact of the information would have been a deterrent to the enemy rather than being helpful to them.'

'That is not the question I asked you. Please answer the question. If the enemy didn't have this information available to them, you took a risk in reporting it?'

'No, I didn't consider the information was risky.'

Treacy clasped his hands behind his back and focussed his eyes on some distant point. 'Do you not think that a member of the Portuguese Government, reading that report, would think that the Rhodesian Government had officially released this news?'

'No,' I replied, 'because the story says the Rhodesian Government has officially not done so.'

Mr Hamilton asked: 'But you are talking in terms of a leak, presumably an inspired leak?'

'Yes.'

'Is it not then, your argument that these were inspired leaks from the Government?'

'My argument is that I understand them to be inspired leaks from the Government, but I was not in direct contact with the military source, therefore I had no way of telling who he was, or who had inspired him to do it.'

Treacy said: 'The information regarding Rhodesian troops in Mozambique – wouldn't that information give one the impression that Rhodesian troops were there because the Portuguese forces were unable themselves to cope with the situation?'

'Not necessarily unable to cope. South African forces are in Rhodesia, but no one has suggested Rhodesia is unable to cope,' I pointed out.

'That is not the question I asked,' Treacy shouted again, although he probably meant "That is not the answer I want." 'Would it not give the impression Portuguese troops were unable to cope with the position themselves?'

'No, I don't agree.'

'Why should Rhodesian forces be there?'

'Because Rhodesia is being affected by the crossing of her border by terrorists operating in Mozambique – both FRELIMO and Rhodesian guerilla bands.'

'And the Portuguese are unable to control the situation?'

'No. It is a fluid movement across the border. It would be reasonable for a neighbour to help.'

'Do you think that the information regarding the disposition of Rhodesian troops in Mozambique would have been useful to organisations such as the United Nations Organisation, or the OAU, the Organisation of African Unity?'

'No, I don't. Both the OAU and the United Nations have very sophisticated information networks. All the information which had previously been published about Rhodesian troops being involved in Mozambique and about the various attacks and so on would be very well known to them indeed.'

'You don't know that they personally had this information?'

'I don't know personally that they had this information, but I would be amazed if they had not.'

'My point is, if they had not this information, don't you think it would give them another platform on which to attack the so-called illegal regime?' He looked furious at the thought.

'No,' I said. 'If it had been said officially, if the Government had given it out and said it, probably they could have. I would hesitate to imagine the reports would be sufficient for them to launch any major attack on Rhodesia, or even a minor attack.'

Treacy said: 'You made no attempt, I think you said yesterday, to verify this information?'

'Previously, after it had been originally published, I had verified it with my sources. I didn't reverify it because I knew it to be true, and because I thought it had come from a Government leak. I also thought that the Government had no objection to this information going out, and would not have found it embarrassing because of the terms of their earlier denial of Mr Doublet's article, and because if they had found it to be embarrassing, they simply had to pick up the phone and say: "We find this embarrassing, would you please not use it."'

'Were you surprised, on the 16th November, the following day, when you did get a phone call?'

'I was quite surprised.'

Hamilton leaned towards me and said earnestly: 'But by that time the damage had been done.'

'But by then the story had gone out,' I corrected him. 'But I can't accept it would cause damage. It was certainly never written with the intention of committing the slightest damage to Rhodesia of any description.'

The assessor, Mr Coleman, took over. 'In your evidence yesterday, you mentioned that these reports you made could act as a deterrent to any enemy of the state.'

'Yes.'

'Is that your opinion on reflection now, after what you heard?'

'No, that was my opinion at the time I wrote it.'

'What was the object of your writing it?'

'It wasn't deliberately written as a deterrent, but I would not have written a story that was an invitation to terrorists, or which . . .'

'I don't suggest it is an invitation at all,' Mr Coleman said mildly. 'What I am suggesting, or asking you, is this: was it as a deterrent to whoever in ZAPU headquarters, or ZANU headquarters may be contemplating an attack on this country?'

'Its primary objective was simply to put the true position as far as Rhodesia was concerned, to say . . .'

'So it wasn't written as a deterrent?'

'It wasn't written primarily as a deterrent. It was written as a straightforward news story.'

Then it was Mr Hamilton's turn, and he appeared to enjoy himself. 'Did you get the entire content of the Schedules from the one informant, the one source?' he asked.

'Everything that is quoted, that is tagged to a military source, including the FRELIMO attack, all came from the one informant, although most of it was a re-statement.'

'What is a re-statement, apart from "In August, Rhodesia's Minister of Defence, Mr Jack Howman, said . . ."?'

'The re-statement is: "Rhodesians are watching the security situation in Mozambique with growing concern."'

'Yes?'

'Rhodesians are already taking an unofficial part in the Mozambique guerilla war.'

'Well no,' said Hamilton, 'You say you got that from a military source, your informant, on this one occasion?'

'Yes, but I had verified that earlier, after the original reports had been published.'

'Who did you verify it with?'

'I verified that with my own source.'

'Your own sources were what?'

'In Rhodesia.'

'Oh?' Hamilton's eyebrows raised, and his mouth opened as if to laugh heartily.

'And it was confirmed. I didn't use the story, because it had already been used.'

'What were these sources?'

'They were military sources.'

'Of what standing?'

'Special Branch, and . . .'

'Do you mean to tell me that members of the Special Branch told you that?' Hamilton's eyebrows had nearly vanished into his hairline.

'Yes.'

'If they told you, surely it must have been in the greatest confidence?' Eyes wide, mouth poised for mirth.

'No.'

'Do you mean to tell me that they spoke to you, giving you information that you could freely use?'

'I went to them and said "Is it true?" and my contact said "Yes, that's what's happening." '

Hamilton made a disbelieving face at me. 'Do you think he gave it to you for publication, or did he give it to you in confidence? I realise people do deal in confidence with the Press, but surely the Press must understand it is in confidence, especially if it comes from the Special Branch, and suchlike.'

'Well, I . . .'

'Surely they are giving you the greatest confidence?'

'Your worship . . .'

'And not for publication,' said Hamilton in a pantomime whisper.

'When people give information in confidence, they always preface it by saying "This is absolutely off the record" and they make it quite clear that . . .'

'Do you think that a member of the Special Branch was then leaking information?'

'No, he was confirming. I asked him about the story.'

'Oh, he was confirming it. Did you think then you were free to publish it?'

'I was not told not to.'

'Yes?'

'I was not given to understand it was in any way embarrassing to the country. It was . . .'

'Do you really expect Special Branch men to come out with that sort of information, and tell you that it would be embarrassing?'

'Well, I should think, if . . .'

'This was a friend in the Special Branch?'

'Not a personal friend.'

'Did you think he confirmed that, and therefore on his confirmation you were free to publish it?'

'Well, I didn't publish it at that stage.'

'Nor at any stage, bearing in mind your source?'

'Bearing in mind my source, I would have felt, after that confirmation . . .'

'If it suited you, would you have rushed off and published that?' Hamilton's face was a study in childlike surprise.

'If it was new information, I would have taken it to the Ministry of Information for comment.'

'Yes?' His eyes encouraging.

'It was not new information. They had already commented, and it had been confirmed. That is all. I was never given any warnings of any sort about this.'

'This informant of yours, he is your military contact, and that sort of thing,' Hamilton said. 'Also he is your Rhodesian intelligence source. Who did he imply to you that he was dealing with?'

'There was no implication at all. My immediate contact simply came back and gave me the information that . . .'

'Weren't you interested to know exactly where you got this information?'

'I would never ask someone to divulge a source.'

'Where did you then imagine he would get this information? At what level approximately?'

'At a fairly high level. I imagine it was an official leak.'

'Do you think leaks are pushed out through military sources?'

'Yes, they are pushed out through very wide sources.'

'Is your informant of the bar-keeper, taxi driver, waiter variety?'

His face begged me to say 'yes'.

'No. I never use barmen, taxi drivers or waiters.'

'What is he therefore?'

'He is a responsible Rhodesian.'

'Do you still think so?' asked the magistrate, eyes wide in disbelief. If I had any lingering doubts about the verdict, they were gone now.

'I have no reason to suspect that the information was in any way embarrassing,' I said.

'Both your colleagues said that if they received this information that Rhodesian forces were operating in Mozambique they would wish to verify it first.'

'If it had been new, I think they would have. But it was not new. I had verified it.'

'You only verified it from what is commonly called a delicate source, isn't that right? You were dealing with Special Branch people.'

'Not that delicate.'

'Why did you go to the Special Branch to verify it?'

'Because I thought they would be in a position to know immediately.'

'Isn't it because they know, or have more confidences and secrets in their possession than other people, so you go to someone who possesses that sort of information, such as the Special Branch and ask him?'

'But the Special Branch . . .'

'Otherwise I can't imagine why you went to the Special Branch and didn't go to the Information Department.'

'The Information Department had already been approached. They had already made their comment, and they said they didn't know where it could have come from.'

'You went one better.' No more smiles from the magistrate.

'I wanted to find out if . . .'

'Having been told by the Information Department they didn't know, you then went to this other source where it was given to you, you say?'

'Yes.'

'Surely, bearing in mind the source, how can you claim that it had already been stated?'

'Well, it was published in the *Rhodesia Herald*.'

'What do you mean? These articles?' Hamilton gave a contemptuous wave of his hand towards the exhibits.

'Yes.'

'They weren't admitted.'

'They weren't categorically denied.'

'Didn't that put you on your guard?'

'No. I . . .'

'Bearing in mind you are experienced in these matters.'

'I would have been on my guard had there been a categorical denial,' I said. 'If they had said: "This is absolutely not true, this is absolute rubbish," I would have been on my guard. But as they said "We don't know where you got the information from," this is something commonly done by Governments. They won't deny or confirm.'

'If they won't deny or confirm, there is a third reason.'

'They don't want it known that they officially say so.'

'Quite.'

'Not that they don't want it known.'

'Quite. And the only way you could get this confirmed was by asking someone in Special Branch.'

'I am sure there would be other ways I could get it confirmed, because I heard this from a number of purely private sources.'

'Yes,' said Mr Hamilton. 'In view of the fact the Government had never announced it, you only had these negative attitudes to the Press reports which have appeared, and it was bar talk. Surely you would be on your guard?'

'No, there was nothing to put me on my guard. Had the Government considered it a delicate matter, I would have expected them to phone up and say "Don't use it." '

'They didn't know you had it, did they?'

'Well, when the *Rhodesia Herald* phoned them up and read them Mr Doublet's article, they did not immediately say "Please don't use that." At no stage subsequently . . .'

'They just said "We don't know where you got it from." '

'But they didn't deny it,' I said. 'Had they emphatically, categorically denied this, then one is in a different position. But if the Government is lukewarm over a matter, in my experience although they don't want to say so officially, they admit it is so.'

'Tell me,' said Hamilton, leafing through the Schedules, 'when you wrote these reports, why did you say "According to Rhodesian intelligence reports" as though the report was available to you when, in actual fact, it was not a report to you at all, it was a confidential source?'

'A confidential source in my . . .'

'You said: "Military sources said the Rhodesians . . ." Why didn't you say you understood from a confidential source, as you expressed it?'

'Most newspapers and agencies, United Press International is one of them, will not accept a story which does not have the area of the source at least defined. They won't accept "reliable sources". They won't accept "well-informed sources". They say, if they were not reliable and well-informed, you wouldn't use them.'

'Were you bringing one over the *Guardian* or the BBC?' asked Hamilton.

'I beg your pardon?'

He spelt it out: 'Were you defrauding the BBC and the *Guardian* by giving out, or pretending, or implying, that the source was available to you and you didn't get it through this confidential source?'

'I don't think I defrauded them.'

'You say they wouldn't have accepted it if you had simply said: "I understand from a source", "a secret source", or a "confidential source", or just a plain source that – which was the true position.'

'I trusted my source to give me the correct information.'

'You have already said, if they understood it came from this confidential source, we will call him, that they wouldn't have accepted it. Is that why you implied that this was available to you direct from these sources?'

'No. I had got from my source what the military source had said, and I trusted he was correct.'

'You didn't even pay him, you say?' asked Hamilton.

'No, I didn't.'

'He was what is basically just a common informer?'

' "Informer" I think implies in that context someone who deliberately gives out information which is harmful or hurtful, or something like that. In this case, I didn't believe . . .'

'Do you still say that if you set out the true position, that this information came through this confidential source, it would probably have been rejected?'

'No, I think it would have been accepted. I have a certain reputation with my clients, and they would have accepted it. United Press International would not, unless I had said "military sources", because that is where I got it from. It was via an intermediary.'

'You got it from an intermediary?'

'But I had no reason to suspect it was not originally from a military source.'

Hamilton put his final question: 'When you sent these reports to the *Guardian* and to the BBC, am I right in assuming you intended they should be read by their readers or listeners?'

'Yes, I did,' I said.

Brendan Treacy and Michael May took about an hour over summing up, quoting precedents out of British, South African and Rhodesian law reports, while in a corner, the prison officer found difficulty staying awake. His eyes kept closing, and his head lolling forward.

Hamilton set the judgment date as 30 March, in the new Magistrates' Courts on the outskirts of Salisbury. As Brendan Treacy left the courtroom, he remarked to an official: 'A minor matter – deserves a suspended sentence.' We were all surprised, therefore, when Mr Treacy returned to the Regional Court for judgment and sentencing, a three-page typewritten speech in his briefcase, which called it 'an extremely serious offence' and added: 'In the interests of society, a sentence of deterrent length should be imposed.'

chapter 12

The photograph in the *Herald* that morning had stung the prisons department into action, and while I was undergoing final cross-examination and the European on escort duty in the court was falling asleep, plans were being made to evade the Press.

When the court adjourned, I was kept waiting in the building for more than half an hour, while journalists and cameramen staked out both the front and rear entrances. Finally with a great show, a prisons Landrover was driven up the sanitary alley behind the court, and my colleagues clustered around it to wait. When those at the main door had all rushed away, I was escorted quickly out of the front, and across the road into the Magistrates' Court where I was locked in a cell for three hours until every journalist had gone.

It was filthy – worse than the Bridal Suite – with yellow walls and a non-flush concrete toilet pan in the corner directly opposite the spy-hole in the steel door. The walls were covered with graffiti scribbled by prisoners awaiting sentence, or who had just been sentenced. 'There is only one judge,' one man had written, 'and He is certainly not of *this* world.' Someone else had scrawled in large letters: 'Cancel my subscription to the resurrection'. There were some dirty rhymes, but mostly just names, dates and offences charged. Along one wall ran a wooden bench, and a podgy white man in an open neck shirt sat, his head hanging. He was about thirty, and obviously scared. We didn't speak for some time, but both stared into the distance. He lit a cigarette, smoked it and lit another, then prowled to the opposite wall to minutely examine some scribbling, and prowled back, shaking his head in disbelief, although I gathered it was at his predicament rather than at what he had read. He seemed to me typical of many white Rhodesians: despite his relative youth, too much beer and nothing to do had given him a spreading gut –

young whites proudly call it their 'Rhodesian Front' – and he did not look especially intelligent.

Finally he said: 'Jesus!' and shook his head again.

I noticed he had a watch, so I asked: 'What's the time?'

'Twenty past twelve.' Then: 'I don't know what that magistrate is up to.'

'Why, what's happened?' I asked.

He offered me a cigarette but I declined. 'I was sitting at home last night having a beer and minding my own business,' he said, 'and I saw this police Landrover drive in. I thought maybe they wanted to ask directions, but this cop said: "We've got a warrant for your arrest." "What for?" I asked. "Non-payment of alimony to your wife," he said. I told him I could fix it all up, and he said he wouldn't take me to jail, but I should come to court this morning. I'll tell you, last night my heart was just pounding! So I come today, and I give documents to the magistrate, and he says "I don't know anything about this. We'll adjourn until this afternoon," and they come and lock me in here! I've got a cheque in my pocket to pay the arrears in full!'

'Too bad,' I said sympathetically. 'How much do you owe your wife?'

'About $180.' There was a pause. 'What are you here for?'

'I'm a detainee, but I've also been charged under the Official Secrets Act.'

He looked blankly at me, then comprehension dawned. 'You're the bloke in the paper today?'

'Yes.'

'Jesus.'

He fell silent again, and despite our comradeship in sharing the dirty cell, there was suddenly a distance and an air of hostility between us. When I was taken out, he did not look up to see me go.

I was led through a large African cell, where about one hundred black prisoners sat on rows of benches in handcuffs, with numbered boards hanging around their necks. If you're an African going to court, you have a number to show who you are. You all look alike. A black prison truck was parked in the entrance to the Magistrates' Court and I was escorted into the middle section with the blinds drawn, and driven back to Salisbury Jail.

The days stretched slowly out. I read, played solitaire, and listened to the radio.

Nonie meanwhile resumed her fight for better visiting arrangements. From week to week, she watched as solitary confinement sapped my morale. The Special Branch were told of the problem. They were very sympathetic, and wrote a letter to Supt Ruff at the Remand Prison, indicating that as far as they were concerned, we could have daily visits. The letter said: 'Permission is hereby granted for Mrs Oenone Niesewand to visit her husband Peter, who is currently detained at your prison *once daily* subject of course to any provisions or requirements you may have.' The letter was given to Nonie, who took it up to Supt Ruff at once.

Ruff turned her down flat. The Special Branch permit, he said, tapping his swagger stick in the palm of his hand, made no difference to him at all.

Nonie wrote to Desmond Lardner-Burke:

Since your detention order was served on my husband over five weeks ago, I have had to face a lot of difficulties, not the least of which is the financial strain of trying to keep our newly-purchased home, Peter's business and our family afloat despite a drastic cut in our livelihood. As you are aware, at no stage have I asked for your assistance on any matter, despite my firm hope that you will resolve this distressing situation in which you have placed Peter and me as quickly as it is within your powers to do so.

But there is a matter which I am referring to you, as it concerns the prison authorities under your control. I have exhausted every other avenue, and now need some authoritative ruling on their actions.

I am allowed to see Peter for half an hour a week, according to the prison authorities. In the circumstances – and I cite Peter's solitary confinement, my pregnancy (I am now in my sixth month), the decisions I've had to take regarding the sale of our house, the foreclosing of insurance policies, fund-raising for expenses, and the administrative problems connected with running the office – I feel the decision is unjustified.

She mentioned the letter she had written to the Director of Prisons, Mr Patch, and the reply received from the Assistant Director, and attached copies of the correspondence.

Then Special Branch, distressed at the conditions under which I have to operate, and knowing that there was no security risk attached to my visits, gave me a letter authorising me to have a visit once daily. I enclose a copy herewith.

I was very happy when I received that letter, and the same day, presented it to the officer in charge of the Remand and Detainees section, Supt Ruff. I explained that all I wanted was to see my husband for half an hour, three or four times a week.

He claimed that the letter from the Special Branch counted for nothing. Then I need to know what does count.

Initially, Supt Ruff said it was the Emergency Regulations that ruled his decision. He showed me the relevant section that says a detainee may only receive one half-hour visit a week. 'What,' he asked, 'is so special about you?'

I explained firstly that as Peter was in solitary confinement (or 'isolation' as I believe prison authorities term it) and had no human contact apart from his jailers and a half-hour visit a week, he does differ from other detainees. I think this should have some bearing on the case.

Supt Ruff replied that the prison was understaffed, held a lot of maximum security prisoners, and that he did not have the time or facilities to grant extra visits. This surprises me, as the Remand Section in Salisbury is surely organised to have facilities for remand prisoners to receive frequently both legal and personal visits.

This last explanation seemed to abandon reliance upon the Emergency Regulations and in any event, they only give the 'Protecting Authority' power to restrict visits – which has not been done: witness the letter herewith from the Special Branch.

I then pointed out that in Gwelo Prison, Peter had been allowed an hourly visit every day.

I didn't tell Supt Ruff, but it is worth mentioning here, that the contrast between his attitudes and the humanitarian treatment received from Supt Durand, officer in charge at Gwelo, is quite marked.

Special factors influenced the extra visits at Gwelo, according to Supt Ruff. Firstly I was pregnant, and secondly, I had a long drive-through. What that had to do with daily visits as opposed to extended visits, he did not explain.

I am still pregnant. I asked Supt Ruff whether, if I lived far from Salisbury, he could grant me extra visits. Oh yes, he replied, you could have two hours with him.

The Prison has staff for a two-hour visit once per week, but not for visits of half an hour per day.

So what is the real reason behind refusing me extra visits?

It's not, as Supt Ruff originally claimed, the Emergency

Regulations, as we see they can be interpreted by whoever is in charge. Nor is it for security reasons, as Special Branch are as disappointed as me that visits have been refused. Nor is it the lack of facilities, as Supt Ruff can avail himself of two hours' visiting time if I were to move out of town.

Finally Supt Ruff threatened that he could require visits to Peter to be behind a glass wall, speaking to each other over a telephone. And, he threw at me: what will I do next month when my husband is a convict, and I can see him for only half an hour a month?

I await the decision of the court, and think Mr Ruff's advance expectations on the matter are unnecessary.

So what was the purpose behind these veiled threats? Are they aimed at me, or at Peter? In the light of them, and the stalemate now reached, I have written to you, outlining the problems with the prison authorities I've had to face.

I can't believe that it was your intention to make detention a punishment for Peter or me, but in the light of Peter's isolation, my very restricted access to him, and the very many pressing financial and business matters on which I require Peter's guidance and help, that is how it is operating.

Nonie mailed off the letter to the former family friend, and waited for a reply. Meanwhile, during a weekly visit to me, she discovered that none of the letters she had written had reached me – although even under strictly-interpreted prison regulations I was permitted one letter a week. She spoke to Supt Ruff, who said he was holding the letters in his office, until they were checked by the Special Branch. She phoned the Special Branch. 'Honestly,' said the officer on duty, 'we will read the mail any time. It's just that we haven't been asked to. We didn't know it was there.'

A Special Branch man went directly to the prison to censor my letters, but it took Mr Ruff some days after that to get round to passing them on.

I did get a letter from Nonie on Monday, 26 March which did not have the Special Branch stamp on it. Even if I was found guilty under the Official Secrets Act, almost everyone expected me to be given a suspended sentence, and released from detention on condition I left the country. A friend in London wrote to Nonie offering to sell us his houseboat on the Thames, but wanted a quick reply. Nonie wrote a letter to me, and delivered it personally to Salisbury Prison on a

Saturday morning. She handed it to Prison Officer Dennis Smith, and asked him to let me have it that day, as she wanted me to think it over and give her my reply during her Monday visit.

Dennis Smith came to my cell on that Saturday and stood in the doorway.

'Your wife's brought a letter for you, but you can't have it until Monday,' he said.

'Oh,' I said, and after hovering a while, he went away. I thought nothing of it, because all mail had to be censored, and Supt Ruff was not on duty.

Smith returned to my cell on the Sunday. 'I don't know why your wife is panicking,' he told me. 'But my advice to you is to tell her "no".'

I could feel my stomach tightening. 'Tell her "no" about what?'

'That I can't say.'

'Well, what's she panicking about?'

'I can't tell you.'

'Is she in trouble? Is she sick?'

'She's not sick.'

'You can't just leave me like this. Why should I tell her "no"?'

'I don't think it's a good idea.'

'You don't think what's a good idea?'

'I can't tell you. It's in the letter.'

'Is it financial?'

'Yes.'

'Well, can't you just give me a hint?'

'No. I'm sorry.' He went away, and the door to the compound crashed shut. I lay staring at the ceiling, wondering what had gone wrong at home, and my imagination raced.

At midday on Monday, I was handed her letter. The 'panic' was that she wanted my reply during the next visit, to the 'financial' offer of a houseboat. The line between thoughtlessness on the part of prison officials, and actual vindictiveness, is indeed thin. I was not the only prisoner on the receiving end of such questionable treatment.

In the adjoining compound, a Portuguese man called de Sousa was held on remand, charged with strangling a woman to death. It was alleged that he had killed her, and then tried to commit suicide by jumping from a second storey window in a block of flats. He had received back injuries, and had just been released from hospital. One afternoon, I went to my compound door to get my supper, at the same

178

time as de Sousa was standing at his barred door, arguing with the prison officers about the food, which he was refusing to eat.

A white officer, a thin smile on his face, said to de Sousa: 'Eat, you cunt. We're fattening you up for the rope.'

I went back to my cell, wondering at the unkindness, and late into that night, I could hear de Sousa beating with his fists on the thick wooden door of his cell and crying out in anguish.

I wondered also at the treatment which must be meted out to Africans. If this is how Europeans are treated – a privileged class even in prison – then how do black Rhodesians fare?

I did not have to wait long to find out. Even in solitary confinement, I established a rudimentary system of contacts with the rest of the prison. I never saw an African detainee, but I heard of them – and in particular of one man, Enos Nkala, a former leading official of the outlawed ZANU. Mr Nkala had been taken from the company of other detainees some three months earlier, and thrown into a solitary confinement cell. It wasn't as luxurious as my own: no daily pint of milk for the black man, no bed, or radio, or food parcels from home. Every day he was taken out for exercise, and one afternoon when he was being returned to his cell, he baulked at the door. Enos Nkala turned to the white warder escorting him back.

'I have a knife in my pocket,' he said, 'and I will kill the first man who tries to get me back in there. I will not go back into that cell. It doesn't matter if I kill you, because I've got nothing to lose. I'm dead already.'

Nkala spoke in a low, measured voice – a man at the point of desperation, and not to be trifled with. The prison officer did not know if he had a knife in his pocket or not. Certainly, it was possible he had. His lips were tight, and his eyes, wide and staring.

'Get back in there,' said the warder nervously, his fingers closing around the solid wooden truncheon in a clasp round his waist.

'I want to see Ruff,' Nkala demanded. 'I've asked to see him for weeks, and he's refused to talk to me. Now I will see him. You go and tell Ruff that I want to see him.'

The warder sent word to other prison officers that he was in trouble, and five or six whites from the Reception block came up to the detention cells to muscle Nkala through the doorway and slam the door shut behind him.

But he did get to see Brian Ruff. Nkala stood eyes blazing before the Superintendent on his government-issue carpet and swore loudly and solidly at the man. Ruff rose immediately and went across to the windows, to close them and prevent the sound reaching the alert ears of other prisoners and warders.

His precautions were in vain. Before nightfall, every prisoner – including myself – knew that Enos Nkala had called the Superintendent every barrack-room name known to man, and had warned Ruff to beware for the future. Did he think he was safe? Nkala wanted to know. Did he think Africans would not get revenge for the injustices they had suffered?

Ruff's low-voiced replies are not on record, but before long, Nkala was released from solitary confinement and allowed to rejoin the other detainees. Ruff's reaction was that of a bully. Faced with a challenge, he retreated.

Unfortunately, the authorities are not often challenged, either by those who are free, or those detained.

They deliberately set out to punish, and humiliate, without trial. Early in 1972, Josiah and Ruth Chinamano, staunch African nationalist supporters, were arrested by the Special Branch. The Chinamanos are very cultured people, with university degrees and a western standard of living. They were not illiterate tribesmen, dragged suddenly from a remote mud hut, yet the Government, who knew their background only too well, treated them with vindictiveness.

Although husband and wife, they were placed in solitary confinement in separate jails. Although entitled to Scale 1 'European' conditions, they were given felt mats on the floor instead of beds, and sadza (thick porridge) and beans to eat. Although Josiah Chinamano, who suffered from hypertension, collapsed at his home when he was arrested, the police made only a brief stop at an African hospital before taking him on to jail. His wife was driven directly to jail, and left there, fearing for her husband's health, and for their young children, and for their own futures. At the time of writing – June 1973 – the Chinamanos are still in detention, although they have been reunited at a camp near Marandellas, and their conditions have been improved.

It took strong representations from the British Government's Pearce Commission before the Rhodesians made the changes. If no one had complained, the Chinamanos might have been in solitary confinement under tough conditions to this day.

Other black detainees fared as badly. Automatically a black man or woman is given the worst possible deal, regardless of their backgrounds or standards of living. It's up to them to apply for improvements in their conditions, if indeed anyone bothers to tell them they are entitled to improvements.

Once a year, the detainees have their cases reviewed by the tribunal, consisting of Judge Harry Davies and two government appointees.

The tribunal is usually very pleasant to those who come before it. The detainee arrives perhaps an hour before the hearing is due to begin, and is given the Government case against him. The dossier he is handed contains his full name, where he went to school, and other background material. But the good bits – the allegations which led to his imprisonment without trial – are blacked out on his copy, and he cannot read them. He then goes, with his lawyers, into the courtroom assigned, where the tribunal offers him a cup of tea, and Judge Davies says: 'Well, what do you have to say?'

No allegations are made, no evidence presented, no witnesses questioned. The tribunal is not precluded from relying on rumour or hearsay. It need not even see the detainee himself, but it usually agrees to do so as a matter of form.

The Government is understandably modest about the workings of this impartial body, and there is a penalty of five years' imprisonment for anyone talking about it.

Most white Rhodesians have little knowledge of the actual machinery of justice, and law and order, in their country. Africans are not, in my experience, surprised at the operations of the white government against their fellow men, but Europeans generally do not know, or will not admit, what is going on in their own country, and are unaware of the sweeping security legislation which can be marshalled against any one of them at the whim of the Government.

Black detainees and their families know, and so do the few white detainees there have been. I was in the position of seeing not only the security regulations in action against me, but also the way the Government was prepared to use the courts of law in an attempt to railroad through a flimsy case against someone who, quite simply, had become unpopular with them.

I prepared myself mentally for the judgement. By the Thursday night, I was feeling quite tranquil about it, and lay in bed listening to the Rhodesia Broadcasting Corporation. With a shock, I heard on the news that judgment had been postponed for another week. I found it difficult to stop shaking, but one thought ran constantly through my mind – they're really trying to break me.

The following morning, I was again loaded into the middle section of a black prison van with the blinds drawn and twelve others squashing in and complaining at the lack of air. Across from me sat another remand prisoner – a young, thin white man with LOVE tattooed across the knuckles of one hand, and a thin scar on his other wrist, marking a recent suicide attempt. I didn't feel much like talking.

The new Magistrates' Court building had not yet been completed, and the remand was to be at the Harare court, in an African township. A tall, sinewy prison officer – an immigrant from Britain – led me into the court building past a photographer. The officer held out his hand – 'no photographs, no photographs' he ordered.

'No photographs?' asked the cameraman, looking straight back at the officer, while his Leica hung by his waist on a cord, and his fingers worked busily – click, wind-on click, wind-on. . . . It was a professional operation and the officer, caught up in his self-importance never knew he and I were being photographed.

There was more than half an hour to wait before the court began sitting, and I asked if I could see my wife. 'Yes,' said the officer, 'I'll fix it,' but he locked me in a cell and went away. I was brought into the courtroom a minute before the magistrate entered, and just had time to greet Nonie and my younger sister Wendy before I had to go into the dock.

Hamilton entered and bowed. Then he looked at the public gallery, crowded with journalists who had simply come to say hello to me and give me moral support during the formal remand. 'The position is that we are still *in camera*,' Hamilton said.

Anthony Eastwood rose. 'Your worship, as I understand it, no judgement is to be given, and nothing is to be said about the facts of the case. Perhaps this would be a suitable moment for an exception to be made, as intimated by Mr Treacy at the previous hearing.'

'No,' said Hamilton with a weak smile. 'I think if we are *in camera*, we are *in camera* for all purposes.'

As the court was cleared, I thought of the crocodile tears Hamilton had shed at the beginning of the trial about his opposition to secret hearings: 'The courts are never very sympathetic to proceedings being held *in camera* . . . if at a later date in the course of proceedings the court has reason to change its mind then I will be the first to do so.'

When only court officials and prison officers remained, Hamilton said: 'I wish to give further consideration to the question of judgment, for which reason it will be necessary to further remand the accused to next Friday at the Regional Court, and the accused will be remanded accordingly.'

And that was that. I was taken back to the cell, and again I asked the prison officer if I could see my wife. 'Yes,' he said, 'I'll fix it,' but I knew he wouldn't. A few yards from the cell, I could hear Anthony Eastwood asking to speak to the officer-in-charge to arrange access to me, and I could hear him being told 'No you can't speak to the officer-in-charge. He's not available' and a steel door slamming shut.

Finally the officer unlocked the empty cell in which I waited, counting spiders, and said 'Come along quickly'. He led me through the courtroom, down a corridor and then held my arm and bustled me out through a side entrance into a waiting Landrover.

It roared away, and he said: 'How was that? Pretty good? I used to be with the Metropolitan police in London.'

'Were you indeed?' I said coldly, and we completed the journey in silence.

I was learning about waiting: about how to pass interminable hours sitting in empty cells. Count the spiders. Read the graffiti. Remember poetry. Pace out the size of the room. Don't think about pleasant times in the past, and on no account think about the future.

For judgment in the new court building, I felt certain I'd be left waiting for hours, so I took a paperback copy of Hammond Innes's book *Campbell's Kingdom* in my pocket. The new Magistrates' Courts are a nightmare of corridors, lifts, staircases and barred windows and doors. The prison truck drives down into the basement, which is arranged rather like the check-in counter of an airline with a new building and a low budget. Prisoners are checked in, and then taken to the row of cells set aside for their particular Scale.

I sat on a hard bench along the wall of a cell, looking out through the floor-to-ceiling bars which covered the whole side leading to the passage. A flush lavatory was in a door-less recess of the cell, also looking onto the passage. I read, and wondered dismally why it was so many novels concerned people who were either in, had been, or shortly would be, in prison.

When the time came for judgement, I was taken to a lift which carried my escort and myself to the third floor of the building, and then we walked along a huge circular corridor, up some stairs and through a door which led straight into the dock of the Regional Court.

Nonie was in the courtroom waiting for me, and we had a short time together, talking over the wooden sides of the dock. There was a small demonstration outside, she said – about fifty people carrying placards denouncing the concept of secret trials. They were outnumbered by police and Special Branch men, and all had their photographs taken by police photographers. All of them now have files in the Special Branch offices, and no doubt are subject to scrutiny from time to time. Police had also sealed off the entire third floor of the new building, but had permitted Nonie, accompanied by Anthony Eastwood, to pass through the cordon.

As Hamilton and the assessor entered the courtroom, Nonie left and took up a position in the corridor outside, watching through a glass panel in the door. She waited for two hours, relieved only by a meeting with Supt Ruff who remarked on the length of time it was taking. 'But,' said Ruff, 'one thing you can say for Hamilton, he's fair. If there's anything that can be said in favour of a prisoner, Hamilton will find it.' Nonie remained silent – wisely, as it turned out.

Sitting on a large red-upholstered seat beneath a green soapstone carving of the Rhodesian coat of arms, Hamilton went through the allegations against me, and noted that although I admitted sending the reports, I had pleaded not guilty.

'The despatches, by implication, make reference to official sources for their contents,' said Hamilton, reading from the hand-written judgment, 'by mentioning Rhodesian intelligence reports and military sources and suchlike. The impression given by the despatches and this the accused admitted in his evidence, is that the author, that is the accused himself, had recourse to, and was quoting Rhodesian intelligence and military sources for his information.'

I had declined to disclose my source of information on journalistic ethical grounds, Hamilton said, but had said that the source had been found reliable in the past. I had also presumed, but did not know, that the source had access, through contacts, to military and intelligence information.

Hamilton turned to the problem of establishing whether my purpose had been prejudicial to the safety or interests of Rhodesia; unless my purpose was prejudicial there was no offence. He said: 'It is clear that once any purpose is established, the question of whether or not it is prejudicial to the safety or interests of Rhodesia is for the Courts to decide, applying an objective test. . . . It was clearly the accused's purpose to obtain, collect and communicate information to both the *Guardian* and the BBC. That is not in dispute.

The evidence must show that it is information which is calculated to be, or which might be, or is intended to be, useful – directly or indirectly – to an enemy.'

The word 'enemy' in terms of the Unlawful Organisations Act, included ZAPU and ZANU. But, said Hamilton, looking sternly down at me, the ordinary and common meaning of 'enemy' also applied, and it was the prerogative of the state to decide who was an enemy. 'In this regard, Mr Fleming [The Secretary for Law and Order] included as enemies of Rhodesia the Front for the Liberation of Zimbabwe, known as FROLIZI, the OAU, the United Nations, Zambia and Tanzania. And his evidence in this regard is in no way challenged by the Defence.'

Hamilton said the Defence had cross-examined Mr Fleming to show that, in fact, my conduct was not useful directly or indirectly to an enemy. 'The purport of Mr Fleming's evidence is that throughout 1972, Rhodesian forces – that is military and air forces – have operated in Mozambique against terrorists on an off-and-on basis, as he expressed it. By that, we understand that Rhodesian forces were not there all the time. That the forces were so operating in Mozambique was classified by the Government as Top Secret,' and again, the stern look from the bench. 'This information or knowledge had never been announced publicly by the Government.

'The Defence cross-examined Mr Fleming to show that in spite of the Government's attitude, it was common knowledge that Rhodesian forces were operating in Mozambique. I might say he denied that it was such common knowledge, although he admitted that soldiers returning from duty could not be prevented from talking about their operations.'

Hamilton said that in my evidence, I had referred to reports in local newspapers concerning Rhodesian involvement in the neighbouring territory, and he added that I had claimed it was common knowledge amongst journalists in Salisbury that this was happening. 'The accused seemed to take it as an admission by the Government that Rhodesian forces were operating in Mozambique, because they never categorically denied those newspaper reports,' he said.

'Without a doubt, those concerned, both military and civilian, were, of course, aware that Rhodesian forces were in Mozambique. For the rest, it must have been a matter of deduction, or speculation, based on unofficial statements of various kinds, and some of them no doubt possibly convincing statements, such as a possible statement by a soldier who had himself taken part in the operations. However, all such statements were private as opposed to coming from an official source, and the accused had no reason to suppose otherwise.

'It is true,' said Hamilton, 'that the Government did not positively deny the Press reports to which I have referred. On the other hand, they did nothing to confirm them. Neither is it possible to presume confirmation in what was said by way of official response. One might be suspicious that the reports bore some background of truth, but that is all.'

Hamilton said that in my evidence, I stated that I thought the information regarding the use of Rhodesian forces in Mozambique had been an official leak. 'These were simply the accused's thoughts,' he said. 'They had no special or factual basis. That is the accused's own evidence.

'We have to decide whether or not the obtaining or collecting of the information set out in the Schedules to the charge was calculated to be, or might be useful, directly or indirectly to an enemy. Mr May argues that the information could not be useful, because it was already known that Rhodesian forces were operating there, because of the rumours, and further any enemy would have been engaged by Rhodesian forces, and thereby have the direct knowledge of their presence in Mozambique.

'There is force in Mr May's arguments,' Hamilton said, a little grudgingly, 'because it is possible that any enemy's intelligence service – that is, if they have one, of course – may well be able to obtain this information in the field. But it would also be very important to know if the Rhodesian forces are openly in Mozambique with authority or not. For instance, an army which is prepared to let its presence be known might well be expected in greater force and to attack more boldly than one which wishes to hide its presence. And it is not difficult to think of other reasons why this information could be useful.'

He paused to shuffle his papers, and it seemed he had lost a page. But finally he found it.

'The accused's despatches,' said Hamilton, 'give out that the information contained therein originates from an official source. Anyway, that part which relates to the presence of Rhodesian forces in Mozambique. Such a statement could be of great value to an enemy, especially bearing in mind Rhodesia's international position. So that we are satisfied that the information contained in the Schedules to the charge is information which was calculated to be, or might have been useful, directly or indirectly, to an enemy.'

I glanced out through the glass panels of the door to the courtroom where Nonie was standing motionless, watching the silent movie version of Hamilton dispensing justice.

'I now deal with the point made by Mr May that Mr Fleming's evidence to the effect that Rhodesian forces are operating in Mozambique is inadmissible as being hearsay,' he went on. 'Mr Fleming admits that as a member of the Defence Council he receives reports informing him of what occurs, including that relating to Rhodesian forces in Mozambique. However, the matter does not end there. He not only visited the border areas between Kariba and Kanyemba, but he has also visited the joint operations command in the north-eastern area of Rhodesia. He has therefore had an opportunity to verify the contents of the reports he received. For these reasons, Mr Fleming's evidence on the point in question can be accepted.

'We are satisfied, for the reasons I have given, that the accused's purpose was prejudicial to the safety or interests of Rhodesia, and consequently find him guilty of the principal charge. There is therefore no need for me to deal with the alternative charge.'

Treacy stood up and said: 'The accused has no record.' So far, it was as we expected: a guilty verdict. The question of sentence had to be dealt with next. Michael May had gone on leave and Anthony Eastwood rose to make a statement in mitigation.

He said that my arrest on 20 February had completely deprived me of my livelihood – I was self-employed – and it was unlikely that I could re-establish myself in Rhodesia. I had a young child, and a pregnant wife.

'His acute financial embarrassment has meant that he has had to surrender insurance policies and arrange the sale of his house to enable him to make some provision for the maintenance of his wife,' Anthony said.

I had also been detained in isolation which had 'operated with most unpleasant effects upon the accused'.

'It has undoubtedly affected his psyche and his sense of judgement,' Anthony said. 'He has also lost some 20 lbs. in weight.'

He recalled the evidence of David Williams that I was a responsible journalist, and the evidence of Michael Keats and Anthony Ryder. 'They were speaking primarily in the sense that his reports were reliable, he did not send speculative material, or biased, one-sided material. That is how journalists would tend to judge each other, as Mr Williams would tend to judge a journalist,' Anthony said.

'In the present case, there is no suggestion that the accused's information was incorrect or wrong, or insufficiently canvassed by him. The nub of the state's case has been that the evidence was only too true. In that sense, there can be no criticism against the accused. The criticism, as I understand it, against the accused is that he should have ascertained that this information was not to be disclosed so far as the Government was concerned.'

The court, said Eastwood, had found that the reports might have been useful to an enemy. 'The fact of the matter is that it appears the enemy has been able to make very little use of these reports,' he went on. 'Outside of this court, and the Ministry of Law and Order, there seems to have been no particular interest or attention paid to the reports of Rhodesian troops operating in Mozambique. There was no suggestion by Mr Fleming of any resulting embarrassment that, in fact, arose.'

Hamilton said: 'Well he did. He mentioned the diplomatic embarrassment with the Portuguese.'

'I didn't understand him to say the Portuguese were an enemy,' said Eastwood. 'I am saying the enemy has not made any particular use of this. So far as Mr Fleming's evidence goes, and so far as one can see, there has been no particular interest or outcry that Mr Fleming referred to, or that has come to anybody's attention arising from the presence of Rhodesian troops in Mozambique.'

The Government had not attempted to warn journalists not to publish this information, and even since this case, had still not issued any warnings.

'Although these charges have been brought,' said Eastwood 'the Government does not seem to have taken a particularly anxious view of these reports. After all, they were known on the 15th or 16th of November. All the material necessary for the charges was available on the 28th of November to the police but the accused was not arrested until the 20th of February and was not charged until March. There was a period of two and a half months in which no action was taken.'

Anthony Eastwood submitted that any sentence should be wholly suspended because of the circumstances of the case.

Brendan Treacy then rose, and pulled from his briefcase the typewritten speech. A conviction under this section of the Official Secrets Act was 'extremely serious', he began, and carried a maximum sentence of twenty-five years, without the option of a fine.

'In my submission,' Treacy read: 'there are several aggravating features about this offence. Firstly, the information was given wide publicity over the vast network of the BBC and the *Manchester Guardian*. Secondly, the accused did not seek to confirm his information, or obtain approval from an official body such as the Department of Information before disseminating it. He acted recklessly, regardless of the consequences, in my submission.

'Thirdly, the accused has not been frank or co-operative in regard to his source. He has refused to reveal the identity of his source. He has put himself above the law, although he has no privilege in law in this regard. His source has also, *prima facie*, contravened the provisions of the Act and he is at large, and his identity is unknown to the authorities.

'The probabilities are that his source had access to Top Secret information, and that the source is probably a state servant. This is a most serious aspect of this case, in my submission,' Treacy declared.

'It follows from this that the accused has shown no contrition or remorse. He has put his own interests before or above the security of the state.

'Fourthly, the information was true. In my submission, this is an aggravating feature. Of course, the accused's whole evidence was based on the assertion it is true. To publish true information regarding the disposition of our troops is, in my submission, far more serious than publishing information which is untrue.

'In my submission, in imposing sentence, the Court must have regard to the deterrent effect of the sentence. It is respectfully submitted that the deterrent effect of the sentence in this case is of particular importance.' (I'll bet it is, I thought.)

'It must be brought home to the accused, and other journalists like him, that reckless reporting of matters which are prejudicial to the interests and safety of Rhodesia will not be tolerated,' Treacy read.

'Contraventions of the Official Secrets Act of this nature could be gravely damaging to the security of the country,' Treacy continued, turning over a page, 'and could well tend to endanger the lives of members of the community.

'No direct link has been established between the publication of the information and the first terrorist attack in December of last year,' he read. 'It is not known what number of terrorists entered the country after publication of the information or the number that were here before it was published. But one factor does stand out: in recent months the dangers of loss of life at the hands of terrorists have been increased. If such information was in any way useful to our enemies in their incursions into this country, then there is a grave need to protect society from the publication of such information.

'In the interests of society, a sentence of a deterrent length in my submission, should be imposed.'

He cleared his throat and read on: 'The sentence which should be imposed has a three-fold purpose. It must be punitive, it must be designed and calculated to deter others, and it must be meant to be a safeguard to this country.'

Treacy sat down, and stared at the paper in front of him. Then he put it back in his briefcase, and zipped it closed.

The court adjourned to consider sentence, and I was led down to my cell to read another chapter or two of *Campbell's Kingdom*.

Hamilton giving judgement and passing sentence was a sobering experience: he was often wrong on matters of fact, and interpretation – as the Appeal Court was to find later. But there was no way of correcting him at that stage.

Passing sentence, Hamilton also read from a prepared address: 'The accused obtained his information from an undisclosed person: a person he continues to decline to disclose, who, according to the accused, did not give out that he had received information from any official or military source,' he said. 'On this basis, he wrote his despatches in the form he did, implying that he himself had received this information from military and security sources.

'The accused admitted in his evidence that if he had disclosed the truth in his despatches as to the origin of his information, reputable institutions such as Reuters and United Press International, would not have published them. Further, the two journalists who the Defence called as Defence witnesses, that is Keats, the manager of United Press International for Southern Africa, and Ryder, the Central African representative of the South African Morning Group of Newspapers, both stated that they would not have published the information contained in the accused's despatches without first checking with the authorities, or obtaining official confirmation. . . .

'Quite clearly, the accused was called upon to act with the greatest circumspection, and this he did not do at all, especially knowing the wide distribution that would be given to his despatches. . . .'

Hamilton, reading from sheets of paper and jabbing his finger at me to emphasise points, declared: 'It would be obvious to anybody that the publication of the fact that Rhodesian military forces were operating in Mozambique, when that information is alleged to come from military sources inside Rhodesia, could seriously embarrass the Government, bearing in mind Rhodesia's international position, and thereby be prejudicial to the interests of Rhodesia.

'Obviously, it could be of use to an enemy, not only in the field, but politically as well, and thereby, of course, be prejudicial again to the safety and interests of Rhodesia.

'It must be borne in mind that Rhodesia has forces operating in the field, and they were operating at the time in question. Of course, it is in the national interest that nothing should be done that could possibly prejudice their safety. In fact, it is the clear duty of this Court, to make certain that nothing is done which will ever prejudice the safety of forces operating in the field.'

Anthony Eastwood's statement in mitigation was brushed aside by Hamilton. 'No doubt the accused has suffered as a result of his arrest, but that is a feature almost to be expected, and is certainly not uncommon. Persons and their families frequently suffer grievously as a result of having been arrested.'

The sentence, said Hamilton, would be that I undergo two years' imprisonment with hard labour.

'However,' he said, 'because the accused acted openly and not in secret, it will be ordered that one year of that sentence be suspended for three years, on condition that the accused is not again convicted of any offence under the Official Secrets Act, committed during that period.

'There is one further matter which I would like to deal with,' Hamilton went on, 'and that is the question of these proceedings being *in camera*. It does occur to me that possibly the fact of conviction and the offence with which the accused has been convicted, and also the sentence, should properly be announced.'

'I agree,' said Brendan Treacy.

Anthony Eastwood rose, his lips tight. 'It occurs to me some indication should be given of the nature of the offence. Does your worship mean just the details in the summons, or reference to the Schedules, or what? Or just the sections of the Act?'

'No,' said Hamilton. 'Just the sections of the Act. In fact, I will tell you what may be published, unless you have any further comment.'

So it was that only the section of the Act under which I was convicted and the sentence were allowed to be made public.

Anthony Eastwood immediately noted an appeal against conviction and sentence. He added: 'I would apply for an order from this

Court that the sentence of imprisonment passed by this Court be suspended, pending the noting of an appeal and the prosecution of the appeal so long as the accused remains in detention. So that should his detention order be lifted, then he would automatically revert to being convicted in the ordinary way.'

An unmistakable expression of disappointment crossed Hamilton's face, as if Anthony Eastwood was interfering in some carefully worked out plan.

After some resistance, Hamilton finally agreed to hold up the operation of the hard labour sentence, pending the appeal, for bail of ten dollars, providing I remained in detention. But if I was released from detention, bail would become $20,000 – one of the highest in Rhodesian legal history. I felt flattered that Hamilton should consider in my case that a two-year prison sentence, with one year of it suspended, was equivalent to a $20,000 bail, instead of the usual $2,000.

The court rose, and Nonie immediately walked in, but I was being hustled out through the prisoners' door by my escort. Before I disappeared down the stairs, I had time to see Nonie say to Anthony Eastwood: 'What did he get?'

'Two years,' said Anthony, 'One suspended,' and she started to cry.

As my escort and I walked along the corridor to the cells, he said cheerfully 'If you started your sentence today, you could be out by Christmas, with good behaviour.'

chapter 13

I did not want to start my sentence at that stage. If I had, the Minister of Law and Order could have revoked the detention order before the Tribunal was obliged to review my case, and then re-detained me after the Official Secrets matter had been dealt with – thus stalling on the possibility of my release being recommended. I preferred to remain for the time being in detention, and give the authorities a deadline to work against. I was entitled to a review within three months of my detention without trial.

Also, Nonie's letter to Desmond Lardner-Burke had borne fruit. She had received a reply written on 3 April.

'Dear Nonie,' said the Minister. 'Thank you for your letter of the 28th March 1973, and I do appreciate your problems. I have taken the matter up with the Secretary for Justice, and I hope that you will now come to a more satisfactory arrangement with the Director of Prisons.'

Nonie had also received a call from the Director himself, Mr Patch, who had suddenly become available to her, and was charm itself. It's amazing what string-pulling will do to apparently immove-able prison regulations. Nonie would be allowed to visit me twice a week, and my mother and mother-in-law could share a visit once a week: a three hundred per cent improvement on the previous arrangement.

Outside the prison, my conviction and sentence sparked off an international uproar, and although a few words of this reached my ears, it seemed rather remote from a solitary confinement cell. But it was pressure on the Rhodesian Government which finally persuaded them to release me.

In London, the *Sunday Telegraph* reported that Britain's Foreign Secretary, Sir Alec Douglas-Home, had sent a message to Prime Minister Ian Smith through the British Embassy in Pretoria, telling him that 'great concern' was felt in Britain over the sentence, and pointing out that the court case could not improve the climate for any future political negotiations between the two Governments. Britain's shadow Foreign Secretary, James Callaghan, was more forthright: 'This tainted conviction makes a mockery of any fresh efforts by Mr Smith to effect a settlement,' he said.

The London *Sunday Times* called the sentence 'savage'. In an editorial, the paper added: 'That a man should be so sentenced in a so-called democracy which pretends to be the guardian of Western and European culture against the dark hordes of barbarism is perhaps the most graphic illustration yet of the real character of the Smith regime. It illustrates not simply its tyrannical nature, but also its blind stupidity ... Sir Alec Douglas-Home ought now to say, once and for all, that the Government has ceased to have any wish to deal with a regime which to describe as medieval would be to insult the Middle Ages.' The Guild of British newspaper editors sent a cable to Mr Smith saying that the sentence was a 'negation of democracy and interference with the freedom of the Press'. Ken Morgan, General Secretary of the National Union of Journalists, thought it was 'bloody diabolical'.

In Rhodesia itself, the *Herald* roused itself to mild protest. 'We do not defend Niesewand,' an editorial said. 'What we are dealing with here is the manner of the trial. Secret trials in Russia are what we have come to expect. Secret trials in Rhodesia are alien to the Rhodesian way of life – alien to the way of life Mr Smith and his Government are pledged to defend.'

Pat Bashford, a Rhodesian farmer and President of the multi-racial opposition Centre Party, said the outcome of the trial was 'horrible'. He added: 'I feel that, considering the size of the bail, they are trying to intimidate the Press.' Sir Roy Welensky, former Prime Minister of the defunct Central African Federation, added his voice to the chorus of protest. 'This,' said Sir Roy, 'is the darkest hour for Rhodesia since UDI.'

In the House of Commons, British Premier Edward Heath said his Government had urged the Rhodesian authorities to lift the detention order on me and allow me to leave the country. They had not yet received a reply. Parliamentary criticism came from other members of the ruling Conservative Party – people the Rhodesian Government had previously counted on as being their friends. Tory MP David Crouch said that any settlement must now 'protect legal British citizens against the repressions of an illegal police state.' Tory

MP Nigel Fisher urged Mr Heath 'to proceed with the utmost caution in any future negotiations with Mr Smith.' Alan Haselhurst, another Conservative MP, said future settlement terms must become 'more severe than we have hitherto contemplated'. Premier Heath himself agreed that my sentence and other detentions in Rhodesia had 'damaged the possibility of getting a settlement'.

In Salisbury, the Rhodesian Government issued a statement saying it had 'noted' the Press criticism, but added that the matter was *sub judice*.

The Rhodesia Broadcasting Corporation also noted the criticism. A commentary prepared by the RBC newsroom said: 'International relations are being bedevilled more and more by an insufferable impertinence demonstrated in a crusading view which amounts to nothing less than interference in the internal affairs of sovereign states. . . . This holier than thou attitude in a matter which is still before the court is a blatant attempt to subvert the course of justice.'

In the London *Daily Express*, John Monks reported that the charge and sentence had been based on a *Guardian* despatch 'reporting a fact of which Rhodesians were aware and mostly very proud'. He added: 'Rhodesian troops, said Niesewand – as did several other correspondents – were operating in neighbouring Portuguese Mozambique, aiding Portuguese forces hard-pressed by FRELIMO terrorist groups. For saying what was certainly no secret, Niesewand is now in prison awaiting an appeal against his conviction and the astonishing sentence.' John Monks wrote the report from Salisbury – a brave act in the circumstances, and a healthy sign that journalists working out of Rhodesia were unlikely to be intimidated into silence by the Government.

In solitary confinement, my newspapers – when I received them which was not often – were cut to ribbons. Any item about me, or Rhodesian security, or any other prisoner, was scissored out, but I read the small-ads and the entertainments page. On her visits, Nonie tried to impress upon me the volume and depth of the outcry, and although it cheered me up temporarily, she would have to leave after a few minutes, the cell door would shut behind me, and I would sit listening to the African hard labour prisoners returning from the fields while around them, guard dogs bayed and snarled. It was a sound I came to hate.

Anthony Eastwood sent a formal Notice of Appeal to the Regional Magistrates' Court, and the Appellate Division, appealing against the conviction on nine grounds, and against the sentence on eight.

Some were on points of law – definitions of words in the Official Secrets Act which the magistrate had got wrong – others were not.

The Defence argued that the magistrate had misdirected himself:

● In finding that my reports conveyed that the Government of Rhodesia officially admitted that Rhodesian military forces were operating in Mozambique.

● In failing to find that proof of a subjective and conscious purpose to achieve the prohibited objectives on my part was an essential element of the offence, and that I had such a purpose.

● In finding that any of the reports were prejudicial to the safety or interests of Rhodesia, and in particular that the reports gave confirmation by the Government of its military presence in Mozambique, and that such confirmation was intended or might be useful to an enemy.

● That the definition of an enemy in the Official Secrets Act in any way rests upon a prerogative decision of the Government.

● In finding that the allegedly offending matter in the reports had not previously had wide publicity.

● That the sentence was manifestly excessive and induced a sense of shock.

● That the magistrate failed to take into account that there was no suggestion on the evidence or otherwise that my reports had had any adverse consequences for the security of Rhodesia, or that any of Rhodesia's enemies had made any use of the reports or of the information in the reports.

● That the magistrate had misdirected himself in taking into account any question of political embarrassment to the Government.

● That the magistrate misconceived the duties of the court in saying that its duty was to see that nothing was done which might prejudice the interests or security of Rhodesia, when in law it was the duty of the Executive and the Legislature to safeguard the security and interests of Rhodesia, and the duty of the court was only to enforce the law.

● That the magistrate was wrong in holding that the evidence of Mr Fleming as to Rhodesian military forces operating in Mozambique was admissible, and was not inadmissible as hearsay.

When the Appeal judges received the Grounds of Appeal, they wrote to Hamilton asking him to submit Reasons for points in his judgment raised by the Defence, and when he had done so, they asked him to submit Further Reasons.

Hamilton became understandably modest about his Judgement and Sentence, and wrote to the judges describing them as *ex tempore*, whereas in fact he had considered the matter for seventeen days, and had read from a prepared speech.

In prison, my spirits were low. Even with an hour and a half's worth of visits each week, I had a lot of time on my hands, and the uncertainty and solitude weighed me down. A study of men in solitary confinement has found that after only a few days, they tend to suffer hallucinations, depression and paranoid symptoms. After about six weeks, prisoners experience mental dulling, weeping, the need for companionship, and are highly suggestible and easily grasp at any help. Men in solitary confinement need to talk, and crave human association. Warders and interrogators can capitalise on this state of mind to cement a bond of apparent friendship, which they can then use as a tool. My solitary confinement conditions were luxurious in comparison to some: yet the essential elements of loneliness and uncertainty were there.

My emotional state was very changeable. I feared for Nonie's safety, and for her health. There seemed no apparent end to the ordeal. Even if I became a hard labour prisoner, the prison authorities said I would probably be transferred to Marandellas Jail, about forty miles from Salisbury, where I would be the only European prisoner, and so effectively still on my own, as there is no racial mixing in prisons. Then I learned unofficially that I might be transferred to the mountain town of Umtali, on the border with Mozambique – far from Nonie and the Defence team. The appeal date had not been set, and it seemed unlikely the judges would be able to fit my case into their schedule for nearly two months.

Into my unhappy cell came the Chaplain General, Father Bill Clark. I was glad of the company, and I thought him a likeable man. During earlier meetings, he had impressed on me that my duty was to my wife and family – and that, above all, I should think of them. I confided to him my fears for Nonie's safety, and my regret that she should have to go through the ordeal with me, which seemed to be stretching endlessly ahead. I said I'd even be prepared to admit guilt of the Official Secrets charges, despite my innocence, and leave the country never to return if I could get her, and myself, out of the nightmare. Father Clark agreed it would be a Christian thing to do.

A few hours later he was back: the Government was interested in such a deal. Anthony Eastwood was summoned to the prison, and I instructed him to go ahead. I wouldn't disclose my sources, I said, but other than that, I'd be prepared to sign anything. Anthony attended a meeting at Milton Buildings during which the Government expressed interest, and invited him to submit a draft undertaking to be signed by me together with a memorandum of advantages which would accrue to the Rhodesians by the deal.

Nonie was horrified at the idea, but she could not get to me to tell me to stop, and in any case, she was concerned at my mental state. Anthony Eastwood's job was simply to carry out my instructions.

Our impression from Father Clark was that time was of the essence, and the matter became more urgent when the Appeal judges – because of the international publicity – decided they could squeeze my case in on the final day of their scheduled series of sittings, on 27 April, just over a fortnight away. Anthony wrote formally to the Government, underlining the importance of a settlement to them, and the international repercussions of the case.

He also disclosed that the Defence would be applying for the admission of further evidence during the Appeal hearing, including evidence that the reports of the presence of Rhodesian troops in Mozambique had been widely published in South African papers more than a month before my reports were written, and also a Press Statement by the Commander-in-Chief of the Mozambique armed forces, General Kaulza de Arriaga, which was published in the *Rhodesia Herald* shortly after my conviction. If information about Rhodesian involvement was still considered Top Secret, no one had apparently bothered to tell General de Arriaga.

The *Herald* report said: 'Turning to his relationships with Rhodesia, General de Arriaga said he was on the best of terms with the heads of the Rhodesian armed forces. "We have an agreement with Rhodesia that troops may only cross the border from either side when they are in hot pursuit of the enemy. Otherwise there is no involvement in each other's campaigns whatsoever."'

Anthony Eastwood's letter said: 'We feel that there is a good prospect of Mr Niesewand's appeal against conviction being successful, and an even better prospect of the prison sentence being substantially reduced. There is a risk so far as the Government is concerned that the appeal will be wholly successful, and an even greater risk that it will be partially successful.' The undertaking I would be prepared to sign acknowledged guilt of the charges under the Official Secrets Act, and accepted that the court case was justifiably held *in camera*. I would also undertake to keep silent about Rhodesian military matters, my detention and trial, and the circumstances surrounding my release and departure from Rhodesia. In return, the Government would permit me to leave with my wife and family, and would allow me back into the country for a two-week personal visit each year.

The Government replied eight days later. 'I am directed to inform you that Government considers there should be no attempt to avoid the ordinary process of the law following upon Mr Niesewand's conviction,' wrote an official in the Ministry of Justice. Anthony told me of the letter, and I felt a twinge of disappointment, and then later, relief. Admitting guilt stuck in my throat. Imprisonment seemed preferable to such unjust humiliation.

Anthony wrote to the Government: 'Our client is disappointed at the Government's view in this matter. My approach to you and my letter on 11 April were made at the invitation that we understood to emanate from the Government via the Prison Chaplain.' And he added: 'We are instructed that our client is surprised that the Government considers there should be no attempt to avoid the ordinary process of the law following upon his conviction. The courts have allowed our client bail pending appeal, but our client remains in detention only by reason of the Order of the Minister of Law and Order.'

There was an immediate reaction from Milton Buildings. The Ministry of Justice wrote to deny that any invitation concerning a deal had been made by the Government.

'Any such communication from Government would have to pass through the Minister of Justice to myself,' wrote Mr M. F. Garnett, 'and thence to the Prisons Department. There was no such communication, and the first this office heard was a message from the Director of Prisons that your client had made an enquiry through the Prison Chaplain about possible negotiation. It is your suggestion that an invitation to your client emanated from Government "via the Prison Chaplain". The Prison Chaplain has been questioned in this regard, and he denies that anything he said could reasonably have been construed as an invitation emanating from Government. Accordingly, I wish to leave you in no doubt whatsoever that your understanding in this regard is entirely wrong.'

Father Clark came to my cell. After a lengthy talk, and reference to my Christian integrity, he dictated to me a letter, addressed to him, thanking him for approaching the authorities 'at my request' about a deal. I had no recollection of making any such request to Father Clark, merely of discussing the idea of negotiations in general terms. But I did not have the mental reserves to resist his pressure, and I wrote the letter he wanted, in my own hand. Solitary confinement is very weakening.

Had the Government accepted the deal, which they in any case apparently initiated, I should have been bound to keep silent. Apart from the undertaking, I had also given Father Clark my personal assurance that I would not renege on the deal. But it was a deal: Nonie and I would be let off the hook without going through the ordeal of the Appeal hearing, and the Rhodesian Government would bring the adverse publicity to a halt.

After I had won the Appeal, and there was a clamour for my immediate release, the Government came back asking me to pledge my silence if they set me free. It seemed to me there was no longer any question of a deal. I had won my case fairly and decisively. Their piece of paper was a document I signed under duress, and therefore had no legal validity. If I had not signed it, they would have returned me to solitary confinement. When I signed, I was sent into exile. It was an example of modern Rhodesian justice.

The Appeal went ahead. Anthony Eastwood contacted one of Southern Africa's most respected legal brains, Israel Maisels QC, a leader of the Bar in Johannesburg, and a former Rhodesian High Court judge, who agreed to take on my case. Maisels, a tall, spare, stooping man of sixty-eight, has a reputation for thoroughness in preparing his cases, and has been involved in some of South Africa's major legal battles. He headed the Defence team in the Republic's longest-running trial, 'The Great Treason Trial', which lasted from 1959 to 1961, and he defended David Pratt, the wealthy farmer who attempted to assassinate South African Prime Minister Hendrik Verwoerd in 1960.

I was not allowed to attend the Appeal hearing – it is not customary for an appellant being held in prison to do so – and I never met Mr Maisels. But I received a copy of the Heads of Argument he prepared for the Appeal, and a fairly full verbal report of his performance in court. After a thorough reading of all documents, Maisels discovered that the magistrate had found me guilty of something I had never ever been charged with – publishing information 'intended to be' useful to an enemy.

In his Heads of Argument, submitted to the appeal judges, Maisels said the real question was whether I knew, or must have known, that the act of collecting and publishing information on Rhodesian involvement in Mozambique was prejudicial to the safety of the state – that is, that my probable purpose was prejudicial.

My actual purpose, he said, was stated during my court evidence: '. . . to show that the security situations in the two countries are closely linked . . . that Rhodesia is taking steps to contain the situation. . . .' Maisels observed: 'This is nowhere dealt with by the magistrate.'

Hamilton's finding that the information was 'calculated to be, or which might or is intended to be useful, directly or indirectly, to an enemy' was disputed, he said. 'It should here be observed that the appellant was not charged with the obtaining, collecting, publishing of information which was "intended to be useful" and this was not suggested to the appellant, let alone proved against him. This finding by the magistrate is a serious misdirection, and is perhaps indicative of his whole approach to the case. . . .

'The only part of the Schedules to the charges which were found by the magistrate to be objectionable is that part which contained information that Rhodesian military and air forces were operating in Mozambique.

'This fact was found by the magistrate to be a Government secret, classified as Top Secret, and that it had not been published by the Government.

'The mere fact that something is classed "Top Secret" by some administrative official as was the case here does not mean that it is in fact "Top Secret", and still less that its publication is prejudicial to the safety or interests of Rhodesia. These are facts to be determined by the Court on proper evidence. The magistrate seems to have been influenced by this classification. . . .

'The magistrate held further that the disclosure that the Rhodesian forces were operating in Mozambique has embarrassed the Government with its relationship with the Portuguese Government, a friendly power.

'This, in fact, was the only evidence led by the state as to prejudice, if it can be called prejudice.

'The magistrate says the embarrassment caused by the disclosure must therefore be contrary to the interests of Rhodesia. But the Government is not the state. . . .

'Cross-examination of Fleming shows that it does not embarrass Rhodesia at all. The answers given by Fleming in cross-examination show that this cannot possibly be so.'

Maisels said this was not a case where I had intended the information I published to be useful to an enemy. 'He was not charged with this, and there is no evidence to support it,' Maisels went on. 'None the less, this was found to be so by the magistrate.

'This finding by the magistrate on no evidence may explain the vicious sentence. In this connection, the attitude of the magistrate throughout the trial in coming to the aid of Fleming when he was in difficulties and his cross-examination of the appellant is not irrelevant. This attitude of the magistrate is also shown by the bail which he fixed of $20,000.

'The magistrate misquoted the evidence as to the necessity of checking information with the authorities, and the gloss which he has put on this evidence is significant. The evidence of Michael Keats on checking information must be read in the background that he was referring to fresh news and not to something previously known.'

Maisels recalled that the police had taken a warned and cautioned statement from me on 27 November 1972, but no charge had been framed until 9 March 1973.

'It would seem that although the authorities knew in November what the appellant had done,' Maisels said, 'they could not have regarded his actions as anything really serious.'

Before the Appeal Court sat to hear the matter, private meetings were held between the judges, the Defence and the Prosecution to decide whether the case would be held *in camera*.

The three judges, Sir Hugh Beadle (Rhodesia's chief Justice), Hector Macdonald, and A. J. A. Goldin, agreed to a Prosecution application that some of the Appeal should be held *in camera*, but that edited versions of Hamilton's judgment and sentence should be made public immediately.

On the day before the Appeal opened, Prime Minister Ian Smith spoke in the industrial city of Bulawayo, and discussed the security situation in the north-east.

Mr Smith said: 'We will have to go on living with this sort of thing until we have completely cleared out terrorism. And tragically, it is something that stems from across our borders. This is where they have their so-called strongholds, their bases, and until we can clear those out, no matter how successful we are in pushing them back to our borders, there will always be leaks in the dyke from over the border, and we must expect these incursions, while they still have their footholds across the border.

'Don't let us delude ourselves on this problem,' Mr Smith declared.

'That is the ultimate object – to clean them right out! Then I believe we can ensure security, but not when the imaginary line on the map is the border, and they can transgress this border as they do at the moment.

'Anybody who believes that simply because we clean up a certain area and push them across, the danger is over, is indulging in wishful thinking and indeed, he has his head very high in the clouds. I hope I make myself clear on that point.'

Mr Smith did indeed make himself clear, and Israel Maisels QC read his words on the front page of the *Rhodesia Herald* on the morning of Friday 26 April. Mr Maisels carried a copy of the newspaper into the Appeal Court.

The Rhodesian courts had never before held an Appeal *in camera*, and in open session at the beginning of the sitting, when the edited charges and judgement were released, Justices Beadle, Macdonald and Goldin made it clear that they disliked setting a precedent. They proposed hearing sections of the Appeal in public.

Brendan Treacy rose immediately. 'M'lords, I have taken advice, and the Minister of Law and Order is prepared to issue a Certificate in terms of Subsection 2(A) of Section 403A of the Criminal Procedure and Evidence Act,' he said.

Israel Maisels was on his feet at once. 'Then I want to see it!' he declared. 'I want to see the Certificate! My lords, I submit this is most improper.'

The three judges stared disapprovingly down from the bench at Treacy, and a court official rushed away to Milton Buildings to fetch a Certificate overriding the judges' wishes on the matter, and ordering the Appeal Court into secret session. Maisels challenged the validity of the Certificate, and said he was presenting new evidence – that morning's *Herald* – by which the charge against me 'ceased to be secret by an act of Government itself'.

At length, the court official returned, with a piece of blue paper in his hand, and approached Treacy's seat. 'Is this satisfactory to your purpose?' the official asked in a loud voice. Maisels, who was in the process of arguing a fine point of law, paused in full flight, to look inquiringly at the Director of Public Prosecutions. So did everyone.

With all eyes upon him, the perspiring Treacy shifted uncomfortably and muttered something gruffly. He handed the Certificate across to Maisels, and it was then passed up to the Bench. Sir Hugh Beadle looked at it and said: 'Our hands are tied.' The court was cleared, by order of the Government.

In secret session, Maisels produced the *Herald* and drew attention to the Prime Minister's remarks the previous night. Two further Certificates were served on the Court that day by order of Desmond Lardner-Burke and there was no doubt that, for the first time, the state was interfering in the judicial process.

But the Appeal went well. The judges sat until 6.30 p.m. on Friday, and then agreed to resume on the Monday although it was the official court vacation.

The evidence of John Fleming, the Secretary for Law and Order, caused mirth in court with its contradictions and backtracking, and it became apparent that no weight was being attached to his contribution. At one stage, even Brendan Treacy laughed as Maisels took the court in detail through the evidence and highlighted its absurdities.

On the Monday afternoon, the appeal judges announced they would deliver their verdict the following day, and Anthony Eastwood sent word to me in Salisbury Jail that we looked certain to get an acquittal: on the evidence presented, and on the points of law, the state did not appear to have a case.

Chief Justice Beadle delivered an edited judgement in open court. In simple terms, he said, I had been charged with 'spying for the enemy', and it was as well to bear this in mind when considering the nature of the alleged offence. There were three hurdles that had to be overcome in order to achieve a Guilty verdict. First, the state had to prove that what I published was information which 'might be useful, directly or indirectly, to an enemy'. The proof of this was objective, said Sir Hugh, but it must be proved beyond reasonable doubt by reliable evidence.

Second, the state must prove that I was 'not a person acting under lawful authority' when I published the information, and thirdly, if these earlier hurdles had been overcome, the court would presume that I published the offending information for a purpose prejudicial to the safety or interests of Rhodesia, unless I proved to the contrary on a balance of probabilities.

Sir Hugh said that in his opinion, it was essential that both the Defence and the trial court be informed by the Prosecution of the precise purpose on which the state relied as being a purpose prejudicial to the safety or interests of Rhodesia.

Sir Hugh pointed out: 'Before the trial in this case started, the appellant asked formally for particulars of this, but the prosecutor refused to give them saying that it was a matter of evidence and argument. We think that this may have prejudiced the appellant in the preparation of his defence.

'Furthermore, not only were particulars not given, but the evidence on this aspect of the case was vague and almost invariably a matter of opinion, and not of fact.

'Factual evidence of actual prejudice as opposed to opinion evidence was never given.

'I apply these principles to this case: In the main charge, the first hurdle which the state must overcome is to prove that what the appellant published was information which was, directly or indirectly, likely to be useful to an enemy, the enemy here being the terrorists and the hostile organisations which support them.

'This is a question of fact to be determined on the evidence.

'It cannot be emphasised too strongly that under the main charge, it was essential to prove that the information was "useful, directly or indirectly, to an enemy", and that to prove that such information might embarrass the Government of Rhodesia in its political relations with States which are not "enemies" within the meaning of the Act does not assist the Prosecution, since causing embarrassment of this kind does not constitute a contravention of Section 3(c)(ii) of the Act.

'Nor does the mere fact that it is contrary to the general interests of Rhodesia necessarily mean that it is useful to an enemy,' Sir Hugh went on. 'To publish something contrary to the general interests of Rhodesia is a different offence.'

The Chief Justice said that the Minister's Order did not permit the court to make any reference to the facts of the case. 'But I may say that, after anxious consideration of all the evidence led, and having heard the very full argument addressed to it, the court has come to the conclusion that the state has not overcome the first hurdle, of showing that the information which the appellant published falls within the meaning of Section 3(c)(ii) of the Act – that is, information which is likely either directly or indirectly to be useful to an enemy. In the circumstances, the decision of the court on the main charge is that the Appeal against conviction is allowed, and the verdict on that charge is set aside.'

Sir Hugh said that in conformity with Rhodesian procedure, Magistrate Hamilton – having found me guilty on the main charge – then declared me not guilty on the alternative. But the Appeal Court, having set aside the verdict on the main charge, had to examine the alternative to see whether or not the evidence established my guilt on that charge.

The alternative charge alleged that I contravened the Official Secrets Act in that, having in my possession information relating to a military matter, I published such information for a purpose prejudicial to the safety or interests of Rhodesia.

'It was the case for the State,' said Sir Hugh, 'that the information published by the appellant was true, and related to a military matter relevant to the safety or interests of the State.'

He ruled that Treacy had proved I published information concerning a relevant military matter, and that it had not been published 'under lawful authority' – in other words, the State had got over the second hurdle.

But they stumbled at the third: Sir Hugh said that although the court then presumed that my purpose was prejudicial to the safety or interests of Rhodesia, the onus rested on me to prove the contrary, on a balance of probabilities.

'Whether or not the appellant succeeded in doing this is again a matter purely of evidence which cannot be divulged,' the Chief Justice said. 'However, the court is satisfied, on a careful examination of the evidence, that the appellant did succeed in showing on a balance of probability that the purpose for which he published the information was not a purpose prejudicial to the interests or safety of Rhodesia.' The court was also satisfied, Sir Hugh added, that the information itself was not in fact prejudicial to the interests or safety of the country.

Just before lockup at 4.30 p.m. Anthony Eastwood rushed to Salisbury Prison to give me the news. 'I wish I could tell you you're a free man,' he said, 'but I can't.'

It was a sweet victory – an outright acquittal, not a matter of winning on a technicality, and as I lay in my cell later, staring at the ceiling, I felt exultant.

I thought: I'll bet the Government are kicking themselves that they didn't go through with the deal.

Nonie drove from court to the prison immediately after the verdict and asked if she could see me briefly to congratulate me. Supt Ruff said: 'No you can't. He's locked up for the night.'

Telegrams began arriving at our home. BBC Television News cabled: 'BBC Television newsroom staff stood and cheered upon hearing that Peter's integrity had been completely exonerated – not that we ever had any doubts. We now press for his release from a detention designed only to silence a reporter who has earned the respect and admiration of all his colleagues.'

The British Foreign Office said it 'warmly welcomed' the news, and added that Whitehall had urged the Rhodesian authorities to lift the detention order and allow me to leave the country. The *Daily Telegraph* reported that the Rhodesian Cabinet met in emergency session a few hours after the Appeal Court's decision to discuss the implications of the acquittal. Desmond Lardner-Burke promised publicly to re-examine the detention order. The *Telegraph* added: 'Mr Lardner-Burke and the Cabinet are keenly aware that, if released, Mr Niesewand would be in a position to expose fully the details of the charges which were made against him. These are of such a flimsy nature that the Government could face a reaction of incredulity in the country.'

To my surprise, the *Rhodesia Herald* even had a kind word to say about me: 'There could not be a more complete legal vindication of a man's honour,' said a *Herald* editorial. 'He should be released without further delay.'

Centre Party President Pat Bashford commented: 'Three cheers for the judiciary, and three regretful sighs for the Rhodesian Front comic opera approach to the maintenance of law and order. The RF have left no stone unturned to demonstrate to the world at large their unlimited capacity for earnest stupidity. I can only hope that the Minister will see the absolute folly of detaining Mr Niesewand any longer.'

I sat in my cell wondering what would become of me. Every time footsteps approached my isolation block, and the key rattled in the lock, it could be someone coming to tell me I was free. Or it could be a warder bringing my food. I tried not to listen, and I tried not to care.

At midday on Wednesday, 3 May, I was taken to the visitors' room where Anthony Eastwood sat with some papers before him on the table. The Government, having lost their case and come under severe political pressure, were back with a deal. If I agreed not to mention anything about the Official Secrets Trial, or Rhodesian military matters, I could leave the country.

I signed. Anthony Eastwood took the undertaking back to Milton Buildings, and the warder locked me in my compound. I did not feel excited: rather I was filled with a sense of anti-climax. I packed my cases, and stripped the bed, revealing again the filthy mattress. Nonie came to the prison in the afternoon, to discuss arrangements with me. I would be taken to Salisbury Airport by the Special Branch, and put on board a TAP Portuguese Airways flight for

Lisbon and London. We had to pay for the one-way ticket to exile. That afternoon, when other prisoners were locked into their cells, the authorities returned to me my watch and rings, and I had a short meeting with members of my family in the visitors' room. For once, no warder was present censoring the conversation.

The Special Branch man assigned to put me on the plane was a friend: Assistant Commissioner Brian Chalk. He drove Nonie and me out to the airport, and into the transit lounge through a side entrance, avoiding journalists who had been tipped off that I was leaving. There was a visitors' book in the Transit Lounge, with a sign saying 'We hope you have enjoyed your stay'. I signed my name, and under the space reserved for 'Comments', I put a question mark.

Brian Chalk bought me a farewell beer, and escorted me onto the aircraft. Three colleagues caught the plane with me, and we had champagne and quails for dinner, while thousands of feet below us, more than one hundred African detainees slept on felt mats on the floors of their cells.

I was lucky. I was white, and a journalist: I had an attractive and articulate wife who knew how to use publicity, I had colleagues in many countries who fought hard for my release, and there were many ordinary people in Britain who had been angered at my treatment and at the fact that a source of their information had been suppressed.

Inside Rhodesia, a smear campaign was launched. The Government alleged that I had been acquitted on a technicality. Premier Smith said publicly I had been guilty of contravening the Official Secrets Act. Rumours went round that I had operated a Communist radio station from my Northwood home, and that I had a list of names of Centenary farmers who were to be killed by guerillas. The rumours said that Nonie was equally guilty, but the Government had not taken action against her because she was pregnant.

Nonie remained in Salisbury for a fortnight after I left, selling the house, shipping furniture, and dealing with Income Tax. One night some young white Rhodesian men drove to our home and painted the word 'TRAITOR' on the roadway. They also erected a sign saying 'For Sale: Traitors Gate'. But not all white Rhodesians believed the smears. Some were extremely kind, generous and thoughtful, but it appears they were in the minority. It was easy, and comforting for many Europeans to accept the rumours, and focus their dislike, and in some cases hatred, on us. This did nothing to improve the security of their position in the country.

There is no substitute for truth. White Rhodesians need to take a long hard look at their Government and their legislation, at the policy of detention without trial, and the treatment of Africans. Rumours, half-truths and wishful thinking may make life temporarily more pleasant for them, but it does not avert a revolution. Whites are fearful of the future, and insecure. Blacks are resentful of the present, and confident of their long-term future.

In Rhodesia, there are men and women of both races working genuinely in the hope of creating, without bloodshed, a just society. There are not very many of these people, but I hope they succeed.